THE
BEAK BOOK

Understanding, Preventing, and Solving Aggression and Biting Behaviors in Companion Parrots

Written and Illustrated
By Sally Blanchard

with a Special Section on Medical Care for Parrot Bites
By Ellen Selden Schreiber, M.D. and Brad Selden, M.D.

Published by the PBIC, Inc. (Parrot Behavior Information Council)
Sponsored by the Companion Parrot Quarterly

Blanchard, Sally 1944 -
The Beak Book by Sally Blanchard
Illustrated by Sally Blanchard

ISBN 0-9671298-1-8

Library of Congress Control Number: 2002108317

1. Companion Parrots
2. Parrot Behavior
3. Aggressive Behavior and Biting

Printed on Recycled Paper by Dakota Press, San Leandro, California

ALSO PUBLISHED BY PBIC, Inc.
Companion Parrot Quarterly - Published since 1991
        Edited by *Sally Blanchard*
Sally Blanchard's **Companion Parrot Handbook** -
        The definitive book on Companion Parrots. Published May 1999

Planned or in Process
*Companion Amazon Parrots: The What You See Is What You Get Parrot - *Sally Blanchard*
*Grey Matter: Living with an African Grey Parrot - *Sally Blanchard*
*Caiques: The Bird Who Would Be King - *Sally Blanchard*
*Parrot Personality Profiles - *Sally Blanchard*

The Companion Parrot Behavioral Solution Series
The Beak Book: Understanding Biting & Aggressive Behavior - *Sally Blanchard*
        the first in a series of in-depth publications to help people understand
        the behaviors of their companion parrots. Other publications will include:
*Winning the Trust of Rescue Parrots - *Sally Blanchard*
*Understanding the Basic Needs of a Companion Parrot - *Sally Blanchard*
*Understanding Excessive & Manipulative Screaming- *Sally Blanchard*
*Behavioral Feather Picking: Understanding Causes, Prevention & Solutions - *Sally Blanchard*
*Understanding Phobic or Fear-related Behavior- *Sally Blanchard*

(*not yet available in 2002 - check our web site for publication dates)

Wholesale prices are available on all publications to legitimate retail outlets.

PBIC, Inc./Companion Parrot Quarterly
PO Box 2428, Alameda, CA • 510-523-5303
staff@companionparrot.com • www.companionparrot.com

TABLE OF CONTENTS

The Beak Book is the first in a series of comprehensive publications intended to help caregivers prevent and solve the behavioral problems that people are most likely to encounter with their companion parrots. In this series, I eventually hope to cover all of the important issues involving companion parrot behavior.

Over thirty years of studying and working with birds, I have advised many clients and written many articles about aggressive behavior in parrots. This publication contains a great deal of new material plus revised, rewritten, and updated versions of several previously published articles from the Pet Bird Report, The Companion Parrot Quarterly, The Companion Parrot Handbook and Bird Talk Magazine. There may be some repetition but I believe certain concepts are worth repeating from different perspectives so that they become reinforced in the reader's mind.

The goal of this publication is to help people get the information they need for understanding, preventing, and solving their companion parrots' biting and aggressive behavior. Don't give up without giving your parrots the chance they need for a quality life in a nurturing home — reading this book and following its advice can make the difference!

For more information on living with companion parrots, please refer to my Companion Parrot Handbook and our web site at www.companionparrot.com. Don't forget to subscribe.

FUN AD by Sally Blanchard

(This cartoon advertisement is only for fun and NOT for a genuine product or service.)

Sally Blanchard

My thanks and appreciation to the people and parrots who have helped me with this book: Gayle Reece, Maggie Rufo, Sandy Black, Dr. Ellen Selden Schreiber, and Dr. Brad Selden

and, of course, my avian artist models who include: Bongo Marie, Paco, Rascal, Pascal, Spikey LeBec, Whodeedoo, Twiggy, Bosco, Molly, Josey, Miracle, Skippy, Gracie, Bojo, Rosie and all of the other parrots who taught me how special they can be ... even if they aren't perfect.

ARTICLES ON COMPANION PARROT BITING & AGGRESSION

Too Aggressive to Handle?

Most of what I have learned about biting has been from working with countless parrots who were too aggressive for other people to handle. In the beginning I was bitten often but as I began to understand why these parrots became aggressive, I was bitten less and less. I could even handle parrots who were considered to be exceedingly aggressive. Only a very few of the parrots I worked with were so aggressive that I felt their behavior couldn't be managed if the caregivers utilized the rules and techniques of *Nurturing Guidance*. Even overly-aggressive rescue parrots who have lived miserable lives will respond positively to the nurturing influences of a knowledgeable and patient caregiver.

All animals mature and some people have to face the fact that many parrots do not keep the delightful, malleable, and cuddly personalities they had as bappies. This is not to say that they still can't be delightful and loving — it means that the relationship has to mature just as the parrots have. Caregivers need to learn to understand and respect the moods of their parrots and even understand that there might be times during the year when their avian companions can't be trusted enough to be handled. In the majority of situations that I felt were hopeless, it was the people who I believed would fail their parrots. Usually it was because they were looking for "quick-fixes" — miracles that would suddenly and effortlessly make their parrot behave. "Quick-fixes" rarely, if ever, accomplish anything — particularly on a long-term or permanent basis. Caregivers need to consistently change their own behaviors if they expect their parrots' behaviors to change.

When I first started working with parrots, the advice given for changing behavior was often too aggressive and absolute. Over the years, I have determined that the best way to deal with companion parrot aggression is based much more on empathy than dominance. Successfully reading body language and cajoling parrots into doing what is needed is far more successful than being "the boss." While it is critical for caregivers to establish enough authority for parrots to perceive them as a "flock leader," absolute rigid authority is likely to create more problems than it solves. For example, aggressively "laddering" a misbehaving parrot from hand to hand as punishment, is likely to bring on more aggression from that parrot. Most parrots reflect the mood and energy of their caregivers and aggression is usually met with increased aggression from the parrot. On the other hand, if the caregiver regroups and calms down he or she will be more likely to achieve positive results. All of the articles in this publication have been updated to reflect these changes in my thinking.

In working with parrots who have become aggressive, the four most important characteristics the caregivers can exhibit are:
- Determination
- Dependability
- Patience

and most of all
- Forgiveness

Getting angry, taking it personally, and punishing the parrot will guarantee future problems. While it is true that some companion parrots become very willful, they rarely bite to "get even." Biting often starts out of a confused combination of fear and territorial defense. People have to believe that they can be successful in changing their parrots' aggressive behaviors. They also have to understand that there may be times when parrots rightfully become aggressive no matter how trainable and sweet they are most of the time. Observing, predicting, and avoiding situations that cause aggression are the best ways to prevent problems. Caregivers need to be dedicated to following a patient long-term approach rather than expecting dramatic quick-fixes to permanently change their parrots' behaviors.

Beak Basics

The Anatomy of the Beak

Another name for parrot is hookbill and it is the beak (or bill) that is the most identifiable characteristic of the parrot's anatomy. Although they are similar, parrot beaks vary from species to species. The beak is not simply a chunk of dead plastic-like material but a constantly growing organ whose structure is actually a continuation of the parrot's skull. The upper beak covers a bone called the premaxilla, while the lower beak covers a portion of the mandible or lower jaw. The part that is visible is the keratin covering called the rhamphotheca (ram-fo-THEE-ka from the Greek *amphos, beak* and *theka,* sheath). If we realize that keratin is basically the same material in the parrot's toenails and our fingernails, it becomes more obvious that the beak grows. As a parrot chews and grinds, the tip of the beak wears away but there is continuous growth that maintains the proper shape and functionality. If the growth areas of the beak become damaged through injury or disease, it may become misaligned. In some cases, this problem can be serious enough to cause starvation. This is particularly true with birds such as parrots whose beaks are used to manipulate and process food before it is swallowed. Beak notching is a despicable way to try and prevent biting behaviors. It is an abusive quick-fix attempt to solve a problem without any consideration of the parrot's needs and well-being.

If a parrot stays healthy, eats a nutritious, balanced diet that includes high-quality proteins, calcium, and vitamin A and has lots of fun "stuff" to chew on, the beak should never have to be trimmed. If it does need trimming, a competent veterinarian or groomer who understands the beak's anatomy and physiology should do it. As a living organ, the beak has pain receptors, sinuses, a nerve supply, and blood vessels. A damaged beak can bleed! It is painful for a parrot when someone grinds the tip back too far, especially the improper use of one of those motorized tools that can also make the beak intolerably hot. Often, if the beak is groomed improperly, it can become sore enough for the bird not to touch anything for days — including food.

A Zillion Uses

Parrot beaks are not proportionately used as weapons any more than human hands are. The parrot beak is an incredibly versatile instrument with a zillion uses. Human lips and teeth are pretty much useless compared to the versatility of a parrot beak. The beak serves the purposes of lips, a mouth, and a hand. The beak is used to manipulate and process food to prepare it for digestion. Parrots use their beaks to slice, dice, shred, rip, tear, and demolish almost anything faster than any other animal can without extra tools. Beaks are used to play-wrestle for fun or even to show affection in courtship. Bonded parrots use their beaks to preen and caress each other. Too many parrot caregivers think that just because parrots reach out with their beaks that they are going to bite. This is a common misconception with novice and uneducated caregivers. Beaks are used to explore and a parrot often reaches out with his beak for balance. When a parrot touches a person's hand with his beak, it is to test the stability of the perch. Beaks are not usually used as a weapon unless the parrot is seriously threatened or given mixed messages. Some parrots, whose human friends don't set rules for them or do not read their body language properly, do learn that their beaks are powerful tools for getting their way! If a parrot does use his or her beak aggressively, it can do some serious damage!

Parrot beaks have a great range of dexterity and can also be incredibly gentle. Beaks are used to preen, clean, and re-zip feathers together to keep them in tip-top shape. If a parrot has an itch, the beak can be used to scratch just about every part of his or her body. The beak can shell the smallest seed or even feed the tiniest chick. The delicacy with which a Hyacinth Macaw uses her *humongous* beak to feed a chick is amazing. The parrot beak can crack the hardest shell of the most protected nut and delicately pick out all of the nutmeat or carefully snip a delicate flower blossom from its twig. A group of parrot beaks working together can quickly and indiscriminately rip and shred almost all the foliage and flowers from a rain forest tree. In Costa Rica, I watched a flock of Mealy Amazons do just this to a flowering tree just outside a village. The beak can carry and hold food or nesting material while a parrot flies or climbs through the trees or around his or her cage. The beak tip has something called a Herbst's Corpuscle. This is an encapsulated bundle of highly sensitive nerve endings. The tongue is equally sensitive and combined with the beak, the parrot senses as much about what she is touching as a human can tell by touching something with his finger. Whenever you do anything to a parrot's beak, remember how sensitive it is.

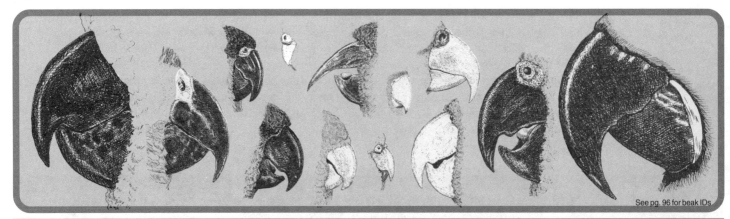

See pg. 96 for beak IDs

The Beak As A Tool of Defense

Defensive Weapon

Despite the fact that beaks have many more uses, when a parrot is threatened or pushed hard enough, he will use it as a defensive weapon. Parrots can also be patterned to bite for less obvious reasons. Before they actually bite, many parrots start out with negative body language or a fairly harmless warning bite that some people don't take seriously. If their more gentle warnings are continually ignored, the warnings can become far less subtle. Parrot beaks come in different shapes and sizes. Almost everyone who has been bitten swears that his or her own parrots have the absolute worst bite. That, of course, is a subjective opinion. I think the parrot who has the worst bite is the one that is biting you so I hate the idea of judging parrot species by which ones are the worst biters. I am not bragging when I make this statement, but I have been bitten by just about every species of parrot commonly kept as a human companion and they all have their bad "points." Some parrots pinch, some pry, some poke, some grind, some gouge, some slash, some clamp, and some are stubborn enough to hang on until they are pried off. A few will sucker you in with a sweet "I love you" before they chomp down. I have been told that because of the grinding action of the beak, the huge beak of a macaw can't possibly be used to bite your finger off but this is little reassurance when one who is upset has your digit firmly clamped in his beak. I suppose the bigger parrots can cause more damage but even little parrot family birds like Cockatiels, Budgies, Lovebirds, Lories, and Parrotlets can provide painful bites. In fact, it seems like the little guys keep their beaks extra sharp. Over the years, I gradually became stoic about being bitten and actually learned to show little, if any, reaction. For a long time, I have taken full responsibility for the vast majority of the bites I have received but hopefully, I know enough about parrots to avoid being bitten unless I forget my own advice and get sloppy.

Looking back ...

I think the most painful bite I ever received was from a wild-caught Military Macaw. He had been imported at least three years before I was called and no one had ever handled him. They called him "Slasher" in the pet shop because he lunged at anyone who came near the cage. They wanted him tamed and my first job was to get him out of a large cage with a very small door. It was next to impossible and I finally had to use a glove, a towel, and a stick. I hated to approach him in this manner but I had little choice. True to his nickname, he slashed my left index finger to the bone as I brought him out of the cage. Once I got him out of the cage there was no way I was going through that hassle again despite the fact that my finger was bleeding profusely. Believe it or not ... within less than a half an hour he was stretched out on his back in my lap all fluffed up with me skritching him under his wings. The short

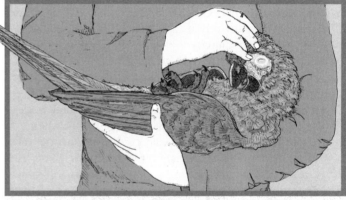

Parrots are very empathic and usually reflect our energy when we are with them. Learning to lower your energy and become calm with a parrot so that he doesn't sense aggression or fear is one of the best ways to win his trust.

version of this story is that I lowered my energy to the point where he could sense neither aggression nor fear. I gently put the heel of my hand against the top of his beak and was then able to start skritching his head and neck. Parrots are very social and physical with each other and he hadn't experienced any pleasure in years so he just melted into my hands.

...or maybe the worst bite was the Yellow-nape who bit clear through that sensitive fleshy area between the index finger and thumb. That one was absolutely my fault. I had been bird sitting and taught him several new tricks. When his caregiver came to get him, I wanted to show off his new tricks but the "love triangle" was more than he could handle.

... but perhaps the worst bite was from a wild-caught Moluccan I kept for a few years after rescuing him from a place where people mostly sat around and did drugs. When I first started working to win his trust, he put his whole beak around my wrist and clamped down. My fingers were numb for several days. I think the funniest bite I ever received was the time I was working with another wild-caught Moluccan. As I laddered him slowly from hand to hand, every fiber of his being screamed that he wanted to bite me. Despite this, he wasn't going to bite me as long as I was making eye contact with him. I put him down beside me on the couch and leaned forward to talk to his caregiver. At that moment, the cockatoo lunged at my backside with his beak and then took off running across the room squealing with delight. He didn't really bite but I ended up with quite a blood blister where I sit down. The bite that hurt my feelings the most was many years ago when my beloved Double-yellow Head Amazon, Paco, who was then 3-years-old, preferred my blonde friend. I was jealous and puckered up to ask Paco for a kiss ... after five stitches in my lip I knew that I would never let that happen again!

I can't possibly remember all the times I was bitten when I first started working with parrots but each bite taught me something important about parrot behavior ... and I still have the use of all of my fingers. After awhile, I was rarely bitten unless I forgot one of the lessons I had learned the hard way from the parrots. I think the most important lesson I learned was that if I thought a parrot was going to bite me — he usually did. If I calmed myself down, focused completely on what I was doing and convinced myself that I wouldn't be bitten — I rarely was.

Fundamentals of *Nurturing Guidance*™

Nurturing Guidance™ is the umbrella term for the theories and concepts I have developed over more than a quarter of a century working with companion parrots. (For more specific information, please refer to The Companion Parrot Handbook.) The following are fundamentals of this theory:

◯ All interaction should be trust-building — not trust-destroying.

◯ Parrots are more comfortable with people who are comfortable with them.

◯ Parrots are capable of bonding and re-bonding on many different levels throughout their lives and they can form different types of relationships with both people and other parrots. The concept of the one-person bird is often a self-fulfilling prophecy.

◯ Realistic expectations are critical. We must accept the basic personalities of our parrots and their limitations.

◯ It is our responsibility to protect our parrots as much as possible from threatening, dangerous, and traumatic situations.

◯ Punishment, abandonment, aggression, quick-fixes, and physical abuse of any kind destroy trust and are not effective toward changing behaviors in a positive manner. Aggression and punishment is most often met with aggression and negative behavior.

◯ Quick-fixes do not create long-term behavioral solutions and are often trust-destroying.

◯ The best way to stop negative behavior is to spend more time giving focused attention time your parrot — particularly time spent in instructional interaction.

◯ The foundation established with a domestically-raised parrot by the early caregivers (including the breeder, hand-feeders, and new human flock) is the greatest influence on lifelong pet potential.

◯ *Behavior* is a response to a situation (also known as a stimulus) occurring in a companion parrot's life and home environment. Without guidance, responses are unpredictable and often create negative behaviors.

◯ Parrots are instinctively wild birds and need our guidance to adjust to life in our living rooms.

◯ Without positive guidance, parrots will develop substitute behaviors for unsuccessful natural responses. It is the conflict between natural behaviors and an unnatural environment that causes confusion and inappropriate, nonproductive behaviors.

◯ Negative behaviors can be changed if the caregivers have the knowledge to work with their parrots in a positive, consistent, nurturing manner.

◯ Parrots will test their caregivers during behavioral work because the status quo is more comfortable.

◯ Parrots are highly empathic and often mirror our energy and mood. Our high energy and/or bad moods can negatively affect a parrot's behavior. Lowering our energy can help parrots relax and respond to us with a calmer more focused energy.

◯ Parrots are capable of learning throughout their entire lives.

◯ Parrots learn through patterning — the repetition of situations. They can be patterned to negative or positive behaviors.

◯ We actually teach, or at least encourage, many of the negative behaviors our parrots develop as companions. Many problem behaviors are a reaction our inconsistency, mixed messages, lack of focus and other confusing behaviors. If we don't consistently change our behavior towards our parrots, they won't change their behavior.

◯ Parrots are more likely to learn from people and be less territorial and aggressive in a *neutral room*. This is an unfamiliar room (or area of the house) where they can't see their cage and where they have not established a sense of territory or a need to display territorial protective behavior.

◯ Changes are rarely, if ever, linear from step A to step B. They are often 3 steps forward, 2 steps back, 1 step forward, etc.

◯ Losing hand control of a companion parrot is usually the first step in losing tameness. Maintaining the ability to handle a parrot is essential for his or her continued pet potential. Fear of being bitten is the major cause of losing hand control.

◯ Companion parrots can be *drama addicts*, often perceiving any dramatic response, even if it is negative, as a positive reward. We need to be aware of our behavior around our parrots as part of figuring out why they do the things they do.

◯ Aggressive biting, excessive screaming, phobic fears, behavioral feather picking, and other common companion parrot problem behaviors are symptoms of greater problems. These problems may be that a parrot in control of his life is doing a bad job of it, or that a parrot is not receiving proper emotional and/or physical care. Illness and injury often create problem behaviors. Confusion and fear can also influence behavioral problems. Treating the symptoms with quick-fixes only acts as a distraction and does not teach the bird anything about not biting, not screaming, stopping feather picking, or other negative responses.

◯ We must establish ourselves as the *flock leaders* in the cage territory and be able to easily take our parrot out of his cage with the word "UP." If we share the territory as members of the flock, we can avoid aggression due to territoriality.

◯ We must be decisive and assertive with our parrots without being aggressive and overbearing.

◯ We should never force our parrots to do anything that makes them frightened or traumatized, unless it is an emergency situation. We must gradually introduce new objects, strangers, and unfamiliar situations so they become familiar and acceptable.

◯ We must learn to sort through all advice and information with common sense and a cause-and-effect logic. Anticipation and preparation are the best ways to avoid problems and dangerous situations. Think about your parrot's possible response or any potential dangers before you do something involving him. (If I do this ... this could happen.)

◯ Establishing a positive lifelong relationship with a parrot requires the caregivers to take full responsibility for the parrot's behavioral development and for maintaining his or her full potential as a successful companion.

◯ **Behavioral problems are <u>NEVER</u> the parrot's fault.** ✒

The Major Companion Parrot Problem

No Surprise

Since 1999, we have been working on an in-depth survey about companion parrots. We have received thousands of responses and, at this time, we still have a long way to go in entering all of the responses to the Companion Parrot Quarterly Questionnaire. However, there are some aspects of parrot keeping that are becoming very clear. It comes as no surprise to me that aggression and biting are the number one reason that people do not keep their parrots. The following is just a sampling of the responses to the question, "What would be a serious enough behavioral problem for you to decide to find another home for your parrot/s?"

- Serious biting issues.
- Uncontrollable attacks.
- If he went after the kids
- Viciously attacking others.
- If he killed another parrot.
- Biting and aggressive behavior.
- Injuring other birds and people.
- Turning mean towards the kids.
- If I required stitches in my face.
- Excessive, deliberate aggression.
- Only if he became very aggressive.
- If he became dangerous to my child.
- Aggression that couldn't be corrected.
- Injury from a high level of aggression.
- Aggressive biting that I could not curb.
- Aggressive biting when I have children.
- Any bites from the bird that draw blood.
- Vicious, unpredictable attacks on everybody.
- Incurable biting after unsuccessful treatment.
- Aggression to my wife and women in general.
- Very severe biting problem to any family member.
- If he attacked my newborn baby which he hasn't.
- Parrot so untame it would be dangerous to keep him.
- Aggressive biting — I would put parrot in breeding program.
- If I was totally unable to handle him because of his aggression.
- If he drew blood all the time and there was no other alternative.
- Severe biting problems — can't take chances. It could be an eye.
- Severe enough aggression that I couldn't do cleaning and feeding.
- They would have to be pretty damn mean to me — so far so good.

The Importance of Education

Another very interesting aspect of the survey shows that respondents who subscribe to the Companion Parrot Quarterly (CPQ) are more likely to try and work through behavioral problems than non-subscribers. While it would be nice to presume this was only because of all the CPQ's good parrot behavior information over the years, it also has to do with the fact that many subscribers are the type of people who want to learn as much as possible about their parrots. I have always believed that educated parrot caregivers are more likely to find solutions for problem behavior than they are to find a new home for their parrots. I believe one of the major reasons this is true is because educated parrot caregivers have both realistic expectations and a better understanding of the complexities of their parrots' personalities.

Is Parrot Aggression Natural?

Is aggression in parrots natural or do we teach them to be this way in our relationships with them? There is some truth to both of these questions. From all I have learned over the years of working with parrots, I believe they are rarely offensively aggressive. In other words, they rarely attack without provocation. Most of their innate aggression is defensive — a response to a perceived threat or defense of what they perceive as theirs whether it is food, nesting territory, or a mate. Companion parrots have a full complement of these same instinctive behaviors. But if companion parrots do not usually initiate aggression, why do some seem to attack people for "no reason at all." First of all, the parrot usually has a reason even if it is not always apparent to the people in his life. Parrot logic is very different from human logic. If we can't try our best to see life from the parrot's perspective, we will not be successful caregivers. Some "aggressive" actions may actually be your parrot's idea of a game.

I have heard many opinions about parrot aggression. Some people make the absolute statement that biting and aggressive behavior is not natural and others insist it **is** just as emphatically. While one behavioral faction insists that you should never "make" a bird do anything he doesn't want to, another insists that you have to be the "boss." One popular statement is that all parrots, no matter how tame, will (viciously) bite someone someday. Many people who filled out the survey indicated that they were living in fear that someday, somehow their sweet bappy would turn into an aggressive biting monster. One woman said, "Please tell me he won't change!" All young parrots do change but it certainly doesn't mean they all "turn mean."

One Man's Nibble is Another's Bite

When I talk to people with "problem" parrots, the definition of aggression can be extremely varied. For some, biting means a parrot who playfully chews on their fingers and pinches from time to time. The word aggression is often used to describe a parrot in *overload* behavior that is actually excitement and over-stimulation. Hormonal behavior can result in aggression but paying close attention to the parrot's body language can prevent a great deal of overtly aggressive behavior. Overload and hormonal behavior may also result in predictable aggression but it certainly does not come from the same origins as aggression from a "mean" parrot. I don't think I have really worked with a parrot that was innately "mean" and I don't believe that companion parrots "turn mean." Those parrots who exhibit serious aggression towards people have usually been treated in a manner that develops that behavior whether it is a lack of guidance or aggressive behavior from the people in their life.

Information Overload

Often, aggressive behavior in parrots is a result of ignorant caregivers. We used to suffer from a shortage of information. Now there is almost an overload of information that can be very confusing. We all want to keep our parrots as tame as possible throughout our lives with them. How can we know what information will really help our relationship with our parrots? There are few absolutes in parrot behavior because there are so many variables that influence it. The major influences are:
➜ Species characteristics
➜ The individual parrot's personality.
➜ The quality of the parrot's early socialization.
➜ The parrot's life experiences.
➜ The physical environment.
➜ The parrot's individual relationship with each person in the household.
➜ The parrot's interaction with his *human flock* as a group.
➜ The complex personality of each individual in the parrot's household and their interactions with each other.

Our Aggression

Because there are so many variables that affect a parrot's behavior, handling and corrections that seem aggressive to one bird may be effective tools with another but there are limits. I would never handle my grey, Whodee, in the same way that I play with Spikey, my high energy Caique. Some of the things I do with him might seem aggressive to other people. Spike doesn't see them this way because he seems to consider most of life as his own amusement park. He is rarely threatened by anything in his life. He can also be

Biting parrots should not be punished. They don't understand the concept of cause and effect and using aggression creates returned aggression or fear. A distraction and a quick look of disapproval is often the most effective way to deal with biting when it happens.

very willful at times. While I don't believe in punishment, especially aggressive discipline and mistreatment, I do not feel it is abusive to express disapproval to a misbehaving bird. Of course, like so many aspects of parrot behavior, these terms are open to misinterpretation. Words do have power and people seem to have varying concepts as to the definition of words like aggression, assertiveness, control, dominance, discipline, and punishment.

If (I mean <u>when</u>) Spike misbehaves, I try to be consistent in my response so there is no question in his mind that I disapprove of his behavior at that moment. Parrots pick up our body language and energy so quickly; I do not have to do much. I usually say his name quickly followed by the word NO in a firm but not shouting voice. I accompany the exclamation with a quick disapproving look. I call this the "evil eye" but the dirty look I give him takes only a second. He usually gets the message immediately and is not the least bit threatened by this assertive communication. However, if I am in a bad mood or very frustrated with something else and go beyond my normal response to him, my anger is much more about me than it is with what he did. If this happens, he does become insecure and can react with fear. It is not fair for me to overreact to the incident because Spike has no way of knowing that the escalation from disapproval to anger has nothing to do with him. It is as important for Spike to be able to reliably read my body language as it is for me to be able to read his. My response to him should only have to do with what happened at that immediate moment and must be consistent. This seems to be contrary to human nature as so many of us tend to bring all of our baggage into our relationships, even those with our animal companions.

Making Our Parrots Do Something

Among people working with companion parrots, some of the most fanatical and perhaps pointless arguments are often more about the syntax of words rather than behavioral theory. An example is the unequivocal statement that one should **never** *make* a parrot do anything he doesn't want to do. This statement is, of course, open to a great deal of disagreement. Does this mean that we are to ask our parrots if they want to do something first or ask their permission and make a request? Should it then be their decision instead of ours? Perhaps the disagreement is in each individual's interpretation of what "making" a parrot do something means.

There are many times we must "make" parrots do what they don't want to. This is evident to anyone who has lived with a curious parrot. If one of my parrots is chewing on an electrical cord, I am certainly going to "make" him stop whether he wants to or not. I want Spike to be cute, not *electro-cute* (sorry). Obviously, one of our greatest responsibilities is to prevent parrots from getting into trouble by making our household safe and not letting them get into dangerous situations. To me, the idea of making a parrot do something he does not want to do does not carry as much onus as "forcing" him to do something. I don't believe that parrots should be forced to do something against their will unless it in the parrot's best interests or involves a dangerous situation.

Most parrot caregivers know that parrots can be incredibly stubborn if they don't want to do something. An example is the concept of "making" a parrot go back in his cage when you need to go to work or leave the house. People who understand parrots or have read the CPQ long enough know that it can be futile to try to get a parrot to go back in his cage if the caregiver is in a hurry. The more rushed and frantic the person becomes, the less compliant the parrot will be. Trying to insist or force the parrot to comply usually escalates the lack of cooperation. In fact, if this frenzied unsuccessful situation is repeated enough times, the lack of cooperation will become entrenched in the bird's patterning. If this happens, it will become almost impossible to get a parrot back in his cage without forcing him to go. Eventually this type of interaction can create serious problems in the parrot/human bond. It actually will take less time to get a parrot back in his cage if the person retreats and then calmly re-approaches the bird. This usually makes an incredible difference. When we are calm and relaxed, our verbal commands and requests receive much more cooperation because they are not confusing.

I have always liked the word "cajole" in getting parrots to do something I want them to do. Synonyms for cajole are coax, persuade, wheedle, sweet talk, flatter. If I want one of my parrots to do something, I find that flattering him with calm sweet talk and then using a quiet but decisive "UP" command goes much farther than barking a command at them in an aggressive tone.

Bongo Marie's Compliance

As I look back to my relationship with my legendary African grey, Bongo Marie, I realize that we had just about the right balance of asking and making without forcing. She and I shared our lives for over a quarter of a century. She was not a young bird and she was very sick when she came to live with me so I feel blessed that I had so much time with her. Besides being the smartest parrot who ever lived (no bias there, huh?), Bongo was very much in tune to my mood and body language. If she was out of her cage and saw me do anything that looked like I was going somewhere, she would climb back into her cage. She was so well patterned that most of the time, all I had to do was to start looking for my shoes or my car keys and she would take it as a cue to go back in her cage. One time my mother was visiting and Bongo managed to get out of her cage because I had not latched the door properly. I was not home and Bongo started climbing down the cage towards the floor. My mother looked at her and said, "Bongo, you go back in your cage right now." She looked at my mother, froze for a minute, and then climbed back up and went into her cage.

This is not to say that she did not occasionally like to play games with me but we both pretty much knew they were games. If I repeated my request in a gentle voice, she would usually comply. Bongo was usually compliant because our long-term relationship was based on mutual trust. She trusted that I would not do something that was not in her best interests and I trusted that she would not bite me when I picked her up or gave her a kiss. Of course, this was all dependent on how we read each other's body language. She had lived with me long enough to

Creating a balance of mutual trust is the best way to create a well-behaved parrot. I lived with my African Grey, Bongo Marie, for a quarter of a century and, although she had occasional moments of stubbornness, she was a very agreeable parrot most of the time. I believe this was because she always trusted me to be there and do the right thing for her.

pick up many subtle cues from my body language. Over a period of time, many sensitive caregivers become aware of the fact that their parrots become so attuned to them that they often do not have to give commands for their parrots to do something. However, I think that verbal commands (cues) are still important because they add a consistency to both the caregiver's request and the parrot's response.

There are friendly ways we can get parrots to do what we want them to, even if it is not what they want to do, without making them do it. As stated earlier, if I have to leave the house and I have to put one of my parrots back in his cage, I can try various approaches. If I am in a hurry, I simply walk over to the cage and use the "UP" command (or cue — some people prefer this word as it seems to imply less force or "dominance" than the word command.) All of my parrots have been patterned to respond positively to a friendly "Up" command so there is usually no problem. One minor exception is when Spike is eating a special treat like a pistachio nut. If I have to pick him up when he is being food possessive, I have to distract him first. Usually I snap my fingers on my other hand to bring him out of his pistachio nut trance. This brings up a very important point. We have to be aware of what our parrots are doing before we make them (or ask them) to do something we want them to do (or something they may not want to do.) Sometimes you just have to leave a parrot alone and let him do what he is doing if it is not destructive or dangerous to him.

When I use the "UP" command, I say it in a friendly yet firm way. I always try to approach my parrot in an enthusiastic and positive manner even if I am not feeling particularly positive at the time. When they respond by stepping on my hand, I reward them with sweet talking verbal praise — "Oh what a good bird." In return, they reflect my energy and are usually quite cooperative. However, if I am too preoccupied and oblivious to what they are doing, upset or in a hurry, my parrots are not usually very cooperative. This is when trying to make one of my parrots do something leads to my failure. If I become more assertive or aggressive about insisting they do what I want, then aggression can become even more of a problem. It is better for me to just forget it for the moment and regroup. Again, the more I insist and the more it becomes something I am making them do, the less likely they are to do it. At some point this insistence can become aggressive and it becomes trust-destroying.

There are certainly times when we have to make our parrots do something they do not want to do. I know of few parrots who are happy about going to the veterinarian and certainly we must take them there whether they want to go or not. However, we can do many things ahead of time to make the visit much less traumatic. We can get them used to traveling in their carriers in the car with short rides around the neighborhood. We can play with them in a towel so it is not such a threatening means of capture. We can investigate ahead of time so that we know that the veterinarian and staff are comfortable, considerate, and competent with parrot handling. We can introduce our parrots to their veterinarians in a friendly manner and most of all we can stay calm while they are being examined. If we become upset or anxious by watching the veterinarian handle our parrots, it is best to leave the room so no more negative energy is added to what is usually already a threatening situation.

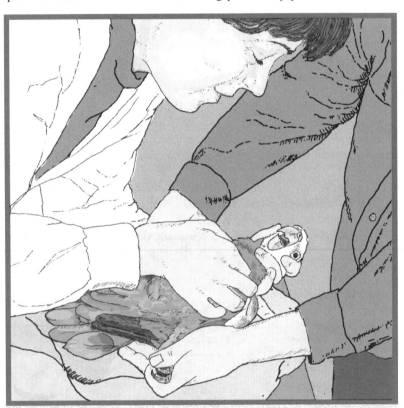

While a veterinarian will most likely have to do examinations, testing, and/or procedures that will make your parrot uncomfortable or even cause him pain, the general atmosphere should always be one that is protective and benevolent towards the parrot. If your parrot becomes stressed or traumatized, it is best just to let him rest when he comes home. Trying to handle him right away may stress him even more.

Lost in Syntax

In the past several years, there has been a great deal of argument about the choice of words behavioral writers have used to describe certain behavioral concepts. Words do have a great deal of power and it easy for a writer to be misunderstood. Behavioral writers need to choose words carefully when we describe human/parrot interaction. However, many of us seem to be lost in the subtle meanings of words when it is our intent, compassion, and energy towards our parrots that is important. For their own good, we do need to make our parrots do things they do not want to do but we can strive to make these situations as pleasant as possible. We can also show them that we are competent in the decisions we make for their lives — that they can trust us to do the right things for them. Although we may not want to **make** a parrot do something he does not want to do, the truth is that our goal is to do something that will result in the parrot doing what we want or need him to. The more we understand ways to win our parrots' trust and then calmly guide their behavior, the more they will cooperate with us. The more we try to coerce them (instead of cajoling them), the less likely it is that they will cooperate. This lack of cooperation can escalate into serious problems for both parrots and the people in their lives. ✒

The Worst Biter Award goes to ....

I have worked with people who have purchased parrots despite the fact that they are afraid of them — especially the parrot-family birds with big beaks. Unfortunately, this can even be true with people who have purchased the most gentle baby parrots. Starting life together being afraid of your companion parrot will create serious problems. Often, because of the parrot's response to mixed messages and inconsistency, the very fear of being bitten will have the direct result of turning a parrot into a biter. Parrots don't bite because they are mean. Most often, they bite because they are confused, threatened or have learned to bite as a communication in certain situations. The more a parrot bites, the more that behavior becomes an established pattern in his behavior.

Certain parrot species have reputations for being more aggressive than others. However, I do not intend to provide a breakdown on what parrot species are more or less aggressive because I believe this has much more to do with the way they have been raised and the guidance they receive than the tendency for a certain species to be aggressive. Often people who say that a certain species or gender of that species is aggressive state this because this has been their experience with their own parrots. It is absurd to jump to the conclusion that all parrots of that particular species are, therefore, aggres-

Even a Budgie can create quite a painful bite if he gets overexcited — especially if he gets one of the more tender parts of the human anatomy. Some of the smaller parrot-family birds can be quite tenacious and may hang on until they are pried off.

sive. For every aggressive parrot I know in a given species, I have known another who has exhibited little, if any, aggression. While it is clear that some species may have higher energy, a bigger beak, or a sharper beak, it does not necessarily follow that these parrots are more aggressive.

Not all parrot bites come from aggression. Some are from overexcited play while others are an immediate response to a threatening or frightening situation. These bites can usually be managed by being aware of the parrot's body language and what is going on in the environment when you are with him. Many parrots clamp or nip as a communication that says, "I am not comfortable with this situation" and these bites are not usually a big problem unless the person being bitten response in a way that causes more aggression. If the caregiver ignores that warning, he or she may experience an escalation of that biting behavior. To me, the worst bites come from parrots who have learned to bite and, therefore, intend to bite. Often this biting has become patterned because of aggression from the people in the parrot's life. The intentional bite is usually a strong message stating, "I am not comfortable with you and/or this situation — LEAVE ME ALONE!"

I think bites from little birds are often unexpected and start as a tenacious "jackhammer" series of bites. Perhaps a series of bites from a small parrot may not be as injurious as one big bite from a larger parrot, but both indicate that there is a problem in the parrot/human bond. In my years of working with parrots, I have met only a few that could not become more trusting and gentle in response to nurturing care and guidance from their human flock.

A playful bite from a Hyacinth can cause quite a pinch. These macaws, the largest of the parrot family, have the most massive parrot beak and are capable of cracking the hardest nuts. However, because the upper and lower mandibles are used together as a grinding tool, they cannot "chop" off your finger.

Basics of Biting & Aggressive Behavior

The Easiest Problem To Solve

Although biting is probably the most common behavioral problem in companion parrots, it is generally the easiest to solve. However, this is only true if the person works with his parrot in productive ways. Some fail in their attempts to stop their parrots from biting because they try to permanently change behavior by using quick fixes, punishment, returned aggression, and/or drama rewards. There is also a rampant misconception that just letting the bird bite and taking those bites without reacting is the best way to teach a parrot not to bite. All this usually does is pattern the biting behavior even more.

Most caregivers identify biting as the behavioral problem but this type of aggression is usually only the symptom of greater problems. Although the reasons that parrots bite can be quite complex, the underlying causes of aggressive behavior are usually the same — *caregivers who do not know how to set rules or provide guidance, and/or confused parrots in control of their own lives and doing a bad job of it because there have been no behavioral guidelines established.*

Baby parrots are adorable and, if raised properly, full of wide-eyed curiosity.

Baby Parrots are Adorable

Once they start getting their feathers, baby parrots are hard to resist. If they are well-socialized, bappies are full of wide-eyed curiosity and eager to learn about their surroundings. Our goal with domestically-raised birds is to insure that they will stay as sweet as possible as they mature. Parrots simply do not make good companions if they are not taught to be good companions. Even human-raised bappies do not know how to adjust to life as a pet without a teacher or surrogate parent guiding their behavior. They are not instinctively prepared to live the life of a human companion, and the behaviors parrots learn from their early interactions with people will be the behaviors they exhibit throughout life, unless work is done to change them at a later time. Because parrots are intelligent animals and are capable of learning throughout their entire lives, teaching new behaviors will require the caregiver to have good behavioral information. Most behavioral changes start with humans changing their behaviors towards their parrot. *Long-term consistency and patience on the part of the owner are essential.*

Proper early socialization with *Nurturing Guidance* is imperative for a young bird to develop into a successful human companion. However, even the pet potential of a chick who has been wonderfully prepared by the breeder/hand-feeder can be seriously jeopardized by a caregiver who cannot or will not provide proper guidance.

Biting Usually Doesn't Start as Aggression

Most biting does not start as aggression. Remember, the parrot beak is not inherently a weapon, but a sensory organ used to touch and explore. Much of the exploration parrots do with their beaks is not even biting. Bappies particularly love to explore everything around them as part of their learning process. If the exploration gets a little rough, and even painful at times, this beaking and tonguing of our skin, particularly our fingers, is still based on play or affection. We need to teach our parrots how far they can go with their *beakiness*. Exploration should certainly not be punished or even discouraged, but working with your parrot to keep his beak manipulation gentle will save you some pinches and little *birdie hickeys*. Most bappies can easily be trained to recognize the pain threshold of their human friends. When a parrot gets too excited or rough and starts pinching with pressure, softly say the word "gentle." Be consistent, so he gets the message that this type of beak exploration is unacceptable. If he is too excited to be gentle, slow things down by calmly removing your hands from his beak area. If he becomes too willful or stubborn, he may need a more assertive response from you in the form of a "No" and a quick disapproving look. If this doesn't work, he may need to go back to his cage or playgym for a time-out — not as punishment, but to cool down.

Unfortunately, many people actually teach their parrots to bite. In the beginning it may be play but dramatically wiggling your fingers in the face of an excited parrot to try to get him to stop chewing on you makes grabbing and biting fingers more of a game. We teach this game of chewing or biting on wiggling fingers, and it is probably one of the most common games excited parrots play with people. Once the game has been patterned, the parrot will often initiate it by chewing on fingers to encourage the person to wiggle them even more. While this may be OK up to a point, this game can become quite intense if the parrot becomes too excited. Keep a foot toy nearby to stick in his beak to give him something else to chew on besides your fingers. A toy made from knotted 100% cotton rope or vegetable tanned leather usually does the trick.

Teaching A Parrot To Bite

Biting aggression in companion parrots is often developed from interaction with the people in their lives. In the wild, parrots are prey animals not predators, and it appears that parrots rarely initiate aggression. However, they can become aggressive as a defense if they are threatened. It is a misconception to presume that most biting in parrots is a result of aggressive behavior. Many people remark that their parrots become *mean*. Parrots are not mean because they bite. Some aggressive behavior is a response to aggression from people but the vast majority of biting I see in companion parrots develops because the parrot is given confusing mixed messages and is then unintentionally rewarded for biting in his interaction with people.

Playful chewing rarely turns into biting unless the person makes a big deal about it. If a parrot is chewing on your fingers and it hurts, calmly tell him to be "gentle." If this doesn't solve the problem, give him a rope/leather knot toy to chew on instead.

Once a parrot is in his new home, he either develops his own behaviors or learns from his owners how to behave. A companion parrot will not naturally develop the traits that will make him a contented companion. The new human flock must show their pet how to behave in acceptable ways. The problem is that many parrot people do not realize that they are teaching their parrots the traits that make them a "bad" companion parrot. A parrot can quickly learn that the best way to get people to leave him alone is to bite them. A parrot who bites actually needs to be handled more, not less! The parrot who bites often does so because his caregiver has reinforced or rewarded the bird for biting. Without realizing it, many people are actually teaching their parrots to bite. A caregiver who is aware of the dynamics of aggression and biting can prevent a parrot from developing these behaviors.

The first step in preventing and solving biting behavior is to understand a bit about what makes our avian companions so special and unique in the world of pets. Understanding that parrots are still instinctively wild animals is the first step in understanding why they act the way they do. Biting, especially of other flock or family members does not seem to be a natural behavior among wild parrots. So why has biting become such a serious problem for so many people with parrots in their lives? Is it natural for a domestically-raised, handfed parrot to become aggressive to people — particularly the people in his human flock? Should every parrot owner live in fear that eventually his tame companion parrot will suddenly turn on him and become aggressive? Can anything be done to prevent this from happening?

Although guiding a parrot's behavior from the time he is young will most likely prevent serious and permanent aggression, there may still be times throughout a companion parrot's life when he may go through aggressive periods. How we understand and manage these periods of aggressive behavior make a major difference in maintaining the continuing pet potential of our parrots. We need to understand our parrots and learn the best ways to react to his negative aggressive behaviors so that they don't become a normal pattern in his life and/or a way to communicate with us.

Reasons that Biting Starts

While aggression does develop in some handfed parrots, I do not believe it is necessarily natural for companion parrots to become aggressive. Aggressive behavior and biting in parrots rarely starts as aggression — normally it starts as one or more of the following:

⮺ Was he just exploring you with his beak and you overreacted, or was he really biting?

⮺ Parrots have no idea how to be good pets and biting is often one of the results of lack of guidance.

⮺ Confusion in response to mixed messages, inconsistencies, or lack of predictability from the *human flock*. Biting is often the result of mixed messages from the human flock.

⮺ A response to changes in life routine — especially a decrease in affection and attention or an increase of stress in the home environment. Parrots often have adverse reactions to sudden changes in their lives.

⮺ The parrot's defense of territory and/or a perceived mate, when he is allowed to control his own life and is doing a bad job of it. Although it may seem illogical to us, often the favorite person receives the aggression.

⮺ A fear or confronting response to threatening behavior from people who handle him aggressively or inconsistently. Aggressive behavior towards a parrot is almost always met with aggression from the parrot.

⮺ Was he trying to tell you something and after exhibiting all sorts of communicative behavior, biting was the only way to get his point across? Was he in pain? Did he hurt himself? Is he sick? Did something frighten him?

⮺ Overload behavior is a major cause of biting in normally tame companion parrots. Most parrots are easily excited and become over-stimulated when playing with people, other parrots, and/or their toys. Interrupting a parrot who is over-stimulated without letting him calm down first is one of the easiest ways to invite a bite.

⮑ Some parrots have one-track minds when it comes to what they want to do. For example, a poorly guided parrot may absolutely insist on climbing up to his owner's shoulder or chewing on a pair of glasses. The aggravation of a person trying to stop this behavior often results in a drama reward increasing the excitable behaviors. If the parrot is so determined to do something he is not supposed to do that he can't be distracted to another more acceptable *project*, it is best to leave him on his stand or put him back in his cage to calm down.

⮑ Some parrots seem to test their human flock to see if they are really "qualified" to be providing guidance. This is the major reason it is so important to provide consistent guidance.

⮑ Sexual bonding and territoriality when a parrot has become too strongly bonded to one person as a mate can initiate a bite. Some, but certainly not all, parrots can become difficult during times of hormonal influence. This is particularly true with what I call "super males." These are cocks (especially cockatoos) who become aggressively dominant during breeding season. Setting a positive foundation, recognizing body language, temporarily redefining the relationship, and being very patient during times of hormonal influence helps caregivers remain lifetime friends with these parrots. Not all males exhibit these behaviors and some hens can be just as difficult during these times.

⮑ Sometimes parrots just go through cranky moods that their owners need to identify and understand if they want to avoid aggression.

When A Parrot Bites You

⮑ Respond as quietly as possible, without excitement or aggression. Reacting with anger or a drama reward can quickly escalate the aggression and reinforce the behavior. Yes, it hurts, but acting calmly helps keep the parrot from becoming even more over-stimulated and biting again. It also does not pattern biting behavior.

⮑ Don't take pride in the fact that your parrot bit you and show off the bite as your "red badge of courage."

⮑ Handle the situation yourself if you can. Don't allow another person — particularly the parrot's favorite person — to rescue you from being bitten. The parrot can quickly learn to bite you in order to go to another person.

⮑ Place the parrot down on a stand or piece of furniture as calmly as possible. If you are too frightened of being bitten again and need someone else to take control of the parrot, leave the room before he or she picks up the bird and returns him to his cage. Then, get past your fear of being bitten so that you can work with your parrot again. But first, calm down your energy by closing your eyes for a few seconds and taking a deep slow breath to relax.

⮑ Try to understand that it's not really the parrot's fault — most biting situations are beyond his control and are responses to situations in his environment he does not understand.

⮑ Don't punish the parrot — a pain response like "OW!" and/or a quick "Evil Eye" (a disapproving look that lasts no more than a few seconds) plus an immediate quick "NO!" are all he needs to know his behavior is not acceptable. Aggressive handling as a response to biting just encourages more aggressive behavior on the part of the parrot.

⮑ As soon as you calm down, use cause-and-effect logic to figure out why your parrot bit you. Most of the time there is a reason, and it often has to do with us not being aware of what we (or they) are doing when we approach them.

➤Did you not pay attention to his body language before you approached him? Was he pinning his eyes, lowering his head, or erecting his feathers?

➤Was he already in *overload behavior* from playing excitedly with a favorite toy or defending his favorite food?

➤Did you move too quickly or approach him when your energy was too stressed?

➤Did you just come back from jogging or were you having a heated argument with your spouse before you tried to handle your parrot?

➤Were you really focused on him when you tried to pick him up, or doing something else at the same time?

➤Did something or someone in the room startle him, causing a fear reaction?

➤Was he protecting you or another person from a perceived intruder?

➤Did you startle him by wearing a red baseball hat or something else you don't usually wear?

⮑ Just because your parrot bit you does not mean he does not "love" you. Don't take it personally. Biting usually means a parrot is reacting with confusion, or in some cases, fear, or hormonal influences.

⮑ If your bird bites you it does not automatically mean he has become a biting bird and cannot be trusted again. Most biting is based on an incident, and does not become a pattern unless you make it one.

Read your parrot's body language before you approach him. Trying to handle a parrot who is pinning his eyes will usually result in a bite!

Parrots are highly empathic easily picking up and sharing our moods. Approaching a parrot when you are exhibiting high-energy will result in a high-energy parrot. When your parrot is "wound up" the best way to calm him down is to slow down your own energy and give him some time to match your energy.

➲ While many parrots are protective of their perceived territory, mate, and flock, they rarely turn "mean." Normally, parrots who become excessively aggressive on a permanent basis do so for a reason. That reason almost always involves the parrot's relationship with the humans in his life.

A Tragic, but Common Scenario

Almost all parrots, at one time or another will bite someone, sometime, somewhere, for some (not always obvious) reason. What we do about it will often determine whether biting will be an incident or become a pattern. If we perceive the parrot as turning "mean" instead of trying to understand the problem, then the parrot/human relationship will suffer. Why does a tame, sweet, bonded parrot suddenly start to bite? The answer can be both simple and quite complicated at the same time. In a common scenario, the parrot, accustomed to a good amount of handling, becomes agitated when his owner does not give him the focused attention needed to keep him gentle and contented. Parrots don't always know how to ask appropriately, and often respond in ways that actually bring about the exact opposite of the nurturing handling they need. Parrots who are not getting enough attention can quickly become apprehensive, insecure, or simply "out of the habit" of being handled, especially when people are in a hurry or stressed, and they don't really focus on their birds. Another example of a first biting scenario is when a parrot is approached in an inappropriate manner. If it was the parrot's caregiver, perhaps he or she moved too quickly, too aggressively, or maybe he or she had been distracted. Whatever the situation, the person probably had a very different energy that threatened the parrot. If a stranger approached the parrot too directly before being introduced, and the parrot was startled or frightened, biting would be his best defense. It is the caregivers' responsibility to protect both their parrot from threatening situations and their friends from a confused, threatened, and therefore, aggressive parrot.

Parrots are highly reactive pets, and a stressed person usually means a stressed parrot. When a parrot becomes petulant, the person becomes less likely to handle him. The confused bird becomes increasingly uncomfortable being handled as the person becomes more uncomfortable. The bird bites. If the person is shocked, takes it personally, and has a dramatic, negative reaction, then the cycle continues with less handling and more biting. Perhaps the caregiver's response becomes more and more dramatic, increasing the excitability of the parrot. The negative behaviors of both the person and the parrot become patterned, and the vicious cycle continues until the owner gets good information on how to get past this cycle or loses patience and *gets rid of the bird*. A great deal of companion parrot pet potential can be lost when a person blames his or her parrot for biting and refuses to accept responsibility for managing the parrot's behavior to prevent future aggression. Unfortunately, too many good parrots are given up because of confusion and lack of knowledge on the part of the people in their lives. ∫

BEAKBITE TIP: Very Similiar Behaviors

A very high-energy man called me on the phone about problems with his Moluccan Cockatoo. He said the bird was fine with everyone else but him. The Cockatoo was a handfed baby who was about a year old. The man stated that he had lots of experience with parrots because his mother used to breed them. As I talked to him, I found myself feeling as if I was being assaulted. As we talked, he became more and more hyper and even, belligerent with me. He acted threatened by every question I asked him and argued with every suggestion I made. I vividly remember this phone call, not only because the man was so difficult to deal with, but mostly because of the irony of it. His description of his Cockatoo pretty much described my reaction to the caller. He told me that whenever he approached the Moluccan, the bird would become agitated, raise his crest, start screaming, and often would become aggressive towards him. He said the bird never acted this way with anyone else, yet refused to acknowledge that his behavior had anything to do with the way the Cockatoo acted around him. The only way this man would ever be successful with his 'too was to stop blaming the bird and to learn to approach the bird with lower energy.

Be Careful What You Teach Your Parrot

Parrots Mimic More Than Words

The more intelligent an animal is, the more it depends on learning to develop its personality and behavior. We all know that parrots are quite intelligent and as human companions, they depend on us, their caregivers, to teach them positive behaviors as they mature. Just as a baby parrot in the wild would watch his parents very closely to learn how to be a parrot, young companion parrots watch us closely and learn from our example and teaching. Parrots are not only capable of learning words from our language but also pattern many of their *actions* and *behaviors* according to what they see and hear us do. It is very important for caregivers to be aware of what they are actually teaching their parrots.

A Very Confusing Life

Life can be very confusing for young companion parrots who grow up without the proper guidance from the people in their lives. In the wild, their instinctive and learned behaviors are in harmony with each other. In our living rooms, instinctive behavior clashes with learned behavior often causing serious confusion as young parrots mature. Serious behavioral problems that may jeopardize the human/parrot bond can develop because people teach their impressionable young birds negative behaviors without realizing it.

Many parrots love to be cuddled and we usually enjoy giving them this type of affection. While cuddling is a wonderful part of living with most tame parrots, we need to encourage their natural curiosity and their sense of adventure and play. It is critical to provide them with lots of instructional interaction to teach them to be independent in such a dependent situation.

One Of The First Lessons

A baby parrot is a most delightful creature. They are soft, cuddly and full of wide-eyed innocence and curiosity. Many people make the mistake of giving their new parrots constant handling. Because of this, the first lesson that many baby parrots learn is that their humans are always available to hold them. Baby parrots, especially between the time they would naturally fledge and wean, can be very insecure and in need of a great deal of nurturing, guidance, and reassurance. This is a time when wild baby parrots would have almost constant supervision from their parents as they learn to explore their rapidly expanding world. The wild parent is not in constant physical contact but gives continual reassurance to the baby that everything is O.K. and that he or she is not going to be abandoned. This is the time that new parrot caregivers need to give their bappies lots of love and nurturing but must also help their parrot develop independence by encouraging them to play by themselves with close supervision and reassurance.

Teaching A Parrot To Bite

The first lesson in biting is usually pretty innocent and is most likely to start after the "honeymoon" period is over. The new caregiver decides that they do, indeed, have a real life to live and need to do something besides just play with their wonderful new parrot. They still want their new buddy to be with them but need to have their hands free for other endeavors so the person places their avian youngster on his or her shoulder.

Two of the most delightful traits of a parrot are his natural curiosity and sense of adventure. However, the person seems to expect this curious active parrot to just sit on his or her shoulder and behave. This is a very unrealistic expectation. The first thing that attracts the young explorer's attention is the "bird toy" hanging from the person's ear or that sort of floppy mole on his neck. The parrot's beak and tongue contain highly sensitive encapsulated bundles of nerve endings called corpuscles that tell the parrot a great deal about what it touches.

So the young bird starts exploring by "beaking" everything that attracts his attention. This is the way he learns just as a small child would explore new objects with his fingers. The person reaches up saying "hey, stop that and behave yourself!" The intelligent young bird may be distracted enough to sit still for a minute or so but soon the loose thread in the shirt collar or the shiny metal on the frames of his caregiver's glasses are too hard to resist.

Again, the previously patient caregiver reaches up chastising the "bad" bird for not behaving. After the third or fourth time he has gotten attention for poking at his owner with his beak, the young parrot quickly learns that each time he "misbehaves," he gets an exciting drama reward from the person in his life!

Being put in his cage is totally ineffective as punishment for the parrot and teaches him nothing about behaving properly. What he has learned from the immediate cause-and-effect is that all he has to do is poke at his caregiver with his beak and he will get lots of great attention. What a terrific game! Instead, people should plan shoulder-time by placing their parrots on the shoulder when there is something for him to do and/or the person has the patience to deal with his inquisitive explorations.

The Independence Stage

At first, the young companion parrot depends on his human flock to protect him and carefully introduce him to his somewhat scary new world. Other lessons in biting are inadvertently taught to parrots by their caregivers who may not have a good grasp of parrot cause-and-effect psychology. As the young bird matures and begins to feel comfortable in his environment, he reaches the natural stage where in the wild he would start to become independent from his parents. Although our pet parrots depend on us to care for them properly for their entire lives, it is still important for young birds to develop some sense of independence from the people in their lives. The "over-dependent" parrot does not learn to play with his toys or to entertain himself and can develop some serious behavioral problems as the relationship between caregiver and bird changes. As a previously docile companion parrot enters the major independence stage of his life, he can become quite willful and sometimes even aggressive to his caregivers. Often, the person, whose feelings are hurt, is shocked by this change and does not know what to do. If the owner has established "nurturing guidance" by consistently using the "UP" command to request that the parrot steps on his or her hand, the stubborn young bird will still be likely to follow the command because he has been patterned to do so. However, if the caregiver has not established this guidance patterning, this can be a very difficult time for the bond between owner and parrot. Tragically, it is often the time when many people lose the tameness of their handfed parrots.

One of the first indications that the independence stage has started is when a previously willing parrot no longer wants to step on the caregiver's hand just because it is there. They may not be as comfortable cuddling since they would rather be expending their energy with other pursuits. The young bird may seem moody and give mixed messages to his human flock. Often if the message is misunderstood, the parrot jabs at their hands for the first time. Again, the person who has established the "UP" command can just give their parrot a split second look of disapproval and use the command decisively to let the young bird know that his behavior is not acceptable. Without that foundation, the parrot will win and quickly gain control of the relationship. This can really be a problem because nothing has prepared this instinctively wild creature to really know how to behave as a human companion.

Typical Bad Advice

If the timid person gives in and goes away when an obstinate young parrot discovers the power of his beak, biting can become a behavior that becomes a part of the parrot's patterning. The confused caregivers don't know what to do when their sweet wonderful tame baby parrot bites them for the first time. Hurt feelings are usually more painful than the bite. Often, the owner seeks advice from a variety of people who may give all sorts of bad information that may make the problem even worse and actually encourage the young bird to become more of a biter.

⊃ "Grab the bird's beak and shake it!," is one that I hear all of the time. This is not punishment. In reality, one of the ways that parrots love to play with each other is to beak wrestle. As they become mature, beak wrestling becomes serious as part of courtship or even sexual foreplay. If beak shaking is done too aggressively it can actually damage the beak. "Pinch his toes," is another ineffective and aggressive piece of bad advice I hear. If the parrot perceives the "punishment" as aggression, it is likely that it will trigger him to be more aggressive.

Quick-fix punishments such as grabbing the beak and shaking it are not only ineffective in solving behavioral problems, they also can be trust destroying or stimulate the parrot to become even more aggressive.

⊃ Certainly, the often heard advice of "pop him one" is aggressive and inappropriate. It can easily destroy the trust and bonding that is so necessary in a good human/parrot relationship. Parrots are highly reflective of our moods and a parrot that is treated with aggression will return aggression.

⊃ A person's natural response to a bite from a beloved young parrot is total shock. The caregiver first reacts with surprise and pain, "OW! THAT HURTS!" This exclamation of pain by itself is not usually a problem and may actually help the young bird to understand that his bite hurt you. Any exclamations such as "why did you bite me like that?, you little monster!, how would you like me to bite you?, who do you think you are?, don't you love me anymore?, or why did you do that?" becomes a "drama reward" and may actually encourage future biting because of the immediate cause-and-effect.

⊃ "Put him in his cage to punish him. The harder he bites, the longer he should have to stay in his cage!" is another piece of ineffective advice given to bird owners whose parrots start biting. It may keep them from biting as long as they are in the cage but it won't teach them anything about not biting.

Parrots learn from immediate cause-and-effect. Just as a small child being punished quickly forgets why he is standing in the corner, parrots have no way of understanding that time in the cage is a punishment. However, consistent "punishment" by being admonished and then placed in the cage may actually encourage a parrot to become more territorial about his cage and, therefore, more likely to bite when someone approaches.

Calling The Bluff

At first, biting may be a bluff from a confused or moody parrot. The caregiver who calls their parrots' bluff in a positive way will continue to have a good companion. I have found that the most successful way to deal with the first bite is to regroup for a minute or so, slow down and approach the parrot more calmly and decisively. A clear "UP" command combined with focused attention and the use of one hand for the parrot to step on and the other as a distraction can be very effective. The caregiver needs to make sure that his or her response is not viewed by the parrot as aggressive. Laddering as punishment usually stimulates the parrot even more, often causing even more aggression from the parrot. If the parrot does not respond positively to the "UP" command, the caregiver should work to reinforce the patterning at another time when both are in a calmer mood.

Often, the first biting episodes are centered around the cage and the young bird's desire to create a territory of his own. As a human companion, the bond between the parrot and his owner should allow them to share the cage area. If the caregiver has established a nurturing authority as the more assertive "partner" in the pair bond, there should be no reason for the bird to be aggressive in this shared territory. If the caregiver successfully evaluates his or her parrot's mood and consistently uses the "UP" command to take their avian companion out of his cage each time, the young bird will be unlikely to establish an aggressive cage territoriality.

A parrot starting his independence stage may need to be reminded or patterned to the "UP" command by his owner. It is best to start this lesson in a room that is unfamiliar to the bird where he cannot see his cage. I call this the "neutral room." This should not be a frightening place for the parrot but one where you both can be comfortable. Most of all it should be a place where the parrot has not established a sense of territory that he feels he must protect. Place the young parrot on a T-stand or the back of a chair and approach him in a friendly, yet decisive, manner with the back of your hand. Press the back of your fingers into the bird's lower belly and say "UP" once in a clear decisive voice — don't yell or try to sound like a drill sergeant. Keep smiling — parrots are more apt to trust us if we stay calm and keep the training sessions friendly. Most young parrots will step on to your hand quite readily if they have been hand trained at all. If he doesn't, gently pick him up one foot at a time.

Slow "laddering" is an excellent way to pattern a parrot to understand that you are asking him to step on your hand. "Ladder" the bird slowly onto your other hand by saying "UP" again and then, using the "UP" command again, have him step on your other hand. When you want to place him back on the stand, use the word "DOWN." Continue the process several times remaining calm and giving your parrot lots of verbal praise when he does what you ask him to do. Make the lesson fun, give your parrot lots of praise, and always end it on a positive note. Most birds learn the "UP" command very quickly. Once the cues are established and used consistently, the parrot will always be given a clear message — an offer that will be hard to refuse. It is important to continue using the verbal commands throughout the parrot's life. This helps guarantee a consistency for both you and your parrot. Without such a clear message, it will be easier for the bird to be confused about what you are asking him to do. Providing clear messages are a critical part of keeping your parrot tame and easy to handle. Remember, you are only as good as your last "UP" command!

Checking Your Reactions

Handfed companion parrots are intelligent animals who depend on us as their "surrogate parents." We need to teach them their life skills and behaviors. Proper socialization prepares them for life with human beings. Since bappies view us as their human flock, the impressionable youngsters will watch us closely and learn from us even if we are not trying to teach them anything at all. Many times, without realizing it, people actually teach their companion parrots negative behaviors by giving them the wrong kind of reward and attention. Certainly the biting behavior of many parrots has been influenced and reinforced by their often-clueless caregivers. The best way to prevent and stop biting and aggressive behavior is to provide parrots with Nurturing Guidance and positive activity so that he does not have to resort to negative behavior to communicate or to keep himself stimulated. Teach and reward positive behaviors.

Think about your reactions to your parrot's negative behaviors. Is your response based on your own moods? Are you confusing him with inconsistency? Is your behavior so capricious that he has no idea what you want from him or what you are going to do in response to anything he does? Are you actually encouraging these problem behaviors without realizing it by making a big deal of his aggression and providing him with a drama reward? How much responsibility do you accept before you blame him for being "bad? Watch your parrot carefully and he will most likely teach you a lot about your own behavior.

Shaking your finger at a parrot and telling him how bad he was because he bit you just provides him with a drama reward and the wiggling finger may just be another invitation for a bite. The best way to deal with a bite is to give the parrot a quick disapproving look and put him down as gently as possible until he calms down and you can approach him again after you have calmed yourself down as well.

An All-Purpose Tool

Nature intended the parrot's beak primarily as a food-processing tool. It rips, shreds, crunches, mashes and delicately dissects the smallest tidbits of food. The sensitive tip sends information to the parrot's brain about the texture of the food or material that is being touched. The beak is also used as a "hand" in climbing, reaching, carrying and holding. I love to watch Rascal, one of my Double-yellow Head Amazons, stretch his body out as long as he can, reaching with his beak for a higher perch. Then barely gripping the perch he is on with his "tip toes," he throws himself up. Making contact with his beak, he chins himself up onto the new perch. What incredible gymnastic ability parrots have, especially considering that they only have one "hand." What is even more amazing to me is that Rascal can do this with his beak stuffed with a pecan half. The beak is also used as a comb or preening tool to clean and align the barbs and barbules on the feather shaft. This is necessary for the feathers to function properly in flying and insulating the body. Beak wrestling is a form of playing in young birds and in adults it is often a courtship activity that precedes mating. The strong powerful beak is used to rip and shred material to build and "decorate" the nest cavity. Once the chicks hatch, the parent's all-purpose beak becomes a delicate feeding instrument. Molly, a talented Blue and Gold Macaw, cracks a walnut removing the skin of each nut meat section without losing one morsel.

Beak-to-Beak Combat

It is my understanding that the versatile and powerful parrot beak is seldom used as a weapon in the wild. Most parrot defense and aggression is channeled into dramatic calls and posturing. The parrot struts and puffs, making himself as big and colorful as possible. Combined with screeching and yelling, the drama is usually effective enough to chase away the intruder. If not, beak-to-beak combat may occur to secure the nesting or feeding territory. Perhaps one of the reasons

Molly loves her walnuts and her beak has the power to crack a walnut shell and the finesse to delicately remove each and every morsel of nut without losing any of it..

that parrots are not physically violent is because any injury sustained in a fight would put them in mortal peril. I have seen photographs of a parrot jabbing its beak at a hungry snake in defense of its nest. Unfortunately, if the snake is determined, the parrot is usually no match for it. Although I don't have the details, one of the most interesting stories that I've heard was about a Blue and Gold Macaw and a hawk grappling in the sky. The Macaw managed to turn the tables on the predator by flying higher and directing a well-placed bite on the hawk's neck. Certainly there are some parrot species and individuals who may have a more aggressive nature than others, but the majority of wild parrots do not commonly use their beak as an offensive or aggressive weapon in the wild.

Parrots Don't Know How To Be Good Pets

If biting is not a common behavior in wild parrots, why is it one of the most common problems with companion parrots? First, neither a wild-caught nor a domestically-raised parrot understands how to behave in captivity. They naturally know how to relate to their own species and on some level to the other animals in their natural environment but nothing has prepared them to relate successfully to a human being. Secondly, most human beings, especially first parrot owners, have no idea how to relate to a parrot. Many new caregivers call me who have no idea how to handle their new parrot. Some frankly admit that they are quite afraid of the parrot's beak — even if their bird is a handfed baby. Once a parrot is in his new home, he either develops his own behaviors or learns from his human flock how to behave. A parrot will not naturally develop the traits that will make it a good human companion. It is up to the new caregivers to show their parrot how to behave in acceptable ways. The problem is that many parrot owners do not realize that they are teaching their parrots the traits that make them "bad" pet birds. The parrot who bites, often does so because the people in his human flock have reinforced or rewarded the bird for biting. Without realizing it, many owners are actually teaching their parrots to bite.

Too Curious To Sit Still

I hear many variations of the following story. Jennifer and Dave Olson purchased a young Yellow-nape Amazon from a local pet shop. J.C. had been confined to a small cage in the store for over three months but was still fairly tame and receptive to handling. Once he established his new home as his territory, there were some problems. The high-energy Amazon liked Jennifer from the very beginning. He would climb out of his cage on her shoulder and the two of them would watch TV in the evenings while Dave was at work. He'd be fine for a while but then he'd start playing with her earring, picking at a mole on her cheek or chewing on her clothes. Each time she would put her hand up and shove his face away from what he was exploring and admonish him, *"J.C. Cool it! Leave that alone!"* He'd sit quietly for a few minutes and then start picking at her collar, *"J.C. Stop it or I'm taking you back to your cage!"* He'd straighten right up and behave for a minute but then that "bird toy" hanging from her ear lobe would be too much for him to resist. Jennifer would brush her hand up again to make him stop, *"J.C. STOP THAT — You're being a bad bird!"* Distracted only momentarily, seconds later, he was at it again! This time when she reached her hand up, he grabbed it with his beak. It wasn't really a bite, more of a communication of annoyance with her, but she pulled away and then started trying to pull him off of her shoulder. *"J.C. You're a bad bird — can't you just sit still and watch TV with me, J.C. STOP THAT — J.C. DO YOU HEAR ME!!*" This was great fun for J.C. — it was the most dramatic attention she had given him all day.

Every time he poked at her with his beak, she would pay attention to him. What a great game it had become with her wrestling with him and carrying on and on. Each time, Jennifer had become more dramatic and each time the game became more fun for J.C.. Finally, he bit Jennifer a little harder and she pulled him off of her shoulder. Pointing her finger at him and waggling it at him, she shouted, *"J.C. YOU'RE A BAD BAD BIRD AND YOU'RE GOING BACK TO YOUR CAGE!!"* Once he was in his cage, the great game was over. But he would get to play it again the next time he was out. Without realizing it, Jennifer had quickly and effectively taught J.C. to get drama and attention with negative behavior. Of course, this was not her intention.

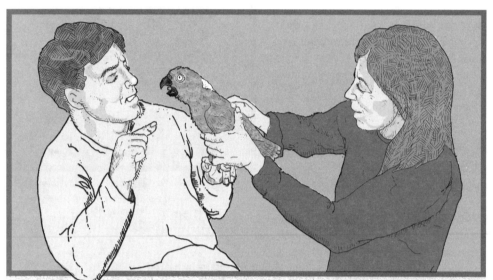

One of the best ways to guarantee that your parrot will bite the other people in your family is to continually rescue the bird or a family member whom the bird bites. Parrots can learn very quickly to bite their less favored person to get to go back to their favorite person if they are pulled away by the favored person after biting. The person who gets bitten should just put the parrot down so that they both can calm down.

The Triangle

There was nothing for J.C. to do when he was sitting on Jennifer's shoulder. The curious parrot found all sorts of things to explore but then learned that the drama was more rewarding than the exploration. Dave and Jennifer inadvertently taught J.C. other negative lessons. The Amazon preferred Jennifer from the beginning. Dave had wanted the parrot but because of his work schedule, he didn't have the time to spend with him at first. After a few weeks, his work schedule changed and Dave was home in the evenings again. He brought J.C. over to the couch and joined Jennifer to watch TV. The parrot started to flutter his wings leaning towards Jennifer but Dave held on to him. Becoming more anxious to go to the person he was most familiar with, J.C. finally reached down and jabbed at Dave with his beak. It wasn't really even a bite but Dave became upset, *"J.C., What did you bite me for?"* Jennifer had mixed emotions, she didn't want J.C. to really bite Dave and she didn't want Dave to get upset with the parrot, so she reached over and grabbed the Amazon, *"J.C. what did you bite him for — you're a bad bird. Don't you want Dave to like you?"* At this point in time J.C. really didn't care if Dave liked him or not, all he knew was he wanted to be with Jennifer. He bit Dave and was rewarded with Jennifer's attention. The Yellow-nape quickly learned that all he had to do to get to go back to Jennifer was to bite Dave. After this happened several times, the Amazon's aggression towards him became entrenched and Dave became insecure about picking J.C. up.

You're All I've Got

When J.C. first came to live with the Olson's, he let both of them pick him up easily. Most parrots, whether with their first owners or previously owned, are quite well-behaved when they are first in a new situation — before they have established their own "territory." The Olson's did not realize that they would have to work with J.C. to let him know they were the ones guiding his behavior. Often he would just hop off of his cage onto Jennifer's shoulder because he wanted to be with her. After a few weeks, Dave had to chase him around the top of the cage until the Amazon consented to get on his hand. But after a few bites, J.C. learned quickly that he had control over Dave. If he didn't want to get on Dave's hand, J.C. just snapped at him and he went away. Sometimes Dave would try and insist but when J.C. came at him with his beak, Dave would hesitate. In parrot training, "He who hesitates is lost." Each time Dave withdrew his hand, the parrot was in control. Occasionally, when Jennifer wasn't around, J.C. would step right onto Dave's hand giving him a false sense of security. It was as if the Amazon was saying, "you're all I've got for now so I guess I'll let you pick me up." Dave never realized that the Amazon was totally in control of their relationship. He just thought that J.C. was moody.

Most parrots do have moods and it is a good idea for the owner to acknowledge that there are times when a parrot may not want to be "messed with." They may be napping, eating or in "overload" from being overexcited. The sensitive bird owner knows that there are times that a parrot should just be left alone. Trying to pick up a bird during these times may be a setup for being bitten. Even my Caique, Spike, can be a real pain when he his being food protective and I know to wait until he is through eating whatever treat he is defending before I to try and pick him up.

One of the rules of establishing *Nurturing Guidance* with a parrot is to never start anything that you don't finish. If it is obvious that the parrot is preoccupied and it is not essential to pick it up at that moment, it is best to wait until it will not be a struggle. If the owner tries and does not succeed and then leaves the parrot alone because he became nippy, the bird can easily learn that biting is a convenient way to be left alone.

Mixed Messages

Once Dave became insecure about J.C., he started using what I call the **"Fish Bait"** method to try and pick the Amazon up. He would reach over to pick the parrot up and if it even looked like J.C. was reaching over with his beak, Dave would pull his hand back. Then he would push his fingers towards J.C. again and back. All the yellow-nape saw was these fingers wiggling around. It seemed like a new game to him. Every time he would take a swipe at Dave's fingers with his beak, Dave would move his hand away. What power J.C. had! How could the Amazon not bite this wiggling finger? Dave was giving J.C. mixed messages and the Amazon was not sure what Dave wanted so he filled in his own rules for the new game. J.C. was becoming quite a biter at a young age and if the

The Fish Bait approach of wiggling your fingers usually says "Bite me!"

Olsons didn't take control and teach the Amazon not to bite, they would have serious problems as the bird got older. Every time a parrot is allowed to bite, a biting pattern is established. If the biting is continually rewarded with attention or drama or leaving, the biting becomes a consistent behavior. The Olsons called me wanting to know how to stop J.C. from biting. Their first question was "what do we do when J.C. bites one of us." Although this is important, the more important question is "how do we guide J.C.'s behavior so that he learns not to bite us?"

Treating the Cause — Not The Symptoms

Treating the biting as a symptom is not usually effective — treating the cause (a parrot in control of his own life) usually is. When the cause is alleviated, the symptoms often disappear. J.C. not only got his own way when he bit but also was rewarded with drama and attention. Punishment is usually ineffective because the parrot often sees what we think is punishment as a reward. Having a "logical" conversation with a parrot about why it shouldn't bite is usually meaningless attention. Yelling and screaming is a drama reward. Grabbing and shaking the beak is a form of play or even sexual foreplay for a sexually mature parrot. Hitting or slapping a parrot is abusive aggression and certainly will not create a trusting relationship. Parrots mimic our energy and aggression is usually met with aggression — sustained aggression results in fear. It is not only tragic for a parrot to live in fear of the people in his life; it also creates serious dysfunctional behavior for the parrot. Putting a parrot in his cage as punishment for biting could only be effective if parrots had a more complex sense of cause-and-effect. Cause-and-effect implies that a living creature is capable of understanding that certain behavior will have certain results. Often the anticipation of negative results will keep a person from doing something. Although a parrot does understand the immediate results of his actions, he does not understand long-term punishment. If a parrot bites his owner and the person swoops him up, telling him what a bad bird he is and then takes him and puts him in the cage to "think about it," the bird only understands the instantaneous drama reaction and not that he is being punished for biting by having to be in he cage. The instantaneous reaction is usually a drama reward that may actually encourage the bird to bite either from patterning or to get his way. Once the bird is in his cage there is usually no correlation between the biting and being in the cage. Adjusting the length of time the bird is kept "locked up" according to the intensity of the bite is not effective since a parrot does not have the same time reference that we do.

Giving The Parrot A Clear Message

The way to stop a parrot from biting is to set rules and provide the guidance to teach him what is acceptable behavior. The first step is establishing hand control by teaching a parrot the "UP" command. J.C. was given mixed messages by both of the people in his human flock. One time Jennifer would present her hand for him to step onto and the next time J.C. could just hop onto her shoulder. Dave was always wiggling his fingers around even if J.C. didn't intend to bite him. The Amazon was clearly in control of his cage territory. If he didn't want to go with either of his owners, he didn't have to. If he took a swipe at their fingers with his beak or went to the corner of the cage, they just went away and left him alone. He had actually become pretty aggressive in or near his cage by the time the Olson's called me to do a consultation.

The first step was to get J.C. away from his cage and onto a stand in a "neutral room" where the Yellow-nape had no need for territorial defense. In the beginning, in order for Dave to work successfully with J.C., Jennifer could not be in the same room or the Amazon would feed off of her energy and still be aggressive to Dave. If he could establish a separate bond with the Yellow-nape without his wife's presence, Dave would have a better chance of handling J.C. when Jennifer was present. Once J.C. was on the T-stand, I showed Dave how to present his hand to the Amazon in a decisive manner. This way J.C. would get a clear message about what was expected of him. Both Jennifer and Dave had allowed J.C. to step on the back of their hands or their wrists. Picking him up this way, neither of them had control over the parrot and J.C. would immediately use the arm as a runway to the shoulder. A parrot should be trained to step on to his caregiver's hand. The hand should be held with the palm facing the person. It is easier to get a parrot to step on the upper ridge of the index finger if the fingers are held together. This way even the largest macaw can be "finger" trained. If the parrot is held on the ridge of the index finger, the thumb acts as a psychological barrier to keep the parrot on his caregiver's hand. If needed, the thumb can be used to gently hold the foot in place. In picking up a parrot, I give the same advice that a golf instructor or a baseball coach gives — follow through. If the caregiver just presents his hand in front of the bird, the parrot may not get a clear message to step up. However, if the owner visualizes the complete action of bringing the hand down to pick the parrot up, pushing gently into his belly and then bringing the hand with the parrot on it up in a complete arc, the parrot gets a clear message that he is being picked up.

Direct eye contact communicates authority to a parrot but has to be used carefully so the parrot is neither intimidated nor challenged. I have worked with hundreds of parrots and am rarely bitten. The times that I have been bitten usually occur because I have diverted my eyes from the bird to the caregiver to answer a question. Direct eye contact keeps the parrot "guessing" about what you are going to do and generally he is more involved with watching you than biting you. Parrots are intelligent enough to understand verbal commands. The "UP" command is the most important because it not only tells the bird to step onto your hand but also establishes your authority. Once I taught J.C. the "UP" command by picking him up and putting him down (with the "DOWN" command) several times, Dave was able to pick the Amazon up easily combining all of the techniques that I had shown him. This was the first step in gaining control of J.C.'s behavior. Both Dave and Jennifer would have to work individually with him on a consistent basis. Gradually they would work with him together in the living room establishing their authority over his cage territory but they would have to set the rules so that the Yellow-nape would not play the same "game" with them. If he does bite, I instructed the Olson's to quickly establish their authority by picking him up assertively with the "UP" command and using the split second "evil eye" (a very quick look of disapproval) Most of all, if J.C. bit either Dave or Jennifer, the other person was not allowed to jump in and rescue either J.C. or their spouse. That would not have been a wise lesson to teach the Yellow-nape.

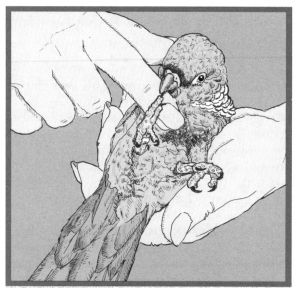

Many of the high energy little parrots need to be given something positive to do when they are with you. Giving them a toy made of rope or leather knots can keep them busy. If they get bored they often resort to bothersome nipping, cuticle trimming, or mole, freckle and scab removal.

High-Energy Birds

As I stated earlier, some species of parrots generally have higher energy than others and some tend to be more aggressive. It is hard to make generalizations about parrot species because there are exceptions to almost every rule. Many of the smaller parrots are high-energy chewers and nippers. The Pyrrhura Conures such as the Green-cheek and Maroon-belly Conure are examples of birds that have to be doing something almost all of the time and so are most of the Lories. Twiggy, my Slender-billed Conure and Spike, my Black-headed Caique, also fit into this category. Usually, they are not really biting but chewing on their owners. It seems to be one of their favorite games. The excited chewing can turn into biting. Sometimes I can let out a short loud yelp and Spike will stop and look up at me as if to say, "I'm sorry I didn't mean to hurt you." But he has a short attention span and goes right back to the chewing. Guidance is essential at this time. When Spike starts chewing on my hand, I reach in with the other hand and say a decisive "UP" combined with a very short look of disapproval. He usually steps right up and stands straight at attention for about 10 seconds and then starts to preen himself as if to show me that he doesn't really care if I am in control. It is critical for the caregiver of a high-energy parrot to establish rules to guide their behaviors. Caregivers often misunderstand the motivation of the beaky little parrots. It is a natural behavior for them to explore everything with their beaks. When the owner lets them chew on fingers or gives them drama, it becomes a game. I know from experience. Spike is a bitey little bird, constantly having to explore everything with his beak. I can't deny him this innate part of who he is. When I want to spend time with him, I always make sure I have a "foot" toy made of knotted leather or rope for him to chew on instead of me. Many of the larger parrots also always seem to need something to chew on. It is a good idea to provide all chewers with something to explore with their beak instead of their caregivers' flesh.

Using a Distraction

Many parrots reach with their beak before they step onto a hand. This is a natural behavior to test the security and/or the balance of the perch and not usually an attempt to bite. But if the person continually pulls back, constantly confusing the parrot, the mixed message could create a biting problem. I can usually tell if a parrot is going to try and bite me from his body language. A perceptive person will notice that a parrot who intends to bite is not relaxed and may precede his attack with eye pinning or posturing. Many times, I will still be able to pick up the potentially aggressive parrot using the "bad hand-good hand" distraction method. I'll take my left hand and bring it up above and a little bit behind the parrot. The goal is not to frighten or intimidate him but simply to distract his attention so that I can just scoop him up on my other hand. In some cases, I will wrap a small towel around the "bad" hand or hold an object in it that can be even more distracting.

Using this method can be an effective tool in changing some aggressive behavior. Often when a parrot becomes a biter, he has established a pattern to bite in certain situations. Not understanding this, the person sometimes becomes a pawn in the parrot's pattern. The best way to change his aggressive behavior is to take control of it by adding a new variable to distract him from the pattern he has been allowed to establish. Holding your hand up or holding an object in your hand can be enough to make him stop and think before he acts in his normal pattern.

When a least-favored person works with a biting parrot, it is essential the parrot is placed away from his cage and away from the preferred person. When I tame wild-caught parrots or work with "good birds gone bad," I always slow down my energy. As I have said before, parrots are highly empathic and mirror our moods. If I am relaxed, they do not sense fear or aggression from me and therefore, have no reason to return it.

Everyone who relates to the parrot should try their best to follow the same procedures and set the same rules. If a parrot is handled inconsistently by different members of his "flock," he may still be confused about proper behavior. Many companion parrots are taught to bite by strangers who try to handle the bird without knowing the proper approach and methods. There are many people who advertise that they tame and train birds but their handling is so aggressive that they may actually

Using a distraction of some kind is one of the best ways to break a pattern of biting in a parrot. Usually the biting behavior has become a habit in response to someone trying to pick up the bird. The bird is not necessarily biting because he wants to, often it is just a habit, or, in some situations, a game or test. Taking control of this habit by adding another variable usually prevents the bird from biting. Sometimes just raising your other hand will work but with other parrots, you may need to hold a non-threatening object such as a remote control, potholder, TV Guide, or just about anything handy. The purpose of this friendly distraction is NOT to frighten or threaten the bird but simply to distract him.

teach your bird to bite. Ask them about the methods that they use before you hire anyone to work with your pet. Teach your friends how to handle your parrot properly before allowing them to pick him up, even if your pet is tame. I've seen many gentle parrots that have been turned into biters because someone has handled them aggressively or ineptly.

The Easiest Behavior Problem To Solve

Out of all of the displacement behavior problems that I work with, I think that biting is the easiest to prevent and solve. Establishing *Nurturing Guidance* with a handfed bappy will keep most parrots from ever becoming aggressive biters. At the age that they would leave their parents in the wild and become independent in the flock, many domestically-raised parrots will start to strut their stuff. The caregiver who has established the "UP" command and has not allowed their young parrot to control his own life, will slide through this time with fewer problems. I have worked with many parrots who are in total control of their own lives because their human flock had not established any rules or guidance. These birds are the ones that end up sitting in their cages because no one can handle them. On a weekly basis, I get several phone calls from people who want to "get rid of" their birds because of aggression problems. If the people are willing to work with their parrots, many positive changes are possible. Once people learn to handle their bird decisively, using the right techniques, biting can be controlled. With consistency, the "UP" command is easy for a parrot to learn. Sometimes it only takes a few minutes but makes all the difference in whether a person can handle their parrot or not. Once people have established a nurturing authority, parrots do not always automatically accept this authority for rest of their lives. There will be times throughout their lives when parrots may challenge the rules set by their human flock. The person who has established and maintained the tools of *Nurturing Guidance* will have a parrot that adjusts well to life as a human companion and knows how to behave.

Skippy has a sweet voice that makes him a delightful little guy. Unfortunately, the cockatoo is easily over-stimulated and prone to aggressive outbursts. Parrots like Skippy can only be managed by caregivers who pay very close attention to the parrot's body language and moods.

Situational Aggression

Most companion parrots exhibit aggressive behaviors from time to time but some seem to be extremely aggressive often and in many different situations. Because they don't have the knowledge or dedication, few people have the patience and emotional flexibility to live with a parrot who exhibits hard-core aggression. The majority of the time, parrots who are aggressive in a home where people have an understanding of their behavior can be worked with to manage that aggression. This is only true if the current or new caregivers take the time to learn about the behavior of their parrots and then work with them in a realistic, calm, and productive manner.

It is important to understand the differences between a parrot who becomes aggressive in particular situations and the parrot who simply IS aggressive. I believe that all parrots, no matter how normally tame and sweet, have a potential for *situational aggression*. This type of temporary aggression can be influenced by many variables in the parrot's life. These include being threatened by strangers and unfamiliar situations, overload behavior from overexcitement, hormonal and seasonal influences, defense of their perceived territory and mate, injury and health problems, confusion from indecisive handling, and aggressive handling in certain specific situations.

Situational aggression is not usually too difficult to work with once the situation is identified. Most parrots who bite do so for a reason even if it may take awhile for us to figure out why they became aggressive. Unfortunately many caregivers take it personally when their parrots bite them. Instead, caregivers need to try to determine why a particular situation threatened or confused the parrot enough for him to become aggressive. They also need to analyze the situation to determine if they have some complicity in causing their parrots to bite and if they are actually encouraging the aggression. Were they too abrupt or unfocused when they approached the parrot? Was he busy doing something else?

Too many people pattern their parrots to become aggressive in certain situations by responding in a way that encourages aggressive behavior. Most situational biters bite because they are threatened by a difference in the what, why, when, how, and who of their environment and handling. Of course, some situational biting has to do with overexcitement and people who approach a parrot too aggressively or clumsily may be bitten.

Biting to Communicate

Some parrots learn to bite to communicate with their caregivers. One of my clients had a Yellow-nape Amazon. Every night the man would watch the news with the nape on his shoulder. The man would doze off and within a few minutes, the Amazon would bite his neck. The man woke up, yelled a bit, and then put the parrot in his cage for bedtime. It became very apparent that this was the way the bird had learned to tell his caregiver that he wanted to go back to his cage.

Some parrots become aggressive when their hormones tell them it is breeding season. People who are aware of this and learn to handle their parrots differently during this time, experience far less aggression. A good example is the person who keeps his parrot on his shoulder. These people may experience territorial aggression if some one else comes in the room. Situational biters are pretty easy to figure out and since they are usually relatively predictable, their biting can be fairly easy for a perceptive caregiver to stop or manage.

Hard-core aggression is a usually different situation. The aggression can't always be related to a specific situation. It is difficult to figure out why the parrot is biting because he seems so unpredictable. There are some parrots who simply can't be trusted without the handlers being totally aware and focused on the bird every step of the way. These parrots are so aggressive they rarely stay in any home. Many of them end up abused or neglected in a back room, garage, basement or, if they are lucky, they go to a quality rescue organization. Only a few parrot lovers are dedicated enough to work with and manage parrots with this type of patterned aggressive behavior.

Reevaluating Expectations

Over the years I have helped people successfully deal with all types of aggressive behavior in parrots — even with some hard-core biters. Success does not always mean that the parrot will never be aggressive again — it means that the aggression can be predicted and managed so that the caregivers can avoid injury and the parrot can enjoy a quality of life. The more unpredictable a parrot is, the more astute the caregiver has to be to avoid aggression. The measure of success with these parrots is having the intelligence to know when the bites are coming and avoid them rather than accepting them hoping the bird will realize biting is not getting his way. Taking the bites is just another way of reinforcing the biting behavior. There are too many people still working with parrots in a trust-destroying, aggressive manner — aggression is met with aggression and becomes patterned.

We all have certain expectations about keeping a companion parrot. We want them to stay cuddly, to talk, to have no neurotic behavior, and so on. This is not always realistic with a domestically-raised parrot who hatches with the instincts of a wild parrot. Much of their success as a human companion depends on quality early development and the knowledge and dedication of their human flock. Unfortunately, if we can't adjust our expectations according to the true behavior, personality, and potential of our parrot, the relationship rarely works. Not all parrots remain cuddly but they may be exceptional talkers. Not all parrots turn into good talkers but they may be great fun to watch as they play on their gyms or in their cages. Even parrots who are never handled by the people in their lives can develop strong bonds to those people and enjoy a positive level of ambient attention. Despite the fact that he may not have optimal pet potential, a parrot who can't be handled or even properly managed still needs a home where he receives good care and some attention.

In some cases, he may be happier with another parrot but parrots who exhibit severe aggression to people may be just as dangerous to another parrot. Many companion parrots develop strange displacement behaviors to help them cope with the alien environment we provide for them. Some of these behaviors may seem pretty neurotic to us. Whether it is genetic or environmental, some parrots develop extremely aggressive and often unpredictable behaviors. Skippy was one such bird ...

SKIPPY'S STORY

Several years ago, an abused Lesser Sulphur-crested Cockatoo temporarily came into my life as a rescue. He had gone through several homes because of his aggression. As soon as I got him home, I skritched his head for a minute or so and then placed him in his cage. While he ate, I talked to him for awhile. He seemed like the sweetest bird I had ever met. His voice was loving and he said several words and expressions besides his name. The next day I let him out and he stepped right on my hand and lowered his head to be petted. He made lots of little kissy sounds. I forgot all the things I had observed about parrots being well-behaved in new situations and couldn't imagine why no one wanted to keep this wonderful Skippy bird.

An Emphatic Reminder

It was about a week later that I began to realize the answer to that question. I was playing with Skippy in my bedroom. He loved to play running all over chasing a ball or a chain I dragged across the bed. It was time for me to run errands and he had to go back in his cage. I was singing to him and picked him up playfully — the same way I had been taking him back to his cage for several days. About half way there, Skippy's posture changed dramatically. Just as I started to react, he lunged at my face and, as I tried to protect myself with my hand, he ripped into both hands over and over in what seemed like some sort of "feeding frenzy." It was all I could do to keep from throwing him down on the floor in self-defense. Within seconds, he was calm again saying his name sweetly. I put him in his cage and stood there bewildered and bleeding profusely from several vicious bites.

By this time, I had worked with hundreds of parrots — a good percentage of them were aggressive cockatoos — particularly wild-caught birds, but this was something new to me. I had worked with some domestically-raised Cockatoos with aggression problems but none had been this quick to become so vicious without a comparable cause. I honestly could not figure out what had sent Skippy into such frenzy. Yes, he could have been in "overload" from playing so hard, and/or his aggression could have been a communication that he didn't want to go back to his cage. Something I didn't notice could have startled him and caused a fear reaction.

I had experienced these types of sudden reactions from parrots before but none of them ever approached the extreme mood change and frenzy that Skippy exhibited. I have often heard people say that their parrots turned "mean" for no reason at all but there always is a reason for aggression. Even with Skippy, there had to be a reason for his sudden violence. I refuse to believe that any parrot simply turns "mean" without reason. The trick was to figure out what was going on in Skippy's exceptionally clever little head so I could try and prevent and protect myself from such severe aggression. →

"When Sally met Skippy" When Skippy arrived, he was the most delightful Cockatoo anyone could imagine. He had the sweetest voice and said many clever phrases. But familiarity bred contempt and it wasn't long before he revealed his Dr. Jekyll and Mr. Hyde personality.

Incredibly Intelligent

Despite his aggression, Skippy was an absolutely delightful parrot. He was intelligent and learned various behaviors very quickly. He was a ham and very fun to have around. He was extremely good at entertaining both himself and people watching him. He could spend hours playing with his toys. In fact, he was the only bird I have personally known who was smart enough to take apart a stainless steel bolt and wing-nut, then place a piece of cloth over the bolt and re-thread the wing nut onto the bolt. The only real problem he had was his aggression. If he could have been happy staying in his cage receiving a lot of ambient attention, that would have been a good solution for him but he also thrived on physical affection and head skritching.

Skippy was a "familiarity breeds contempt" type of guy. He loved to impress strangers with his tricks and vocabulary. Almost any new person could handle Skippy without eliciting any aggression. He was sweet to any stranger who paid attention and laughed with him but once he got to know them, he could become quite aggressive with them. However, I never saw him be as aggressive with anyone else as he had been with me.

Managing Skippy

Skippy was the biggest challenge that I had ever had with a parrot. In the first few months, I came up with some ideas on how to manage his behavior. Collectively I called them "Nurturing Manipulation" — a sort of "Gently do unto them first, so they don't get to do unto you" theory. Many of these ideas are the same concepts used to deal with any aggressive parrot but they become far more important with a parrot who exhibits hard-core aggression like Skippy.

⊃ **Not A Morning Person:** The first and most important aspect was to carefully observe and make notes of Skippy's behavior every day. This way I began to determine specific moods that he exhibited during the day. I discovered he was fairly consistent. He was not a morning person but then neither am I. I discovered that the best time for me to give him physical attention was in the late afternoon or early evening. He also did not do well when there was too much going on so I needed to let him out when the household was calm and quiet.

⊃ **Too Much of a Good Thing:** Skippy loved physical affection but it was purely on his terms within his time limits. I had to watch even the subtlest body language to know if I needed to move to another location on his head or body. For example, if I wasn't focused enough and started to wear grooves in his head, he let me know in a less than subtle manner. He loved skritching but there was a time limitation. He couldn't tolerate it if I went beyond that limit so I had to pay very close attention so that I would notice when he had experienced too much of a good thing. Sometimes he would become a bit rigid or antsy. Often the sign was when he started repeatedly smacking his beak. Other times, if he could, he would reach for my hand to nudge it to pet another place. If I ignored this direct communication, he became very aggravated and I was in trouble.

⊃ **Planning Ahead:** I couldn't just take Skippy out when the mood struck me. I had to plan ahead for just about everything I did with Skippy but it became easier as he became patterned to my consistency. I taught him several behaviors that he learned to do on command. I taught him to spread his wings to the words "Eagle Boy." He learned to shake hands and dance on command. His favorite song to sing and dance to was his own special version of "Skipadeedodah." I would praise him and give him a small treat for his performances. Most of the time, I was able to use these behaviors successfully to distract him when he seemed to have his mind set on something more devious.

⊃ NO **Punishment!:** One thing I learned very quickly was that using something interesting to distract Skippy was the best way to stop him from exhibiting negative behaviors. Saying "NO" to Skippy was like flashing a red cape in front of a bull. Trying to discipline him with an "evil eye" or by laddering him from hand to hand would have resulted in severe injury to my hands. I knew that any kind of punishment would cause many more problems than it could possibly solve.

⊃ **Submissive Calm Energy:** Lowering my energy did help with Skippy so I made a practice of NEVER handling him when I was in a bad mood or hyper for any reason at all. I also found that he was more likely to be agreeable if I acted somewhat submissively with him. I rarely made focused direct eye contact with him unless he was away from me and entertaining himself or others. When I was trying to handle him, I would barely make eye contact mostly looking at a point just below his beak, and then I would lower my head and close my eyes moving my head to the side. I could still observe him with my peripheral vision. When I acted in this manner, Skippy would respond favorably to my calm verbal cues. This made sense to me since I believed that much of his aggression was based on abuse and, therefore, on fear. Animals who have been abused often develop a strong fear of hands moving toward or over them. As we know, parrots are prey animals and the association of hands with the abuse is often too direct to allow handling from a person who approaches them too directly. Biting is usually the best way for a parrot to deal with this fear of being handled.

While being submissive with an aggressive parrot goes against the thinking of many behavioral consultants, it was very effective with Skippy. This is where my concept of manipulation comes in. After several bad bites, I had become afraid of Skippy's aggression. There was no way I could bluff him by trying to be confident and decisive. I knew that any aggression on my part would be returned with increased intensity. In fact any misstep or lack of focus on my part was returned as aggression. I couldn't handle him if I was preoccupied with something or someone else. If, however, I was focused on what I was doing and submissive with Skippy, I found that I could manipulate him into being gentle with me. The more times he was gentle, the more he became patterned to be gentle with me.

⊃ **Self-soothing:** Much of Skippy's aggression seemed to start with and be accompanied with agitation and confusion. The first parrot I ever really tamed was my legendary African Grey, Bongo Marie. Winning her trust was a long-term project but self-soothing techniques were one of the first ways I worked with her. In the beginning she was far too frightened for me to even get her attention. I started out by humming to her when she was relaxed. When she started taking food from my hand, I reassured her with "that's OK." Whenever anything happened that threatened her, I would calmly say, "That's OK." She learned to trust that I would not let anything bad happen to her. Eventually she learned to actually say these words to calm herself when something concerned her.

When I started trying to work with Skippy's aggression, I would watch him carefully. When I saw that he was relaxed and happy I would walk over to his cage, lower my head, and quietly whisper "Skippy, Skippy, Skippy." I would also whisper his name when I gave him his special treats and whenever he was in the rapture of having his head skritched. As he began to associate his whispered name with special quiet times, he would use the words to calm himself down. I could also whisper his name if I wanted to calm him down. It didn't always work but it did enough to make it worth trying in difficult situations.

Teaching something as simple as a basic trick can quickly distract a parrot from a negative behavior. Skippy learned to spread his wings to the command "Eagle Boy" and giving the command often stopped Skippy from completing his aggressive agendas.

⊃Treat Training: Skippy had been quite aggressive when I tried to feed him so I established a feeding routine. I tapped on his top perch through the cage bars. At first when I did this, he would interpret it as a threat but eventually he began to realize that every time he came to this perch, I would give him a pine nut, sunflower seed, almond sliver, or another special treat. Then I would quickly take out the old dishes and put in his fresh food and water dishes which I had ready and waiting. If he stayed on his top perch, he would get another special treat. If he moved, I wouldn't give him his treat or fresh food until he went back up and stayed there until I was through. This also worked when I moved his toys or if I did something else in his cage. My Black-headed Caique, Spikey, is sometimes aggressive when another person tries to feed him, so I have them use this same technique.

⊃ Giving Him a Job: Skippy spent a lot of time in his cage and he did not seem to mind this as long as he had lots to do. Skippy loved puzzle toys so I provided him with several of these high activity toys and rotated them frequently. He also liked cloth and leather mostly so he could jam them into or wrap them around other toys. He was extremely smart and usually played with multiple toys at the same time. He loved foot toys of all kinds but usually found ways to incorporate them with his hanging toys. Skippy's favorite was a plastic bead with multiple leather knots tied around it. He also loved to rip into fresh branches with leaves on them and they could keep him entertained for some time.

⊃ Ambient Attention and Praise: When it was obvious to me that I could not take Skippy out of his cage to handle him, I could still give him ambient attention. I sang to him so he could dance and laugh. He loved it when I laughed with him and praised his dancing abilities. White guys can dance!

⊃ The Security of Routine: Routine became very important to both of us. As long as things remained pretty much the same, he was all right and I didn't receive the brunt of his aggression. If something changed — even something as simple as a large cardboard box being left near his cage — it upset and agitated Skippy. Perhaps this wouldn't be true if he had been well socialized and introduced to new situations when he was younger. It didn't take long for me to realize that a great deal of his biting was fear based. If things were different he was not able to understand his world and became very confused. I don't know if this was a result of his poor early socialization, the fact that he had been neglected and abused, or if was just his quirky personality. Perhaps some aggression was even a way for him to communicate how important this sense of security was to him. Consistency and dependability are essential to the security of all parrots but I do not recommend a strict routine for most parrots. A very strict routine became essential for Skippy and I. We had specific routines for him to come out of his cage and specific routines for him to go back into his cage. I made sure that things were just right before I let him out. Because of his fear and aggressive response to the sight of a stick or dowel, I was not able to stick train Skippy. Every time he saw a dowel or stick, he would raise his crest and try to attack it. There was no way I was going to sneak it in on him.

⊃ Keeping Safe: People who are working with aggressive parrots need to create situations where they are as safe as possible. Since Skippy was not willing to be stick trained, it was helpful that he was not particularly threatened by towels. When I opened the cage door, I tapped my finger on the top of the door. He knew that I expected him to come to the place where I tapped my finger. When he did, I gave him a treat. Although he would step on my hand from the cage door, I found that he was better at doing so if I had a towel draped over my lower arm like a waiter. He had his very own towel that I used to play with him on the bed or couch. The towel gave me a sense of security because I could either use it to shield myself or throw it over his head if he became too aggressive with me. I always had it when I handled him. The towel even seemed to give him a positive sense of consistency — the few times I forgot it, he seemed more apprehensive.

In some cases, using a glove is acceptable to protect your hands from a biting parrot but only if he doesn't see it as a threat. It is important to gradually get him used to seeing a glove on your hand rather than just approaching him with one. Years ago most wild-caught parrots were continually grabbed with gloved hands and many developed a morbid fear of them. Today many domestically-raised parrots don't have this negative experience unless they have been mishandled aggressively with gloves. In this case, use of gloves may exacerbate the biting behavior. The same thing is true if the parrot is afraid of towels. →

⊃ **Understanding Exceptions:** While routine was essential for Skippy in most situations, putting him back in his cage required deviation from routine. The biggest problem was getting him into his cage, not into the cage area. I found that if I didn't try to take him directly to the cage, it was much easier. This was one place where routine seemed to contribute to his aggression. It was easier to avoid upsetting him if I picked him up and put him down somewhere else a few times gradually getting closer and closer to his cage. I would pick him up and put him on a table, the back of a chair, then a T-stand, and then his cage door. Each place, I would give him one of his special treats. Once he was on top of the cage door I would remove the towel from my arm and wiggle it around with my left hand. He learned that was his signal to go back in his cage. Sometimes if that didn't work, I could tap on the closest perch and he usually would swing himself into the cage. He always received praise and a special treat when he went to his top perch.

⊃ **Ambient Attention:** Skippy was a classic "Sentinel Bird." This is a parrot who stays hyper-vigilant to everything going on in his environment. It was important for Skippy to feel that he had some control over what went on. Consequently, he was highly reactive and offered his strong opinion about everything. If I (or anyone) was in the room or nearby, it was imperative that we gave him ambient attention by responding to his contact calls. A simple "Hey Skippy-Do" was sufficient let him know that he had sufficiently warned his flock of any possible threat. It was also important to acknowledge him when I came into the room or when I left. If I was in the living room, I got into the habit of checking in with him at intervals of about 5 or 10 minutes. I would look up from my reading or television program and ask him what he was doing. His response was normally to throw his crest forward and cluck a bit. This seemed to be his signal that the status quo was maintained.

⊃ **Complete Focus:** Skippy had become manageable but I had to stay aware of the fact that I would only be able to manage his aggression successfully if I was willing to take the time and energy to concentrate on the routine we had established. I couldn't talk to someone else, read, or watch TV while he was out with me. If something else caught my attention for too long, I could be in trouble with him. He always let me know if I deviated. Making sure that I gave him at least 5 or 10 minutes of concentrated attention was not that much of a sacrifice to keep him happy enough to relax with me.

⊃ **Patience, Trust, Dedication, Guidance, Forgiveness, and Creative Thinking:** These six absolutes have to be a part of any progress with a parrot who is showing aggressive behavior. What worked for me with Skippy might need adjustment for another parrot's particular situation. In most situations, it may take some time to develop the routines and behaviors necessary to living with an aggressive parrot. With some parrots, caregivers will have to come up with their own methods in addition to or instead of those I have suggested. However patience, trust, dedication, guidance and creative thinking are the essential building blocks for managing parrot aggression. Parrots can't be blamed for aggression and need to be forgiven for their imperfections.

BEAKBITE TIP: Lunge Biting

Several years ago, my Black-headed Caique, Spikey, and I were doing a seminar at a hotel near Philadelphia. We had just finished lunch at the hotel restaurant and I was about to start speaking again. The waiter from the restaurant came in to the room where I was speaking to tell me that I couldn't charge my lunch to my room. His comment was, "Your credit is no good at the desk," and he said this so that at least the first few rows could hear him. There had been a misunderstanding — the seminar sponsor was supposed to pay meal expenses but had not made proper arrangements with the hotel. I was rather irritated that he would come into the lecture room where I was the speaker and make this comment in a loud voice in front of my audience. Spike was standing on his travel cage and quickly picked up my negative energy towards this waiter. As the man realized his mistake and moved closer to me to explain in a quieter voice, Spike launched himself off of his cage over a foot into the air, grabbed the man's nose, and held on tight until I pried him off. Noses usually bleed profusely so it became quite a drama. This was the first example of lunge biting that I had observed but certainly not the last. Although this is certainly not a normal behavior for Spike, I still need to consider that it is a possibility in what may seem to be a similar situation. Spike is normally very friendly to strangers — especially those who have good bird vibes. However, he can have an instantaneous dislike for someone and it is not always predictable who that will be. I have learned to watch Spikey's body language very closely when people are standing over him. I also pay close attention to my energy level since I know that most of the people he has lunged at are people I have concerns about as well. Of course, not all Caiques do this but if your parrot does start this behavior, it will be important to carefully observe his or her body language so you can distract the bird from this behavior and/or prevent anyone from being injured. The warning may seem subtle but with Spike it is fairly predictable — he sways back and forth, thrusts his head up and then leaps.

Spike is not the only Caique I have seen lunge at someone to bite them and I have observed other parrot species exhibit this dramatic sudden aggression. I have heard of several situations where pet shop parrots have jumped off of their cage to attack people who, for some reason not understood at the time, threatened them. Watching body language is always important, especially when trying to relate to unknown parrots in situations where the parrots could act in an unpredictable manner.

Getting Past the Fear

One Biting Incident

My African grey, Whodeedo, came to live with me a few years ago from The Gabriel Foundation. I was told that he had previously lost two or three homes because he had become such a bad biter. From the beginning, I have always approached him in a gentle, calm, and decisive manner. The very first time I placed my hand in his cage, he put his beak around my finger as a test. I didn't pull back and he didn't bite me. Since we have established our bond, he trusts me to handle him with few reservations. He will turn upside down in my hands, hang from one foot, and let me lift his wings and raspberry his belly or under his wings. When Whodee is really mellow, I can nuzzle the skin around his beak with my nose — sort of a psittacine Eskimo kiss. He is a beaky bird and his playful beak is usually all over my hands, but we seem to have an understanding. **If I respect his moods and boundaries, he respects the pain threshold of my fingers.**

Just yesterday, I made the mistake of picking him up right after I had played with my high-energy Caique, Spike. I did not check Whodee's mood first and I moved too quickly for him. He lunged at my finger and bit me. It wasn't a bad bite as bites go, but he did draw blood. I pulled my hand away from him after stating an emphatic exclamation of pain. This was one incident in ten months, and I certainly did not want Whodeedo to get it into his head that this was the proper thing to do. Making a big deal of it or trying to punish him most likely would have reinforced the incident in his mind. The bite did hurt, but more than that, it shocked me that he had actually bitten me after all this time. I admit that it even hurt my feelings, made me a little bit angry, and at least temporarily, made me hesitant to approach him again. Once I thought about it, I knew that my high energy and lack of focus about what I had been doing

Many parrots bite because they are approached in an unfocused, and/or threatening manner. It is less likely for a parrot to step on your hand if you are angry, agitated, or overexcited by something else going on at the time.

when I tried to pick him up had pushed beyond the "boundaries" that Whodeedo and I had established together for me handling him. I did not blame him for biting me. I realized that I needed to be a little more relaxed when I approached him the next time.

I also realized that I had to take <u>ALL</u> of the responsibility for maintaining the positive aspects of the bond that Whodeedo and I have developed. Our friendship is based on trust. If I yelled at him and grabbed him to ladder him, or tried to punish him aggressively, the relationship would be negatively redefined. This would also be true if I allowed myself to become too afraid to handle him again, or if I punished him by withdrawing my attention. I needed to maintain the status quo of a friendship based on mutual trust. To do so, I needed to approach him again almost immediately, but I needed to be very aware of the way I approached him. I took a deep breath, lowered my head, shut my eyes for only a moment to relax, and then, calmly, but decisively, reached my hand towards Whodee. I pressed the back of my fingers gently into his lower belly and said a clear but calm "UP." He stepped on my hand without hesitation and came right out. We went into the living room and had a cuddle-fest and there have been no problems since. For both of us, it is like nothing bad ever happened. By calmly handling him immediately with confidence, I reinforced the previous bond of trust that we had developed and avoided any other behavior that might have "redefined" the relationship toward a more negative plateau.

Twiggy — A Really Bitey Bird

Twiggy came to live with me in 1999 when she was about 7-months-old. She is a Slender-billed Conure — an unusual species that has always fascinated me. Laurie, the store owner was afraid that most people would not be able to handle Twiggy, whose affectionate store nickname was Icepick, so she came home to live with me. I adore Twiggy but she has to be one of the ***bitiest*** birds I have ever met, but it didn't take me long to learn not to take her biting, or should I say pinching, too seriously. She is bitey (nippy), but not a biter, and I have never seen a parrot who can open her beak as wide as she can. It is important for me to stay aware of the fact that her bitey behavior is not usually based on aggression. This behavior seems to be a natural part of her super-wiggly personality — the way she plays and even shows affection. Since she has an unusually shaped beak, she doesn't really hurt when she bites. If one of her beak squeezes does hurt, it is usually just a pinch.

After the first month or so with me, Twiggy finally learned that I don't always appreciate her pinching frenzies. Sometimes I don't mind her excessive enthusiasm, but if I want her to be a calmer bird, I have to approach her in a <u>much</u> calmer manner. I

With her long sharp beak, my Slender-billed Conure, Twiggy, looks like a pretty formidable biter. She is a very nippy bird but she is not a biter — about the most damage she can do with that beak is a good pinch.

need to keep things that way so she doesn't take any rise in my energy level as an opportunity to go into her super-beaky mode. I have also learned a few special handling techniques like gently tucking her in the crook of my arm when she gets too nippy. We also spend a lot of time in high-energy play — she loves to play "ride 'em cowgirl" as I get her hanging playgym swinging or spin the office chair around with her on it when she says, "Ready?"

Ruining the Bond

Recently I talked with the owner of a cockatoo who was still very angry at her bird. According to her, the bird had calmly wandered into the office where her boyfriend was working on the computer. He had climbed up on the man and, without warning, reached up and gave him a nasty bite on the chin. Evidently, the boyfriend had been properly non-reactive and put the bird back down on the floor and then left the room bleeding. However, when the woman saw what had happened, she became un-hinged. According to her account, she ran into the room, scooped up the bird, yelling at him about what a bad bird he was. She threw him back in his cage, took out all of his toys and dishes, and then hit the cage several times with a dustpan.

By the time she called me, the cockatoo had been in this deprivation "punishment situation," being ignored, and I presume not being fed much, for two weeks. This couldn't possibly teach the cockatoo anything about not biting. As she talked to me, it became obvious that she could easily justify almost anything she had done by blaming the bird. I tried to explain that parrots have no way of understanding punishment, especially long-term deprivation. When she argued with me, I explained that even small children do not understand this type of punishment. She disputed any information I gave her and I continued by telling her that her behavior had been very trust-destroying and she would need to diligently work with her cockatoo to win his trust again. She exclaimed, "But I can't trust him!" He certainly could not trust her.

Evidently, he had begun lunging at her when she came near the cage. She would hear nothing I said and I finally gave up trying to talk to her. I could only hope that something I had said would sink in and would make a difference in her attitude and her total lack of responsibility.

I received little background on the cockatoo during this conversation so I do not know what precipitated the bite her boyfriend received. She said that the bird had never bitten before, but then contradicted her statement by saying she had always punished him in this manner whenever he bit her or someone else. My guess is that this extreme situation had been repeated several times. Each time, the bond between the bird and his human flock had been negatively impacted. Because of her horrible attitude, there is no doubt if she had even taken the time to work with the Moluccan, she would probably have experienced further biting situations. Luckily the cockatoo eventually went to live with a new caregiver who was able to work with his problems.

Trust-destroying Cycle

I have now worked with parrots for close to three decades, and during this time I have found that the biggest mistake many people make with their companion parrots is to turn an incident into a pattern. The most trust-destroying cycle in companion parrot behavior starts when a person who has been bitten becomes afraid of his or her parrot. As I have written many times, parrots are highly reactive to the moods and energy levels of the people in their human flock. Although there may be companion parrots who have never bitten (and will never bite) anyone for any reason, the truth is that most parrots will, at one time or another, bite someone. Often a bite is a reaction to something that frightens, confuses, or over-stimulates the parrot. Biting behavior usually starts as a response to a single situation, rather than as a pattern. Unfortunately, biting can easily be turned into a pattern by the owner's immediate and long-term reactions.

The following steps and tips can be used by the parrot owner to get past the resulting fear, once a bite has occurred:
1. DID HE REALLY BITE YOU? Or did he become a little bitey when his energy level increased during play? Lots of parrots go into "overload" behavior when they get excited. During this time, they may get a little rough with their beaks. The best thing to do when this happens is just to return them to the cage and/or leave them alone to let them calm down before you try to handle them again. Getting mad and grabbing them up for discipline or punishment will just escalate their energy level, making them more likely to bite again. Laddering an already over-stimulated parrot will get him even more excited and almost always guarantees another bite.
2. AVOID THE VICIOUS CYCLE. When bitten, some people become apprehensive about being bitten again and, as a result, their attitude and energy changes towards the parrot. The parrot senses this change and may, in turn, become apprehensive about being handled again by that person and bites again. As a result, the person becomes more afraid, and the parrot becomes more confused. The parrot's confusion results in behavior that then makes the person even more frightened of being bitten. This

continuing mistrust escalates until the bond is broken. When a parrot can no longer be handled by the people in his life, his ultimate pet potential is severely threatened. Understanding why and how the situation occurred is the best way to avoid the behavior again and to become comfortable enough to rebuild a trusting parrot/human bond?

3. DON'T BLAME THE BIRD. Biting behavior may become a pattern but it is not a natural behavior unless a parrot is severely provoked. How can we blame an animal that has no idea how to live successfully in our environment? Parrots don't know how to be good pets — we need to teach them how. Often, we are the ones that actually teach our parrots to bite by rewarding that behavior with "negative" drama. Yes, some parrots become willful and stubborn, but blaming the bird will get you nowhere. It will also keep you from taking the necessary responsibility for doing the work you need to do to restore the bond between you and your parrot.

Even a gentle parrot who rarely bites can become excited during play and get a little nippy. If this happens, just slow down your energy and put the parrot down so he can calm down.

4. A BITE IS A SINGLE BITE. Realize that the bite was a single bite… not the end of the world. Most biting in tame parrots starts out as an isolated incident, not as ingrained biting behavior. It is often our reaction to the first bite that turns this behavior into a pattern. An aggressive reaction to a parrot bite is one of the best ways to guarantee that your parrot will bite you again. Even jerking your hand as a discipline when a bird bites can result in another bite when the bird tries to use his beak to get his balance. It is best to pay attention to your parrot and learn to understand him well enough to prevent a bite rather than having to deal with one when it happens.

5. DON'T TAKE IT PERSONALLY. Your parrot neither hates you, nor is punishing you, nor is out to get you. If your parrot has been tame for you, the first bite is usually the most painful from an emotional perspective. Your bird most likely bit you for reasons that have little to do with whether he likes you or not. If he continues to bite, it is most likely because you now approach him differently and you are no longer comfortable approaching him, which makes him less comfortable being approached by you. This can turn into a vicious cycle where mutual trust is lost.

6. WHY DID THE BIRD BITE? Try to figure out why the bird bit you — **DON'T DO IT AGAIN**. This sounds simplistic, but it may be the best advice to follow. Parrots bite for many reasons and sometimes they are not obvious. However, if you can do a quick recall of the situation after a parrot bites, you may be able to make a good guess. A classic example is a strongly bonded bird happily sitting on his caregiver's shoulder. An "intruder" comes into the room and the bird goes into defensive behavior. Although it does not seem logical to us, the parrot often bites their beloved owner in this defensive situation.

Another common example occurs when a bird bites the person holding him when he becomes afraid of something. For example, a person may be too insistent that his parrot goes to a new person that, for some reason, causes apprehension in the bird. Forcing a parrot into a fearful situation often results in a bite.

Some parrots bite when they are approached too quickly, or when they are eating or napping. If you pick your parrot up with what I call the "fish bait" approach by wiggling your fingers in front of him instead of calmly approaching him, he may also be tempted to bite you because he is confused by your indecisiveness. People who approach their parrots too aggressively, in a bad mood, in a hurry, or with scattered energy may also be inviting a bite.

7. DON'T USE PUNISHMENT. Parrots really don't have enough of a long-term sense of cause-and-effect logic to understand that your punishment is related to their misbehavior. The most effective discipline is simply a quick dirty look the minute the parrot misbehaves. This communicates immediate disapproval, which the parrot can understand. Then let it go — nothing else you do will result in negative behavior becoming positive behavior. In fact, if you use trust-destroying, aggressive or deprivation punishment it will most likely damage the relationship you have with your parrot.

8. BE REALISTIC. Don't either insult your parrot's intelligence or expect him to understand something he can't. Having a calm talk with him about why he should not bite you will only work if you use it as a way to calm yourself down. He may not understand what your words mean but he will understand that your calm demeanor makes you more trustworthy.

I once heard a breeder saying that a certain bird couldn't have come from her aviary because her birds never bit people. The truth is that eventually, if the right situation comes along, every parrot, no matter how tame or gentle, will bite. The beak is not innately a weapon. It is used in the same way we use our hands. However, if a bird is threatened or confused, he will use his beak to defend himself. In many situations, a parrot will learn to bite simply because he receives such aggressive or inconsistent messages from the people in his human flock that he doesn't know what else to do to get them to go away.

→

9. GET COMFORTABLE. Remember that parrots are more comfortable with people who are comfortable with them. Making yourself as comfortable as you can with your bird and the situation is the most critical part of being confident that he won't bite you. If you go into the situation thinking he will bite you — chances are he will. You need to "psych" yourself into believing that you are doing everything right to make the situation positive so your parrot will not bite you.

10. PLAN AHEAD. Don't just go and get your parrot out of his cage and then decide what you are going to do with him. Plan ahead to make the situation as positive as possible for both you and your parrot. Get the neutral room ready with a T-stand and your other "props." Make sure there will be no distractions. Pick the time when you and the parrot are the most relaxed. Have anything you will need ready. What about your energy? Make sure you can relax enough to approach the bird calmly and decisively. If it helps you, shut your eyes and say a little positive mantra so that you convince yourself to let go of the fear that your parrot will bite you.

11. WATCH BODY LANGUAGE. Learn to interpret your parrot's body language and listen for verbal communications carefully. There are times when you are asking for problems if you try to pick him up. When my Caique, Spike, is eating one of his favorite treats he becomes aggressive if anyone comes near him. He makes a high-pitched squeal and sometimes mantles his wings over the food as if to hide it from sight. Unless he has something that needs to be taken away from him because it is dangerous, I know not to bother him. I learned the hard way to respect his food possessiveness.

Although there are some classic signs of aggression, many parrots have their own particular ways of letting you know to leave them alone. Increased alertness, flashing eyes, a raised crest, erect feathers on the nape, feathers tucked tight against the body, and beak lunging are usually obvious signs of a bird that should not be handled, but with some parrots the signs are more subtle. Learn to know what your parrot's body language is when he is relaxed or wants your attention, as opposed to when he needs to be left alone.

12. PAY ATTENTION TO MOODS. Know what times of day your parrot's behavior is most mellow. Just like their people, some parrots are easier to get along with at certain times of the day. Some are more receptive in the morning, while others can be friendlier during siesta time in the afternoon. The early evening seems to be the best time to work with many parrots, since this is the time they instinctively wind down from the day. Working with a hungry parrot doesn't make sense, since most birds are more manageable after they have been fed. Trying to handle an over-stimulated parrot is simply bad judgement.

13. IS IT JUST YOU? Is your parrot easier to handle when no one else is around? This is the case with many parrots, and insisting that he comes out when a perceived intruder is in the room is just asking for a bite. Sometimes a spouse or child will purposely antagonize the parrot and if this is true, they should not be in the room when you handle your parrot. Just the sight of

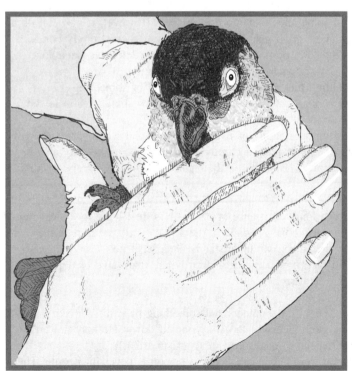

Many parrots love to roughhouse with their favorite people. You can encompass them in your hands and turn them every which way and they love it but watch carefully for signs of over-stimulation and stop before the bird reaches the point of no return.

people like this may make the parrot react with a bite. There are many parrots who become aggressive even with the person they get along with when someone else is in the room. I must again emphasize that if you are trying to work with a parrot who you have become afraid of, you must maximize your situation so there are no distractions and you can focus completely on what you are doing with the parrot.

In attempting to recover the tameness of a companion parrot, it is usually a good idea for everyone in the human flock to work with the bird individually. Once each person develops their own mutually trusting bond with the parrot, he can be worked with and handled by several people again.

14. WORK AWAY FROM CAGE. Many parrots tend to be far more aggressive around their cage territory than they are in a neutral room. A neutral room is one that the bird is not used to being in and, therefore has established no sense of "territory." When the parrot can no longer see the area where his cage is, any need he might feel to be defensive is lessened. Also, when in such unfamiliar territory, he is much more likely to be responsive to the one thing with which he is familiar — you.

If you are afraid to take your parrot out of his cage, you may need to have someone else take him to the neutral room and leave him there for you to work with. If there is no one else who can handle the bird, one of the best ways to get him out of his cage is to bribe him to come out onto a T-stand by placing his absolutely favorite treats in the food cup. Once he is on the stand, move slowly, pick the stand up, and move it into the neutral room. If he flies to the floor, remain calm and approach him slowly. Parrots who are on the floor are often compliant so he should step up to your hand when asked.

15. ARE THERE DISTRACTIONS? Is the dog barking? Are your kids trying to get your attention? Is the television on? Are you thinking about something else while you are trying to work with your bird? If your spouse comes into the room, the kids start roughhousing, or the dog starts barking, it could distract your focus from the bird or make the bird go into a defensive mode that could lead to a bite. It is really important that when you spend time with your parrot after a bite that you focus all of your attention on what you are doing with the bird.

16. EYE CONTACT & FOCUS. In many years of working with parrots, I was rarely bitten when I was totally focused on what I was doing with the parrot. This became evident to me several years ago when I was taming a young imported Blue-front Amazon. After working with him for an hour or so, he was calm enough to sit on my hand. He was a little bit wiggly, but as long as I was making soft eye contact with him, he was OK. When I turned away to talk to the owner, the Amazon reached down and took a chunk out of my finger. When I looked back at him, he straightened and acted like he had never done it. Since that time, I have been very careful to pay close attention to any parrot I was handling, including my own. Unless they are very aggressive, I do not make intense eye contact with them, but I don't take my eyes off of them until I feel I can trust them not to bite me.

17. USING DISTRACTIONS. Many parrots get into the pattern of biting when they get mixed messages from people who try to pick them up. One of the best methods for stopping a parrot's biting pattern is to give him something else to do that breaks the pattern. In this way, you can take control of the biting. If he is in the habit of trying to bite every time you approach him to pick him up, sometimes the appropriate use of non-threatening distractions can attract a parrot's attention long enough from biting so that you can pick him up.

One of the tricks I use to pick up a parrot that I know wants to bite me is to hold something in my other hand. I make sure the parrot can see it but I do not make any kind of threatening gesture with the object. While the parrot is wondering why I am holding a potholder, folded paper, or a remote control in my other hand, I can get him to step up. The object in my other hand provides a distraction that helps to disrupt the biting pattern. If a parrot is not frightened of towels, placing a small towel across your arm like a waiter can be a very effective way to distract a confused parrot away from your fingers. Make sure not to use anything that would frighten or threaten the parrot. For example, I would not advise using a towel to distract a parrot who has become afraid of towels because of the way he has been handled with them.

18. PROTECTING YOURSELF. I believe that all companion parrots should be stick trained when they are young — if possible. Even the best-behaved parrots may go through some difficult stages. However, after a parrot starts biting is not the time to start poking a stick at him hoping he will step on it. Most parrots would be particularly upset by the introduction of such a threatening variable when there may already be problems with aggression. Many people recommend the use of gloves to work with a biting parrot. I usually don't because the vast majority of parrots with whom I have worked become apprehensive about gloved hands. Like trying to stick train a parrot after problems start, wearing a glove just adds another variable that can create even more apprehension in your parrot. If you feel safer wearing a glove and you are positive that it does not negatively affect your parrot, wearing a thin glove on one hand may help you feel more confident. However, a positive, confident attitude with decisive gentle handling will be even more effective.

Many parrots will become at least a bit obnoxious to someone at one time or another in their lives. Because of this, training a parrot to step on a stick or branch will be very helpful in the future. Not only does it make it easier for you to get your parrot out of his cage if he is being ornery but it also allows other people to be able to get him out of his cage if necessary. In the spring, I usually don't want to pick up Rascal, my Double-yellow Head male, with my hand but he readily steps on a stick no matter where he is.

19. THE THREE Ps — Patience, Practice and Patterning. Your ultimate goal is to provide the kind of behavioral guidance that keeps your parrot gentle and tame. It is also critical to develop enough awareness of his moods and body language that you know when he is receptive to handling. There are times when it is simply inappropriate to work with him. Be patient — trying to hurry his progress will actually slow it down.

Start working with your parrot in a nurturing instructional manner as soon as he starts to exhibit aggressive behavior — don't wait until biting becomes an ingrained pattern. It is much easier to work with an incident than it is to change a pattern. Changing a pattern requires a great deal of patience.

Approaching a parrot calmly and using consistent handling techniques such as the "UP" command will help your parrot be much more comfortable with you. Positive patterning is not only important for your parrot, it is also important for you to be as consistent, gentle, and decisive as possible. The more you handle parrots in this manner, the more comfortable the parrots will be with you. If you have become afraid of handling your parrot, it may be helpful to visit a quality bird shop or a friend who has very tame parrots. Practice by handling their birds until you can pattern yourself to become more comfortable picking them up. Then you can transfer that ease to your own parrot. Practice may not always make perfect, but it certainly helps!

20. DON'T GIVE UP! Progress with parrots is never 1-2-3. If your parrot does bite you when you are working with him, go back to step one and start over again. Parrots remember what they have learned and will progress faster after a set back. If you have to, acknowledge your pain with a loud "ouch!" — but whatever you do, stay calm and don't try to punish him aggressively or withdraw your affection. These are not trust-building ways to work with a parrot and everything we do with our companion parrots must work to win and keep their trust. Be patient and consistent.

Don't give up on your parrot. He does not always understand the

As social animals, parrots need in-your-face interaction and attention. A daily affectionate head skritch is one of the best ways to keep a companion parrot happy, trusting, tame and well-behaved. Staying focused on the parrot makes it even better for both of you. Sometimes all a misbehaving parrot needs is reassurance that he is still an important part of your life.

right thing to do. Sometimes he will behave in a manner that is actually counterproductive to what you are trying to accomplish. Take responsibility for being a good teacher. Nurture him — he needs you to show him how to be gentle and consistent. The reward will be a friendship of mutual trust.

BEAKBITE TIP: Don't lead with your face

Facial bites can be a serious problem and may leave permanent scars. A client adopted a second-chance Double-yellow Head Amazon. She knew that the Amazon was wary of hands and because of this, she was wary about approaching him to pick him up. He was a gorgeous, personable parrot with a good vocabulary. As I recall, he had become relatively cage bound because his previous caregivers had not handled him consistently and consequently he would not allow handling. My client had other parrots and genuinely wanted to provide this bird with a good home. Like many people who adopt or rescue previously owned parrots, she was not fully aware of how he would behave under many situations. When he was in his cage, he loved for her to talk and sing to him so she would put her face very close to his cage with the bars were between them. They had become quite comfortable with this interaction so she decided to open the cage door and talk to him with her face in the cage. While it seemed to be the same type of situation for her, it was very different for the Amazon — most likely he was threatened by this new situation. She sustained a serious bite on her lip. Understanding a simple truth about parrot behavior would probably have saved her from this injury — Parrots are more threatened by actions, and new situations and/or objects that occur inside their cages than those that occur away from the cage area. The second rule I told her was "Don't lead with your face."

I do, however, feel compelled to add that many tame parrots can be trusted near the face of their favorite person if the situation is optimal for the parrot to be calm, affectionate, gentle and there is no chance of a sudden distraction. However, before they take the chance, people should know their parrots' behavior well enough to understand when they will and will not be safe.

An Origin for Some Biting Behavior

Parrots are creatures of habit. While it is not a positive step to create a rigid routine for the parrots in our lives, they do thrive on consistency and predictability. The mutual bond between a companion parrot and the person he lives with is the most significant aspect of that bird's life. He needs to depend on that bond and most of all, the consistency of his caregiver's personality. When a person is emotionally undependable and capricious in their behavior towards the parrot, that bird will most likely become insecure in the relationship. This insecurity can create all sorts of behavioral problems with biting being the most common.

Why do insecure birds bite the people in their lives? There are most likely many reasons, but I believe the biting often starts as a way to test the caregiver. This is especially true when there is a change in the attitude, commitment, dependability, and personality of the caregiver.

When companion parrots become insecure, they may start to bite as a way to test the people in their lives. Be sure not to fail this important test!

Many young parrots in a new home will start testing the caregiver when "the newness" wears off and the person's interest is not as strong. The parrot often reacts with an attempt to test the status quo. Is everything the same? Is the caregiver still dependable and capable of being the "flock leader?"

The First "Bite" from Whodee

As many of you know, when my four-year-old African grey, Whodeedo, first came to live with me over a year ago he had a reputation for being a biter. I knew it was important for me to get off to a good start with him so I carefully planned my first approaches to him. When I got him home from the airport, I let him climb from the carrier directly into his cage that was completely set up. I had already placed his favorite toys that Micki Muck, his "foster mom" from the Gabriel Foundation, had sent with him. I did not give him very much direct attention for the first few hours, as I wanted him to have a little time to adjust to his new environment. I did not want to overload him with too much new information at once. However, I also knew that it was important for me to establish a relationship of nurturing guidance as soon as possible. A new home is a "neutral territory" because a parrot has not had a chance to become comfortable enough to reestablish his previous negative behaviors. I wanted to start working with Whodee shortly after his arrival because I did not want to give him the time to establish any of his old routines in his new home. Starting to give him attention right away would allow me to establish new behaviors rather than allowing him to reestablish his old behaviors. After all, these old behaviors were most likely what got him into trouble in his previous homes.

After an hour or so, I stood next to his cage with my head lowered and talked to my new family member quietly for a few minutes. I did not want to be too direct in my approach to him since that can create fear in a parrot in an unfamiliar situation. I came back several times and repeated my quiet conversations for a few minutes until it was time for Whodee to go to bed. After the first few times, he seemed quite curious about who I was and what I was doing. In the morning, I repeated this same process a few times until I felt it was the right time to approach him to handle him.

It is a mistake to approach most birds in a new home too directly — this is particularly true of the generally more sensitive species (Greys, Poicephalus, some macaws, and many rescue birds). It is also a mistake for a new person in the parrot's life to approach too directly without first letting the parrot get used to him being there. Doing anything that seems too assertive on our part may create mistrust of our intentions. At the same time, it is important that we do not project the image of being a pushover. To win the new parrot's trust, we need to establish a positive sense of competency and *Nurturing Guidance.*

I walked up to Whodee's cage and talked quietly with him telling him that I wanted him to be a good boy and come out of his cage without any trouble. Of course, at this point he probably had no idea of what my specific words meant because we had not had this conversation before but he could trust my calm energy. I reached in with my hand with two fingers pushing gently towards his lower belly. As soon as my fingers were close enough, he put his beak around them and applied a small amount of pressure. I knew I had to pass this important initial test. If I had jerked my hand back or responded with aggression, I would have failed. I left my hand in place and quietly said, "That's O.K., I am not going to hurt you." Whodee released his grip on my fingers and, with some trepidation, stepped onto my hand. I had passed the test because I remained calm and my entire interaction with him since he had come into my home remained consistent. →

Since that time, I have always tried to remain consistent in my approach when I take Whodee out of his cage. Occasionally, I am distracted and Whodee responds immediately to the inconsistency with a delicate "test bite." He has lived with me now for over a year and in that entire time, he has only really bitten me once. It was clearly my fault because I had not calmed down my energy from playing with my highly excitable Caique, Spike. I failed Whodee's test by ignoring his gentle warning bite that told me he was not comfortable with the way I was approaching him.

The Human Personality

Many people are not always predictable from one minute to the next and it is often difficult to remain consistent in our busy worlds. Because of the stress of living in the modern world, we often have many variables bombarding us at once. Consequently, we tend to have inconsistent reactions to what goes on around us. Although it is important to be as predictable as possible with our parrots, sometimes it is just not possible. ***The behavior of our companion parrots often acts as a barometer to the ups and downs in our lives.*** During difficult times, many companion parrots will start to test us. These tests are usually presented in the form of inconsistent behavior on the part of the parrot. A normally well-behaved parrot may start exhibiting lack of compliance and some budding behavioral problems such as biting or screaming.

The best medicine for companion parrots during these times is for the caregivers to purposely slow down their energy when they approach their parrots' cages. Predictable increased focused attention on a daily basis will usually provide a parrot with enough security for him to return to his more predictable and usually less troublesome behavior.

Many Life Changes

Parrots can live for a long time if we care for them properly and in this span of time, there are bound to be many changes in a caregiver's life. I lived with my beloved African grey, Bongo Marie, for over 24 years. My Amazons, Paco and Rascal, have been with me since their were babies, almost a quarter of a century ago. Spike has been my Caique companion for a dozen years. During these times, I have gone through many life transitions — moving, travel, life path and occupation changes, illness and accidents, surgeries, and the loss of other pets and important people in my life. Some of these transitions were very difficult for my companion parrots and me. One important aspect of parrot keeping became very clear to me — I couldn't blame my parrots for the behavioral problems they developed during my difficult times. When I become either physically or emotionally absent and, therefore, inconsistent and unpredictable, I need to take responsibility to reestablish the trust in my relationship with my parrots. It is often a simple matter of providing renewed dedication and daily focused attention to get back to the more positive interactions of the parrot/human bond.

Coming Back from Trips

I travel a lot and have found that when I come home from a trip, it is best to go slowly with my parrots. If I immediately rush over to greet Whodee, he seems uncomfortable as if he has to think about it for a while before he accepts me again. If I am too direct with my Caique, Spike, his response tends to be somewhat aggressive until I softly talk him into calming down. My Slender-billed Conure, Twiggy, reacts with overexcitement resulting in overload aggression. My Amazons, Paco and Rascal, are clearly happy to see me but they, too, are excited enough to become aggressive towards me. Pascal, their 12-year-old daughter, is generally such an agreeable parrot that she always seems happy to see anyone. However, I have learned to go slowly with her after a trip because even she becomes excited. One time when I came home, she gave me a fairly painful bite in that web area between the thumb and the index finger. Over the years, I have talked with many companion parrot caregivers who are shocked

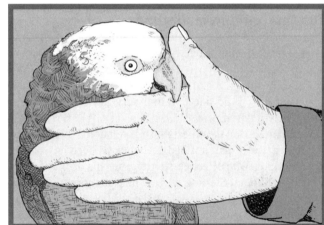

If your parrot bites you when you come home from a trip, don't take it personally. It may just be that your enthusiastic greeting got him too excited. Go slow and greet him calmly.

because their beloved bird bites them with great severity when they returned from being away. Despite my experience with Pascal, there seems to be a disproportionate number of cockatoos who provide their caregivers with this type of surprise greeting when they are so happy to see their parrots.

People have told me that their parrots had forgotten them or were punishing them for being gone. I don't believe either is true. People can't help but take this behavior personally even though it is not a personal statement on the part of the parrot. Since parrots thrive on established patterns in their lives, I think they simply have substituted a new pattern while a member of their human flock is absent. The parrot is simply out of the habit of being with that person. When the person comes in like gangbusters to greet them, the bird is immediately threatened because he is simply not used to being greeted in this manner.

I highly recommend a short period of re-acquaintance before handling the parrot. This can only take a few minutes or a few days. Many people get stressed, tired and irritable from traveling (I know I do!). If they approach their parrot before calming themselves down, the parrot will often respond negatively to that negative energy. The first step in establishing the status quo is to calm down and greet the parrot with a gentle verbal exchange, "I really missed you and I am so happy to see you." Spend a little time around the cage quietly asking the parrot if he missed you or what he did while you were gone. It doesn't really matter what you say as long as the words are spoken in a calm quiet manner to give the parrot a chance to reacquaint himself with you. When he starts to calm down or to respond positively to your presence, bring him out for you normal interaction with him. If a parrot was in a boarding situation, he may need even more time to relax and readjust both to his surroundings and the people in his life.

Our Inconsistent Personalities

Most of us can be inconsistent from time to time but continual inconsistency can lead to serious problems for companion parrots. Most people with substance abuse problems exhibit unpredictable personalities. Some time ago, I did a consultation with a couple who absolutely adored their Timneh grey. Their major concern was that the bird was unpredictably aggressive, moody and had become afraid of both of them although he seemed to tolerate the husband. It only took me a few phone calls and one evening visit to know that I could not give them any advice that would help them with the grey. It was clear to me that both the husband and wife had serious drinking problems. From what I could tell, the man was pleasant enough when he had been drinking although he acted quite foolish. The normally pleasant woman on the phone during the day turned into an angry harridan. They argued and she was quite sarcastic with her husband. He

Companion parrots thrive with dependable caregivers. Most people can be capricious from time to time but those who have problems with substance abuse generally exhibit severe push-pull personality traits that provide their parrots with confusing mixed messages.

became defensive and each one blamed the other for the parrot's problems. Like the parrot, I was uncomfortable being around people who were so out of touch with their own lives and I could understand why the parrot had developed such unpredictable behavior. I could not blame him for biting either one of them but they sure did. My life has taught me that people with this type of problem rarely take responsibility for their own actions. The man often traveled on business and, evidently the parrot was often left out all night to fend for himself when the woman had too much to drink. How could they possibly expect their parrot to have consistent behavior when their own behavior was so capricious and unpredictable? He was living in world of mixed messages and constantly had to test the status quo and his caregivers rarely passed his tests. Companion parrots, like humans, thrive on dependability and predictability. The only way I could help this parrot was to insist that his owners put him to bed before they settled in for the evening. I explained that parrots can become quite grouchy if they are not getting a proper amount of sleep. It didn't matter to me why they stopped handling their grey in the evening, it only mattered that they did.

As long as our behaviors remain unpredictable and inconsistent, we can only expect that our companion parrots will react in the same manner. We all have our human frailties and shortcomings and a certain amount of upheaval occurs in everyone's life. If you know you are in a bad mood, or not yourself in some way that may cause your parrot problems, it is best to give him a break and stay away from him until you can calm yourself down. It is unreasonable to expect our parrots to constantly adjust to our mood changes during these fluctuations in our lives. The key to our predictability for our parrot is to be aware that there is a problem and take responsibility for it. Dedicating some time each day to interact with our parrots in a calm, positive manner will help maintain the status quo for them. If they begin to test the status quo, instead of reacting negatively to their behavioral changes, we need to do our best to pass their tests. Even during times of change such as marriage, divorce, a new baby, and/or a stressful period of life, we can work through them with out parrots and not abandon our avian companions. ⚡

BEAKBITE TIP: Friendly Bites May Still Hurt

Not all bites come from aggressive parrots. Sometimes they come from affectionate play. During play, parrots beak wrestle with each other for fun and communication. If you place your parrot near your face to give him a big kiss or to raspberry his belly, make sure he is in a mellow, affectionate mood. In his excitement, if he wants to play and sees your nose as a friendly beak to wrestle with, even an affectionate nose pinch can bring tears to your eyes!

If a playful parrot becomes excited, his beaky behavior may become too enthusiastic. Even though he is playing, the result could still be an excitable, painful pinch. Eye pinning, feather erection and other very readable body language do not always mean the parrot is acting aggressively. It could mean the parrot has become over stimulated. The best bet is to let him be so he can calm down before you try to handle him again. Handling him when he is still in overload could result in injury.

The First Bite Is Not Forever

Talking with people about their parrots usually helps me clarify my own theories about parrot behavior. A long-term Pet Bird Report (now the CPQ) subscriber called me with a question about her African Grey. For the most part, her grey (who was almost 2 years old) had been a well-behaved, contented parrot causing his owner few behavioral concerns. Her worry was that occasionally, for reasons she could not always understand, the parrot would bite her. These infrequent bites were rarely hard and seemed more like petulant warnings than mean-spirited aggression. In some cases, she had become aware of the fact that he was actually grabbing her finger with his beak to direct her hand because he wanted her to be doing something else. For example, if she was petting him and wasn't paying attention, he would reach over and grab her finger to tell her to pet him more carefully.

If he bit too hard, she dealt with the behavior immediately by giving him a quick disapproving look (*the evil eye*) and saying a firm (but not aggressive or overly dramatic) "NO." Usually the grey would settle down immediately. In some cases, if he seemed over-stimulated, she would quietly place him, without further admonishments or drama, away from her, either on the arm of the chair, his playgym, or back in his cage — not as a punishment but as a time-out to let him calm down.

The reader wanted to make sure these incidents would not become a pattern. Clearly at the young grey's age, the rare biting behaviors were isolated incidents, not part of a habituated pattern. This was most likely true because his owner had dealt with them in a manner that neither rewarded him with drama nor punished him with aggression. My only advice was to try to figure out if there might be some sort of pattern to the biting incidents, keep dealing with the occasional obstreperousness in the same manner, and enjoy her delightful companion.

Prediction, Portent, Prophecy, Prognostication?

Many human beings (not excluding parrot owners) seem to jump to the conclusion that when one bad thing happens, it is an omen of a future full of disaster. (Been there, done that!) Following these prophecies of doom, many a parrot owner goes off the deep end the first time his parrot bites him. Often the first reaction, which is totally illogical, is "my parrot doesn't love me anymore!" The grey's owner had saved her relationship with him by accepting his occasional forays into misbehavior as what they were — simply a part of his independence process or a slightly inappropriate communication. She did not erroneously jump to any conclusion that an occasional bite was the beginning of the end, and was therefore able to deal with the behaviors in a rational way.

Will The Real Drama Addict Please Stand Up

I often write about parrots being "addicted to drama." Certainly many of their behaviors (both wild and domestic) can seem quite flashy. However, it is also important to realize we are dealing with a prey animal (one who can become another animal's lunch at the slightest misstep) who also clearly exhibits the importance of being hidden and unnoticed. There are certainly times when a parrot should be as quiet and unobtrusive as possible.

I would like to make the equally accurate observation that we humans also tend to be drama addicts. And our parrots thoroughly enjoy this aspect of our behavior — up to a point. In fact, our dramatic responses to their behavior are likely to turn an incidental act into a habituated pattern. Our parrots love our drama whether we are attempting to be positive or negative. Providing them with a dramatic response reinforces the behavior we are responding to, and this is often the very behavior we would rather not have repeated. So, in actuality, we are the ones who so often turn our parrot's initial misbehaviors into habituated patterns because we do not deal with them correctly. It is doubtful to me that the grey in this story will ever become a biting bird because at the rare times he does bite only that particular incident is dealt with. He is not rewarded with drama, nor is the single bite responded to as if the African Grey had suddenly turned into a blood-lusting vampire. The incidents will not become a habit. It appears to me there are actually people who seem to have an investment in their parrot's misbehavior. They show off their bites as if they are proud of just how difficult it is to live with such a horrible parrot. They don't want to work to change the aggressive behavior because of the attention it brings them. Perhaps they also love the drama it brings into their lives. Others seem unable, no matter

Most companion parrots love drama and many caregivers love to provide them with the drama that they like. However a dramatic response should be in response to positive behavior and not a response to aggression or other negative behaviors.

how important it is, to set rules and provide guidance for their parrots. Of course, this human behavior is not fair to the parrot and these birds usually end up with serious behavioral problems of one kind or another. Most of them end up losing their homes.

Taking It Personally — Or Unable to Take Responsibility

Another recent call was from a woman whose macaw had *suddenly* become unmanageable at 11 months old. While she could still pick up the bird without being bitten, it had become impossible to handle him around the cage. Her husband had been the macaw's best buddy and now the bird was biting him. This made the man angry, and the macaw's biting behavior quickly escalated in response to this anger. The man's attitude was another I hear too frequently: "For no reason at all, my bird suddenly turned mean." There was no forgiveness in his voice and although he would not admit to it, his feelings had been hurt because the macaw *had loved him best* and now was aggressive to him almost every time he approached the cage. He did not realize that companion parrots often change their bond as they mature ... but they can change it right back if the previously preferred person interacts with the bird in a consistently nurturing manner. Young macaws often bond strongly with a person who just plays with them but as they mature, that bond often switches to a person who provides *Nurturing Guidance* and causes them little confusion.

The man's long-term future relationship with the macaw was being seriously threatened, not because the bird had "turned mean" but because the owner was stubbornly refusing to believe his angry attitude was responsible for the escalation of biting behavior. I explained to him that most macaws go through an independence stage at this approximate age where they might become a challenge for their caregivers, particularly if the birds have had little or no behavioral guidance. While his wife was willing to do almost anything to work on the problem, he was unwilling to accept his complicity in exacerbating the biting patterns. He had discussed the situation with several people who suggested his macaw was exhibiting sexual frustration and needed to be in a breeding program (unlikely because the bird was less than a year old!), a solution he was definitely considering. He also believed, because some "experts" had told him, that he could not change his macaw's recently developed aggressive tendencies because macaws generally turn *mean* and this aggression is engraved in stone. These generalizations are nonsense and people who do not want to work with their parrot grab onto this nonsense as a justification for their own lack of accountability.

I could not understand (and will never understand) why he was so quickly able to dismiss his relationship with a macaw who had previously been his best buddy. In fact, he was more willing to purchase another macaw (most likely from one of the breeders giving him bad behavioral advice) and transfer his affection to that bird rather than working with his previously beloved bird who he thought had "rejected" him. This is one of the most irritating aspects of the "throw away" mentality I see in some parrot owners. I could imagine this man buying a parrot every year, never providing the proper rules and guidance, blaming the bird, and then feeling justified in "getting rid of" him because he "turned mean for no reason at all." Breeding programs and parrot rescue sanctuaries are full of such birds.

Speaking Of Breeding

Does breeding behavior last forever? No. Once a parrot reaches sexual maturity, the bird is not in a permanent, perpetual state of sexual agitation and aggression. People often dread this time because they have heard so many stories, most of which are based on bad behavioral information. Although some parrots slide through the initial stages of sexual maturity without their owners even noticing, others go through periods of time during the year when they do exhibit serious behavioral problems. The only reason these behaviors become a problem for the parrots is because they are a problem for the caregivers. Does this mean a parrot who becomes unpredictable and aggressive during certain seasons no longer makes a good companion? Of course not. Again, the important key is starting out by providing rules and guidance and maintaining this throughout the parrot's life. The other key is accepting the fact that parrots will naturally go through some periods in their lives when they might not be what we humans think of as the *ideal pet.* If people have realistic expectations and provide guidance and instructional interaction, the parrot's negative behaviors will not last forever — live with them, love them, and work with them to get past their moodiness or seasonal behaviors.

Just A Stage?

"Oh, don't worry. It is just as stage he is going through. He'll be fine when he gets through it." While biting, screaming, and other negative behaviors **may** be part of a stage a parrot is going through and he **will** indeed get through this stage, it is important to realize that we will be the ones who determine whether or not he gets through it with his pet potential intact. While some people have an overwhelming and inappropriate response to one or two bites, the opposite also occurs. Too many people wait to work with their parrot's behavior until the problems become entrenched. The longer the person waits to get the right information to change his parrot's aggressive biting, excessive screaming, and/or behavioral feather picking, the more difficult it is to change the behaviors.

I strongly advise parrot owners to take each behavioral misadventure as an event by itself and not go *off the deep end* about them. However, it is also important to know how to deal with these incidents so they won't become repetitive patterned behaviors. If the one or two bites do turn into a patterned behavior with the problem escalating, it is best to get good, trust-building information as soon as possible. The parrot will not change his behavior by himself. It is essential for the owner to start interacting with the parrot in a positive way to change the negative behaviors. *

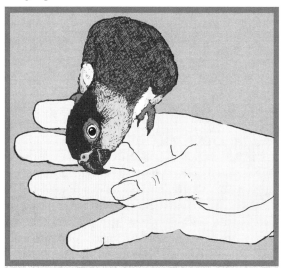

If your parrot goes through a "difficult stage" make sure that you help guide his behavior so he gets beyond the stage with his pet potential intact.

Many small parrots can become very tenacious in their determination to remove fingernails, hangnails, moles, scabs and other such irregularities on their caregiver's skin.

Sharp Beaks and Tenacity

How about aggression from Cockatiels, Budgerigars, Lovebirds, Lories, Parrotlets, Grey-cheeks, and Pyrrhura Conures? Small parrot-family parrots are not that different from the big guys when it comes to aggression. With the higher energy, shorter attention spans, and an element of pinchyness, the bites of the smaller parrots can still cause physical injury. I could include Slender-billed Conures, Rose-breasted and Bare-eyed cockatoos into this group of birds because of their energy and pointy beaks. These are also the birds that need many toys so they can go from one task to another. The beaks of these parrots often seem sharper than those of the bigger birds. They seem to take particular care to hone their beaks so they are as sharp and pointy as possible. What they lack in size, they often make up for in tenacity. Most of the same principles of *Nurturing Guidance* and even *Nurturing Manipulation* apply to these generally high-energy birds. Some of these little guys have reputations for being bitey and, even aggressive, at times. It often seems harder to deal with this aggressive behavior in small parrots because it may seem to be harder to get their attention for long enough to teach them positive behaviors.

Many of the smaller parrots become excited when they are on their caregiver's hands. They quickly learn to play hand games chewing and nipping fingers and they particularly love to explore moles, scabs, and any other irregularity on their caregiver's skin. Most of them can't do as much damage as the larger birds but they do pinch hard enough to be a severe irritant. Because of their tenacity and speed, many of their aggressive attacks consist of multiple bites. Their size seems to make them bite with more of a vengeance to insure their release and escape. The more they get away with this, the more they bite and these little guys can be extremely intimidating when they behave aggressively. Often, these birds are afraid of hands because they are not used to being handled.

If you are working with a parent-raised baby that has never been held in human hands before, it shouldn't take long to establish a calm relationship. The baby just has to learn that the same hands that hold him gently also give the wonderful head skritches. If this is the case, maintain a calm voice and low energy and gently scoop the baby out of the cage to your chest. The small bird will usually calm down when held against your chest. You may want to have a small towel or washcloth to cover him in this position. Talk softly, move slowly, and rub your finger on the top of his head and the back of his neck. After this can be accomplished without much stress or fuss, begin releasing the hold and see if he'll remain on your chest or hand. If he flies down, slowly approach him and ask him to step up to your finger. Many birds on the floor will gladly step to your finger because of their sense of vulnerability on the floor.

Any bird that is displaying aggressive or biting behavior can be more easily handled if his wings are clipped and he is the only bird being worked with in the area. It is difficult to tame or calm a bird that is caged with others or has others in the vicinity to excite his flock instinct. One frantic bird will often stress an entire room of birds. A neutral room is necessary for winning trust if there are too many distractions. If the bird is mature and not used to being handled, the task is more difficult but not impossible. One method that works well in many cases is to take a deep breath, let it out, lower your energy and do the following without flinching. When the bird is perching quietly in its cage, open the door and very slowly approach the bird with your hand in a step up position. The movement of your hand should be almost imperceptible. Do not look at the bird. Go as slow as you possibly can. If the bird seems agitated and ready to flee … stop. Do not retreat but stop momentarily and proceed when he relaxes a bit. You may get all the way to the bird and he may step onto your hand. If he bolts and flies away, wait a moment and start again. Depending on how wild the bird is, you may just want to sit and talk for a while until you can begin again.

If the small bird is fearful and strikes out at you as you enter the cage, you will have to do your work away from the cage. This means you will have to get the bird out of the cage with as little stress as possible. Gloves can be very frightening to a bird so they are not recommended. Gentle toweling is acceptable and sometimes necessary but should be a last resort. Using an old T-shirt or sweatshirt is less intimidating to some smaller birds. Approaching the cage with the cloth casually draped over your arm works best. With the small wild and excitable birds success can be experienced in a dimly lit room in the evening. Again, removing the bird gently from his cage and sitting with him against your chest while you watch TV or just sit and talk softly. The fewer distractions like other people or pets, the better.

Small birds are a little more frantic and, therefore, not as easily tantalized by food, but treats can be tried to coax a wary bird to your hand. Measure your success in small steps and be consistent with your approach. More than one person can work with the feisty bird but be sure that each person is using the same trust building and calm tactics. Don't let someone sabotage your hard work. Little birds seem to get out of the habit of being handled quickly so the more handling, the better. ∮

Are Your Parrots Compatible Or Are They *Combatible*?

We have all seen photographs of multiple parrots of different species playing with each other on gyms and stands. While this certainly is a possibility, talking to almost any avian veterinarian will make it obvious that this compatibility should not be taken for granted. Beak damage, some of it life threatening, is the most common problem in parrot-to-parrot aggression. Another frequent injury occurs when a parrot bites another bird's feet or toes if that bird is on the top of his cage. In situations where bappies have been raised together, the chance is greater that everyone will get along but caregivers should still watch the behavior of their parrots carefully to determine that this compatibility remains as the birds mature.

I am often asked which species of parrots get along best with others. This is an almost impossible question to answer due to the individual personalities within a particular species. It also has a lot to do with the ages and genders of the birds, environmental considerations, and personalities of the caregivers. Sometimes parrots, who seem to be aggressive in many situations, will become very threatened when introduced to another parrot. Most of the time, my Caique, Spikey, seems to strut around as if he thinks he is King Kong. He also reacts very aggressively when another parrot comes near his cage. But is this bravado genuine? One would think that he would be

Pascal was used to being in physical contact with other parrots — Spikey was not. When they were introduced, Pascal immediately moved towards Spike. Spike was quite threatened by this and backed up until he almost fell off of the perch. Although Pascal was not being aggressive, Spike interpreted her attention as if she was being aggressive.

the aggressor when he is being introduced to another parrot but this is not necessarily the case. When I tried to introduce Twiggy, my Slender-bill Conure, to Spike, she seemed to totally concentrate on giving him a frontal lobotomy with her long beak. He was clearly not the aggressor in that situation so I quickly rescued him. I had an idea that this might be the case so I introduced them very carefully. Years before when Spikey met his first hen Caique, they hopped around each other in circles for a couple of minutes and then Spikey seemed to purposefully fall to his back as she kept hopping circles around him. I really don't know what this was all about in the world of Caiques but I am pretty sure that Spike was not being too suave in that relationship. Recently I introduced my mild-mannered Amazon, Pascal, to Spike and the same thing happened. When Pascal moved closer to Spike, he moved away very quickly.

Although many birds adjust to each other if introduced properly, some will remain far more *combatible* than compatible and will never readily share space with others. It is unwise to try to force parrots to get along with each other if they have shown aggression towards each other. Even if two parrots seem friendly at times, there may be situations where they will become aggressive. This is particularly true if they are both bonded to the same person and that person creates a love triangle. One man called me when he couldn't figure out why his head had become a battleground when his two macaws were on his shoulders.

Introducing Parrots to Each Other

Pascal is the daughter of my Double-yellow Headed Amazons, Paco and Rascal. She came to live with me when she was 12 years old. Before that, she had been a good buddy with an African grey. Pascal is an almost totally non-aggressive Amazon. She complains by squealing but she rarely bites. My grey, Whodee, is also a very gentle parrot so I thought they might be able to be friends with each other. I placed one on each hand and talked to them both about the other. Although parrots may not totally understand everything we are saying to them, they certainly pick up on the energy of our words. They knew each other's names and speaking very softly, I introduced them to each other. This showed them that I was there to make sure everyone was safe. I placed them on a stand in my office area and observed them without staring holes in their heads. They moved towards each other. Whodee kept his head low and Pascal moved away but then stretched her head over Whodee's. At that time, Whodee banged a bell and let it do his talking. Whodee's posture showed more threat behavior than Pascal's. She just sat there but fluffed herself after each time Whodee approached her. This didn't surprise me because it was Pascal that was used to interacting with another parrot. I am continuing their introduction but moving slowly by placing them together in neutral situations where they have supervision. Pascal clearly wants to be friends with Whodee but the Grey is still not too sure of the friendship.

The best way to introduce two parrots is to either hold the first bird with one hand and the new bird with the other hand or place them on a T-stand in a neutral area away from their cages. Relax and talk to each of them, reassuring them that everything is OK ... and bring them closer together. It might help to have another trusted person there who can comfortably handle one of the parrots. Watch their body language carefully and don't push the introduction. Let them make the decision to move closer. Supervise but don't overreact to their interaction. Your apprehension could make the parrots more apprehensive of each other. Don't rescue one of the birds from another unless it is obvious that he or she is going to harm the other parrot. Be aware that your relationship with each parrot may influence their introduction to each other. If one of them perceives you as his mate, he may become aggressive to the other parrot in an attempt to defend you. It is important for you to remain calm and friendly since any negative energy from you could cause a problem between the two parrots. Have a towel handy to place over either bird — just in case there is an aggressive altercation. You may have to try several introductions before they become comfortable with each other. A few weeks may pass before they both settle down and relax with each other, so

Since Whodee was not used to physical interaction with other parrots, he did a lot of posturing when he was introduced to Pascal. She just stood her ground while Whodee went through all sorts of display behaviors. Part of his display was to reach up and bang the bell hanging nearby. It took him several introductions before he became comfortable sitting on the same perch with Pascal.

be patient. If one bird is smaller or younger, and therefore more vulnerable, it is critical to be his or her protector. Before any birds are left alone together or without close supervision, you must be absolutely sure there will not be an altercation between them.

Although many birds will adjust to each other if introduced properly, some may never like each other. Others may seem to get along but will not readily share space with each other. Remember to establish rules and provide guidance for all parrots so that they form the strongest bond with you instead of with each other. Whatever you do, don't neglect one parrot in favor of another. Try to provide each parrot in your flock with as much time as possible so one does not feel displaced by the other.

Your companion parrot flock will usually form their own hierarchy. If your parrots are compatible, generally, you can tell who is the dominant parrot in your multiple-bird family. He or she is usually the one who gets preened but rarely returns the favor. They also prefer and usually get the highest perch. Although the people may not always be aware of it, the parrot who perceives himself as being the leader may also have convinced his owner to let him out of his cage first.

If you already have a strongly bonded parrot, it is a wise idea to prepare him properly for the addition of the new bappy. **The major threat to the first bird's security usually has more to do with timesharing than jealousy.** The best way to get the first parrot used to sharing your time is to set the new bird's cage up a few weeks before he comes home. When you clean or service your first parrot's cage, do the same things with the new parrot's cage. Fiddle with the food dishes, the paper, the perches, and the toys on a daily basis. One Pet Bird Report (now CPQ) reader wrote about introducing her new grey into a home with a well-loved Moluccan cockatoo. She fashioned a grey sock and a red sock to look like an African Grey doll, then took it out of the cage on a frequent basis in front of her 'too to help him adjust to the new grey. When the grey bappy actually came home, the cockatoo pretty much took his presence for granted and barely reacted to him. Planning ahead and introducing the new routines gradually, instead of suddenly, prevented some adjustment problems with her cockatoo.

BEAKBITE TIP: Love Triangles

The behavioral dynamics in a home with multiple parrots are different from those in a one parrot home. This is especially true if the parrots have some sort of bond with each other whether they are a pair or just buddies who hang out on a playgym with each other. Caregivers need to recognize situations that may cause aggression and caution should be used in handling these parrots together to keep from becoming an innocent bystander in the squabbles of their relationship. If both parrots have a strong bond with you, they may become upset when you pay attention to the other or they may feel the need to protect you from the other parrot. If my Amazons, Paco and Rascal, are out, I always return her to their aviary first. If I put him in first, he has a tendency to be aggressive towards her and she has to get very bossy to defend herself.

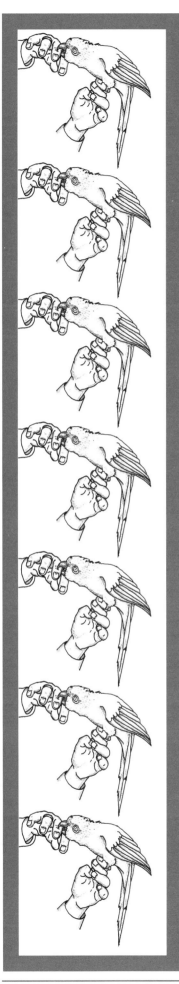

SITUATIONS WITH A POTENTIAL FOR AGGRESSIVE BEHAVIOR

Paying Attention

Once we really start to pay attention to our parrots, their biting and aggressive behavior becomes fairly predictable. Aggressive behavior is often situational and once we begin to realize the type of situations that can excite or threaten our parrots, we can do our best to modify or even avoid those situations.

A classic and simplistic example of this is the woman who told me that her Umbrella Cockatoo loved to be cuddled and petted but if she did this more than a few minutes, the bird would reach out and bite her. She timed the cockatoo and determined that he could only stand about three minutes of petting without getting agitated and then aggressive. The simplest solution to this problem was to only pet him for two and a half minutes but she also needed to watch his body language. As long as he stayed relaxed with the body language of a rag doll pressed against her, he was fine. However, she needed to stay focused on him while she skritched him because he would become irritated if she continually rubbed the same area over and over. As he became older, certain areas became more erogenous and she learned to stay away from these areas when she was cuddling with him. Too much petting under the wing and on the back and tail would stimulate him and lead to aggression on his part.

Many parrots have a threshold for excitement that sends them into an "Overload" situation. My Double-yellow heads, Paco and Rascal, love it when I sing to them. The more operatic I get, the more excited they become and we all enjoy these songfests a great deal. Even though we have developed great rapport during these musical sessions, I have learned through experience that this is not the right time to bring Paco out to give her the big kisses she appreciates at calmer times. When she was a youngster, I also learned that Paco easily falls in love with strangers — particularly blonde or redheaded women. One time I took it personally and decided to show my friend that Paco loved me best. As Paco was cooing sweet nothings in my blonde friend's ear, I picked her up with a assertive "UP" command and asked her for a kiss. That kiss required 4 stitches but I certainly learned my lesson the hard way.

Chances are if you can identify a specific situation as the cause of biting, avoiding that situation, or changing it so it has a more positive outcome makes sense.

The Games

Many parrots love to play high-energy games with the people in their lives. Roughhousing, cuddle-wrestling, gotcha, and hit and run are just a few ways that parrots interact and have fun with their caregivers. Sometimes they start the games and other times they wait for us to start playing. "Keep-away" was the Yellow-nape Amazon's favorite game. He laughed with delight as he chased after the squeaky ball as fast as his short little legs could carry him. Grabbing hold of the soft rubber ball, he rolled over on his back. Squeezing it excitedly, he squealed in imitation of the shrill repetitive squeaky noise that it made. As the ball exploded from his grasp, one of his caregivers

Excited play can put a parrot into Overload. Once he starts to show signs of getting excited, leave him alone to calm down. Trying to handle him could cause injury.

grabbed the rubber ball and tossed it to her friend. The parrot ran after the ball so fast, he tripped over his own feet at least a half dozen times. Just as he got to the person with the ball, she rolled it back to his other human friend. He turned and half running, half flying (almost like a coot running on water) he reached his caregiver at the same time as the ball. She grabbed it first. The Amazon reached out with his beak and grabbed her hand instead, biting her severely. The fun was over and the parrot's caregiver was bleeding and shocked. My client wanted to know why her sweet, tame pet suddenly turned into a vicious, aggressive monster? The Amazon was not being vicious or aggressive. The playful Yellow-nape had reached the level of excitement that I call *Overload*. Many companion parrot species exhibit this reaction to an intense level of stimulation and become excited enough to reach the point when their behavior becomes frenzied. When a parrot becomes this over-stimulated, his actions are not simply behavioral. This is not a time when the **UP** command will work from an assertive owner. I doubt that there is any modification that could change this overload behavior, as it seems to be beyond the parrot's control. However, if the caregiver recognizes the potential of overload as a possibility in certain situations, changes can be made in the way the parrot is handled during these situations. My client doesn't have to stop playing keep-away with her Yellow-nape. She just has to watch closely and notice when he becomes overexcited. When his squealing becomes more intense, his eyes pin and his head feathers stand on end, she has to leave the Yellow-nape to play with the ball by himself and wait for him to play out his energy and settle down. Instead of approaching him, she needed to stop playing the game and calmly wait for him to calm down. She also purchased a net to swoop the ball into if her Nape became totally out of control. In addition, I showed her how to gently throw a towel on top of her parrot from the front, gently wrap him up, and take him to his cage safely for a time-out if she needs to before he calms down.

While some parrot species have a reputation for being unpredictable, my belief is that most are quite predictable in their unpredictability. If caregivers pay close attention to their companion parrots, they will learn to read the barometers of their behavior and prevent situations that create both confusion and overload. Conflict between the natural behaviors and the artificial environment can also create confusion that may result in predictable and therefore preventable, aggressive behavior. Although it is true that an owner who has established *Nurturing Guidance* with their parrot will experience far less aggressive behavior, a parrot in overload or one being stimulated by instincts is not acting in a conscious manner.

Physiological Influences

Overload behavior is influenced by physiological (having to do with body function) influences. Once parrots reached a certain level of stimulation, a change in body chemistry has a strong influence on their behavior. Since the change has strong physical influences, we cannot really blame parrots for their behavior during these times. It is futile to try and get a parrot to pay attention while he is in this hyper state. It can also be dangerous — so much so that trying to pick up a parrot in "overload" would be like "putting your fingers in the garbage disposal." Of course this is an exaggeration but it gets the point across.

We don't have enough pieces of the puzzle about many aspects of parrot behavior. Truthfully, we may never have any absolute answers but only educated guesses. I have spent a great deal of time thinking about why some parrots mutilate themselves or why some parrots kill their mates in captivity. And what about phobic parrots who thrash in their cages to avoid the very people with whom they had such a strong bond? And what about seizures in parrots or what we might term neurotic repetitive behavior that seems to be more common in wild-caught parrots. It has always been clear to me that we can't even attempt to solve these problems if we believe that the reason for various problems is just behavior, or just physical health. The key to many of these problem behaviors is trying to understand the way the emotional and the physical aspects interact with each other.

Basic Biology

At one time or another, all of us have experienced intense fear, rage, or excitement. During these times, there are physiological changes in our brain chemistry and our bodies. We talk about getting an "adrenaline rush" (even though the process is much more complicated than that) to describe a dangerous adventure. We use the expression "scared out of my mind" and other less polite expressions (which may actually be an accurate description for stress droppings in parrots) to describe intense fear. Anyone who has ever been really frightened or enraged knows that it takes time for the body and mind to become calm again. While adrenaline is a factor in a stress and/or fear reaction, there are neurotransmitters and other physiological influences involved that I can't even pretend to understand. One of the aspects of life that we learn in basic biology is that physically and physiologically all mammals (including us) and even birds share many anatomical and physiological similarities. While there are many differences, there are enough similarities to make some assumptions. I don't have enough knowledge about a parrot's physiology to make absolute statements about this topic but I would like caregivers to understand some of the basic concepts so that when their parrots exhibit these behaviors, the people will have a better perspective of the variables contributing to their parrots' intense responses.

The parrot who goes into severe overload is much like the person who experiences strong physiological reactions in an emergency. There is, of course, a major difference in human and parrot behavior. We are legitimately expected to try to control our more negative emotions and physiological responses. It would be foolish to expect this of an instinctively wild parrot with physiological responses that are essentially the same as a parrot in the wild. In reaction to stressful, frightening, or defensive situations, the parrot's brain and system is infused with adrenaline, glucocorticoids, and neuropeptides such as endorphins — his blood sugar rises, his heart beat increases, blood flow is increased to the muscles — the parrot becomes physically "pumped-up." His heightened body response is a natural physiological reaction to what is happening to him. But once he becomes so physiologically stimulated, the natural actions that dissipate this heightened energy are rarely possible for a parrot in a companion situation. What can he do with all of this body chemistry dictating strong physical actions when he lives in the living room? It's like getting all dressed up with nowhere to go. Added to this is the fact that the parrot's caregiver probably exhibits totally inappropriate responses to the bird's pumped-up behavior. Physiological and hormonal overload is also created when parrots are continually over-stimulated sexually by caregivers who don't understand that the ways they are handling their parrots can create continual sexual responses in the birds. I no longer recommend "laddering" a misbehaving parrot from hand to hand because it can be trust-destroying especially if it is done too aggressively with a sensitive parrot. Most of all, if the parrot is misbehaving because he is already over-stimulated, picking him up and laddering him would simply heighten his reaction creating even more physiological and/or sexual responses. A physiologically stimulated parrot in the wild has a strong physical response. He may strut and puff to scare an intruder or he may fly away. The exercise lowers the blood sugar and lessens the heightened physiological response. However, a captive parrot has few opportunities to dissipate this physiologically based energy. Of course, this is another strong argument for providing parrots with a great number of exercise opportunities. In humans, brain chemistry creates changes in the brain. Evidence shows that a chronically stressed and/ or depressed person actually may not be able to remember or experience pleasure because of changes in the way the brain works. On some level, the same may be true for rescue parrots who have been severely stressed by abuse and neglect. If so, this could account for the fact that some parrots recover only partially despite long-term and sustained positive changes in their lives. Permanent changes in brain function could be one factor influencing parrots who continue to exhibit excessive fear and aggressive responses when these behaviors no longer seem appropriate to the situation.

As concerned parrot caregivers, we can add another question to those involving our interaction with our companion parrots — does our handling and/or our response to the behavior of our avian friends intensify their negative behavior by creating *hormonal toxicity* or does it help dissipate these potentially harmful stress and hormonal reactions? 🦜

BEAKBITE TIP: The Big Bluff

Would you approach a parrot who looks like this one? Probably not — he has several of the pre-signs of cockatoo aggression (crest erect, eyes pinned and bugged, beak open, head back, etc.) and will most likely chomp down pretty hard. But is he showing real aggression or just bluffing to get you to go away and what makes one look different than the other? It is almost impossible to say since true aggression and a bluff look pretty much the same unless you have paid close attention to your parrot and his body language. If you have, you might be able to tell the difference with your own parrot. Early in my career as a parrot behavior consultant, I was at a home with two cockatoos. One was tame and the other had never been hand tamed. After talking to the people, it was time to work with the birds. I wanted to work with the tame bird first so I went to the cage and reached in and said "UP." The cockatoo complied and stepped right on my hand. Once he was out standing on my hand, he looked a bit shocked and so did the people. It turned out that I had approached the cockatoo who wasn't tame. They thought I had worked some sort of miracle but I had to admit to them that I had made a mistake and I had just been lucky. There is no way I would even suggest that this would work in other situations, but it did teach me that a good bluff from a person can be pretty effective. Over the years I have seen many people pick up a strutting parrot by just being very direct and confident. This would probably come as quite a shock to a parrot who has been used to showing his stuff and is used to scaring everyone off with his big bluff. In each situation, it was the person's confidence that made all the difference!

Parrots on Shoulders

The Favorite Perch

A classic situation that creates aggression is the parrot who is routinely allowed to climb up on his caregiver's shoulder anytime he wants. Many parrots instinctively defend their territory and mate against intruders. This is particularly true of a shoulder-sitting parrot. Bonding to our heads and perceiving our shoulders and body as some sort of 'moving tree branch,' the bird instinctively will defend its perceived 'mate' and territory from intruders. When a parrot is allowed to sit on his caregiver's shoulder, this confused defense may include a good beak poke or bite at the person's face (most likely to try and make the perceived mate leave the area of danger) when a family member enters the room. I've known more than one person with facial scars and hurt feelings from an otherwise tame parrot. This is not a conscious decision on the parrot's part and should not be taken as a personal attack. It was not the parrot's fault and in truth, the parrot can be trusted again if the owner learns to pay attention to body language and follow some simple rules to prevent aggression. Changing the parrot's instinctive behavior may not be possible if he is allowed to sit on his caregiver's shoulder. The simple solution is to be aware that this can happen and not to allow a parrot on your shoulder, especially if he is strongly bonded to you and has tried to "defend" you from others. If you insist on having your parrot on your shoulder, care should be taken to shield your face when someone (even another pet) who may be perceived as a threat enters the room. By paying attention and understanding "overload" and possible instinctive confusion, the owner can prevent many problem situations. A companion parrot is not bad or mean because he behaves in a natural way in his confusing artificial environment. To guarantee a positive parrot/human relationship, his human flock must accept responsibility in understanding and avoiding the situations that produce this kind of problem behavior.

One of the most significant mistakes people make from the very beginning with their companion parrots is to allow them to run up on their shoulder. Almost all parrots, even handfed babies, like to be as high as they can. This tendency often results in an argument between bird and owner. If the owner does not believe in setting rules or providing guidance, the parrot will easily win and his favorite perch will become the shoulder. This may not seem to be a problem in the beginning but once the parrot becomes patterned, it may become difficult to reeducate him not to run up to the shoulder. There are several reasons why this can create problems. One of the best ways to establish control or discipline a misbehaving parrot is with eye contact. If a bird is on your shoulder, it is impossible to make eye contact without making your face more vulnerable to injury from the beak. Also, a parrot on the shoulder is in a more dominant position because his eyes are usually level with or above the persons.

Letting the bird climb up on the shoulder seems to be a convenient way to spend time with him while the owner can do other things at the same time. People seem to think they can place their parrots on their shoulders and they will automatically behave themselves. One of the reasons we enjoy parrots so much is because of their intelligence and curiosity. These same traits create one of the major problems with shoulder birds. A curious parrot will busy himself looking for things to do. That '*bird toy*' hanging from your ear, or that little mole on your neck with the hair hanging out of it is just too inviting. So he starts poking at it with his beak. You turn and say, "*stop it, do you hear me*?!" He becomes distracted but soon finds the little silver thing on the frame of your glasses or the loose thread on your shirtsleeve. You admonish him again with increased drama. After a second or so, he remembers that mole again. More drama before you finally pick him up telling him what a *bad bird* he is and put him back in his cage telling him to think about what a *bad bird* he is. He has no idea that he did anything wrong. He only knows every time he poked at you with his beak, he was rewarded with a wonderful outburst of drama. Parrots love drama and will learn quickly to turn these behaviors into a game so they can get their owners all excited. As the bird becomes more and more excited, '*overload*' biting can quickly become a part of this game with the bird continually being rewarded with drama. Unless the owner establishes calm, methodical guidance, this bird will become a problem — particularly on the owner's shoulder.

Territorial Protection

Parrots who have been raised with rules and guidance present far fewer problems for their owners when they reach sexual maturity. However, a parrot who has been consistently allowed on his or her owner's shoulder may create serious problems as it becomes more territorial. Parrots bond strongly to their primary person's face. If they are strongly bonded to us and we allow them to sit on our shoulder, I believe their perception is one of sitting together with

Ears are a tempting target for a parrot who has nothing to do when he sits on your shoulder. It can also be a target for displaced aggression if the parrot becomes defensive of his perceived territory or mate. Lacerated ears bleed profusely and may need medical attention.

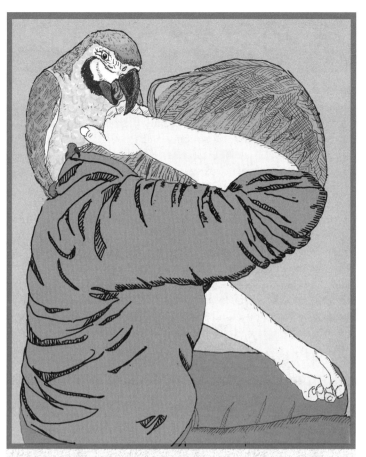

Getting an uncooperative parrot off of your shoulder can be quite an ordeal. They quickly learn about that area on our backs that we can't reach no matter how hard we try. I have watched people try to rub their parrots off of their shoulders onto the cage, roll on the floor to get them to climb off, and even take off some of their clothing so the parrot has nothing to hang on to.

us on a moving *tree branch*. Our body becomes their "territory." If an intruder (your husband, wife, child, dog, etc.?) threatens the perceived territory, it is instinctive for the bird to defend that territory. In the wild, a pair of parrots would most likely become very big by spreading their tails, spreading their wings and/or raising their crests to show off all their color. They would pin their eyes and become as threatening as possible. The pet bird may show the same behavior expecting his or her *mate* (you) to exhibit the same defensive postures to help scare the intruder off, but you either greet them or sit there like a bump on a log. You become part of the problem not part of the solution. The parrot can't defend his mate and the territory at the same time so you have to go! So he takes a swipe at you to get you to fly away so he can defend the territory and you can fly back when it is safe. If a parrot takes a jab at another parrot, he most likely gets a beak full of feathers. If he takes a jab at you, he gets a face full of skin. Facial bites can be quite serious resulting in scarring and even eye injury.

Retraining A Shoulder Parrot

What about the person with the sweet parrot who has been sitting on his or her shoulder for the last twelve years and has never shown any sign of aggression? Does this person now have to retrain his or her parrot not to be a shoulder bird? Probably not — this is the exception. Make sure your parrot can be trusted on your shoulder before you experience aggressive behavior when he is on your shoulder.

Start out by placing your parrot on your knee instead of on your shoulder when you are reading or watching TV. He can play happily and you can establish both friendly and disciplinary eye control with him. If he already has the bad habit of running up your arm, simply bring your other hand down your arm and use the "UP" command to have him step on your

finger. Don't turn it into a game with drama. Do this over and over until your arm is no longer his runway to your shoulder. It may take several weeks to re-pattern him so he doesn't automatically run up your arm. Don't get into the habit of just leaning over to his cage and having him step on your shoulder. ***Maintaining hand control is essential to having a well-behaved parrot.***

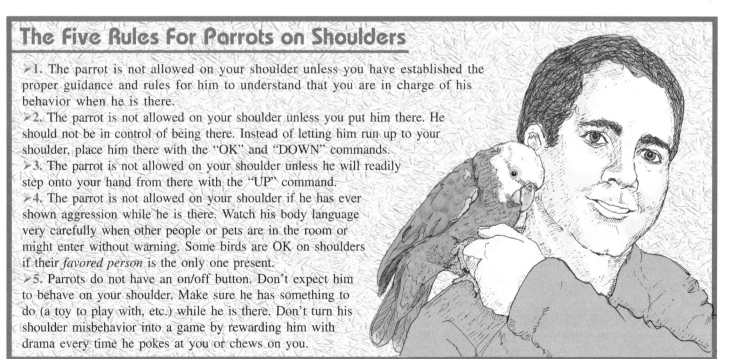

The Five Rules For Parrots on Shoulders

➤**1.** The parrot is not allowed on your shoulder unless you have established the proper guidance and rules for him to understand that you are in charge of his behavior when he is there.

➤**2.** The parrot is not allowed on your shoulder unless you put him there. He should not be in control of being there. Instead of letting him run up to your shoulder, place him there with the "OK" and "DOWN" commands.

➤**3.** The parrot is not allowed on your shoulder unless he will readily step onto your hand from there with the "UP" command.

➤**4.** The parrot is not allowed on your shoulder if he has ever shown aggression while he is there. Watch his body language very carefully when other people or pets are in the room or might enter without warning. Some birds are OK on shoulders if their *favored person* is the only one present.

➤**5.** Parrots do not have an on/off button. Don't expect him to behave on your shoulder. Make sure he has something to do (a toy to play with, etc.) while he is there. Don't turn his shoulder misbehavior into a game by rewarding him with drama every time he pokes at you or chews on you.

How "The One Person Bird" Becomes A Self-fulfilling Prophecy

Several species of parrots are generally referred to as "one-person birds." These stereotypes can keep people from buying a certain parrot who may be the right bird for them. While seemingly true of some individuals, it is usually parrots with whom no one has worked that display this rigid characteristic. Most companion parrots are capable of bonding and re-bonding on many levels throughout their lives. In the wild, the mate bond is not the only relationship a parrot establishes with other birds in the flock. As well-managed pets, most parrots are also capable of bonding on different levels to several people in their lives. Parrots may change their bonding preferences from time to time, but these changes are not necessarily permanent. We may not always understand the reasons why a parrot suddenly changes his allegiance from one person to another but people can work with parrots to re-win their trust and affection. Parrots normally form the strongest bond with the person who provides them the most consistent guidance because these people confuse them the least. Not every parrot bond is the same, just as not every human friendship is the same. Some people are not aware of how strongly their parrots are bonded to them because the bird seems to like someone else better. We need to work with our parrots to establish patterns necessary for multiple bonding. When people are told their parrots will only bond to one person, and they believe it, and don't do the necessary work that allows the parrot to form bonds with other people, the myth becomes a self-fulfilling prophecy. Some people seem to enjoy the fact that their parrots only like them. Some even think it is funny that the bird chases their spouse out of the house and some brag that their parrot refuses to be handled by anyone else. These people are asking for serious problems — both with the people and the parrot in their lives.

Defending The Flock

Most parrots are highly social birds. They form ties with their flock and bond strongly to their mates and family group. They can be territorial in defense of their flock and family members. As members of our companion parrot's *human flock* or even as their perceived mate, we will often be defended from others and intruders whether we want to be or not. When parrots are young, they usually allow most people to handle them, especially when their trusted caregiver and protector is there to provide safety and assurance. As young parrots continue to mature, unless they are introduced safely to new people on a continuing basis, they often develop either a fear of strangers or a need to defend their perceived territory against them.

Parrots who are properly socialized by being safely introduced to new experiences, objects, and people on a continuing basis will usually not shy away or be aggressive in new situations. If a bird only spends his early development limited to attention from his immediate family or single owner, other people may be perceived as intruders until they are accepted into the bird's human flock. Even people who were perceived as members of the flock when the parrot was young, often become intruders unless they work consistently with him as he matures. Therefore, it is essential for all family members and close friends who want to stay a part of the parrot's life to consistently and comfortably handle the bird throughout his life. Using *Nurturing Guidance*, each member of the human flock should handle the parrot both individually and with other flock members. All family members should be encouraged to at least have friendly verbal interactions with your parrot even if they don't want a more defined relationship. These various types of relationships should be encouraged by the "preferred person" who may need to leave the area in order for

BEAKBITE TIP: Dancing With Cockatoos

I did a consultation with a couple who had purchased an Umbrella Cockatoo about a month before they called me. It was actually the husband who wanted the bird, but the wife went along with the idea. In no time at all, the cockatoo was infatuated with the woman and had no interest in the man at all. He was quite upset because he was the one who wanted the bird to be his buddy. He didn't mind sharing the cockatoo's affection but he was a bit jealous that his wife was receiving all the attention. As soon as I met the three of them, I knew what was going on. The woman was quite vivacious and had been giving the cockatoo lots of attention. This attention included singing and dancing. They had even showered together on an almost daily basis. After the cockatoo's shower, she and the 'too would slow dance to soft music while she would hum to him. The husband was as steady as a rock. He was doing the bird chores — cleaning the cage and changing the food and water. He could handle the 'too but the bird acted totally bored with him and wanted to be with his wife. Knowing cockatoos, there was no doubt in my mind why the bird wanted to be with the woman. She was the fun person and she provided him with both great drama and calm affection. The Umbrella loved her singing and he loved to dance and shower with her. The wife could keep doing these things but the husband needed to provide the cockatoo with some of the same stuff and something special that the wife didn't do. Being somewhat reserved, he wouldn't do any of this in front of me. However, with a wink in her eye, the wife confided that her husband could, indeed, be silly. His assignment to win the cockatoo's affection was to be silly with him! And guess what? It worked!

another person to be successful. Timid family members need to at least talk to the parrot directly every day and know the proper use of the "UP" command. Most of all, antagonistic interactions should be prohibited.

Confused Messages From Strangers

A young parrot's mistrust of some family members and strangers is often reinforced by people who don't know how to approach or handle him comfortably, especially when these people have not been around many parrots. When a parrot is continually approached with either fear or aggression, he may become patterned to respond in the same way. The timid person who presents an unclear message for the bird to step onto his hand and then pulls away when the bird responds with confusion may be bitten. This confusion can become patterned into aggression directed towards all people who do not give clear handling messages. This patterning even creates handling problems for previously trusted people. The aggressive person who refuses to listen to the way the caregiver asks them to handle the parrot can also cause serious trust problems — allowing a parrot to be approached by anyone without concern for how they handle the bird can be very trust-destroying. Aggressive handling from strangers may make a parrot mistrustful of all new people in his life.

If You Like Them, They Must Be OK

Introductions are essential. The young parrot per-

Although this woman is not acting in an obviously threatening manner, she may still be approaching the grey too directly for his comfort. If she pushed any harder, she would be forcing the parrot to bite her. Newcomers need to be patient in trying to win the affections of a friend or relative's parrot. It would most likely be more effective for the caregiver to place his or her parrot on the stranger's arm or knee in a neutral room rather than have her reach for the bird.

ceives us as his surrogate parents and looks to us for defense and protection. In order for companion parrots to accept the family and friends of their owner instead of being wary of them, the new person must be safely and gradually introduced. The introduction is gradual enough for the parrot to perceive the stranger as a new flock member and not an intruder. The way to achieve this is for a trusted flock member to introduce the new person to the parrot. This introduction is more successful if it is done in a *neutral room* rather than in the room where the cage is located. Strangers or people who are not considered part of the human flock should never be allowed to approach the cage, nor should they try to handle the bird without first being introduced. When I visit people with parrots, I always take time to observe the parrot indirectly and then ask the caregivers to introduce me to their bird rather than approaching the bird myself.

Becoming A Member Of The Flock

For a stranger to become a member of the flock, the parrot's friends and family must be willing to work both with their parrot and the new person. The bird should already have a positive trusting relationship with his caregivers and understand basics like stepping on a person's hand with the "UP" command. Introducing strangers to a parrot properly is essential even if he is a sweet, tame handfed bappy who seems to accept everyone. You want him to stay that way and an unsuccessful, unsupervised introduction that may not work out well can create serious problems.

First, give new people verbal instructions on how to approach your parrot. Let them watch as you confidently handle him using the "UP" and "Down" commands. Show them how you "skritch" or cuddle your parrot. If they listen carefully, they are good candidates for friendship with your parrot. If they are afraid of parrots, it is not a good idea to have them work through that fear with your pet. If they refuse to listen, perhaps declaring that they don't need to listen to you because they have had lots of parrots, they have no business handling your parrot.

Have the person sit down in a neutral room away from the cage territory. Have them take a few deep breaths to relax. A nervous person will create a nervous, unpredictable response from the parrot. If your friend or family member is frightened or uncomfortable, it is best for them to not handle your parrot unless the parrot is very tame and forgiving. If everyone is relaxed and confident, the new flock member will easily take the parrot from you using the "UP" command. If your friend doesn't feel ready for that step, either place your parrot on a T-stand or your friend's knee. The knee area is the best place for a parrot to sit. The person can talk quietly to the bird, make gentle eye contact from above, and establish friendly control over the situation. Don't ever place your parrot on the new person's shoulder because this position may put them in jeopardy if a problem arises. The next step depends on everyone's comfort level. If everyone is relaxed and confident, your friend can pick up the bird saying "UP." In some situations, you may want to place the parrot on your friend's hand.

If the parrot has a negative reaction and the friend is competent at handling him, the caregiver may leave the room once the introductions have been made. The parrot may still be reacting out of defense for his favorite person, especially if he is a mature bird. However, many parrots who are aggressive around their cage and family become docile when in the *neutral room* and away from their preferred person. It is for the same reasons that some parrots who normally act up at home can be very well-behaved when they go visiting.

Maintaining Flock Acceptance

The parrot's new friend should spend individual time with the parrot in the neutral room. The new person may need to be very indirect until the parrot is comfortable with them. Then focused attention, which is time spent giving the parrot instructional attention, goes a long way in increasing the parrot/human bond. Eventually— whether it takes a few hours or a few months, the parrot should learn to trust the new flock member enough to allow handling near the cage. Once the new person is genuinely recognized as a flock member, he or she should be able to take the parrot out of the cage using the "UP" command. It is important to realize, however, if the parrot's behavior is being controlled by hormones during breeding season, it is best to carefully observe his body language before anyone, even a flock member, tries to handle him.

People with infrequent contact with the parrot, especially if time passes between visits, need to repeat the introductory stages to maintain acceptance. This is also an effective way for people who used to be able to handle the parrot to reinstate themselves as a member of the human flock.

Family members who want the parrot to stay tame to them have to work at it but the *work* can be fun. Playing *warm potato* a few times a week over the lifetime of the parrot is the best way to pattern a parrot to stay tame to everyone. This involves passing the bird slowly around a circle of family and friends (in a neutral room if the parrot is territorial about his cage) with each person giving the parrot a hug, a *skritch*, nutritious treats, and/or verbal praise.

For the parrot to stay tame to them, each person in the human flock must also develop their own individual special relationship with the bird. This involves interactive time spent alone with the parrot doing special things such as showering, teaching fun tricks, playing games, giving nutritious treats, and cuddling. Picking a favorite interaction that only the new person does can help to develop a stronger and longer lasting parrot/human bond.

I have worked with many parrots who seemed to have a strong bond with just one person in the human flock. Using the proper techniques combined with patience and consistent attention, even the most hard-core "one-person" bird has learned to accept and enjoy the company of other human *flock members*. However, it is important to realize that there are occasionally parrots and people who are simply not compatible. But before coming to that conclusion, it is worth giving it a concentrated effort for everyone to get along.

It is certainly easier for only one or two people to care for and train the parrot they love. But in the long run since we do not know what the future holds, it is better for the long-lived parrot to enjoy the companionship of many people by being involved in many human-bond friendships. ✦

BEAKBITE TIP: Taking the Bites

Over the years, I have talked with many people who proudly tell me that when they were working with their parrots, they took the bites. This comes from a philosophy that when a parrot bites you and you keep coming at him, he will eventually learn that biting doesn't accomplish its purpose. This theory states that this will then stop the parrot from biting. While this may seem to be the case in rare situations, I believe that this approach does more to pattern the parrot to bite, especially if the parrot is continually approached in an aggressive manner. Aggression is met with aggression or is some cases, fear.

In the same year, I worked with two separate clients with almost the same situation. Each woman had lived alone with her tame macaw for a few years and now wanted to introduce a new person into her home. One macaw was a Green-wing and the other was a Blue and Gold. In both situations, the new people were not experienced with parrots. The man who was moving in with the Green-wing fancied himself as an animal trainer since he had experience working with dogs. While he was convinced his assertive and even aggressive methods worked well with dogs, they were too trust destroying to use with parrots. By the time his girlfriend called me, he had sustained several serious bites because he was convinced that "taking the bite" would win the parrot's "respect." The macaw had become his personal challenge and he was angry at the bird. The Green-wing had become a bit less aggressive with him but certainly had no affection for him. It was clear that fear was a part of the macaw's body language in response to his attention. Another problem resulted when the previously tame Green-wing started biting the woman. The situation was getting worse and it seemed to me it would reach the point where one of them had to go — the woman was very fond of her macaw. From the very beginning, the situation with the Blue and Gold was much more likely to succeed. This woman's new husband knew how much she loved her macaw. He was not in any hurry to win the bird over but he spent time giving him ambient attention. They set up the neutral room and the woman brought the macaw in after her husband had already prepared the room. The macaw stood on a stand while the man read to him and gave him an occasional treat. Within a few weeks, the macaw took the "first step" and climbed onto the man's hand. The macaw never bit him and within a few months, the bird had established a positive bond with both people.

Height Dominance?

A Barometer — Not An Absolute

The concept of height dominance as an influence on parrots has been debated a great deal in the last few years. Perhaps there is little evidence of this occurring naturally with wild parrots, but I know of no evidence that it is absolutely not a consideration either. However, it has been clear to me that this concept has validity with companion parrots and people should be aware of the concept of height dominance as it applies to their relationship with their parrots. Because of displacement behavior and the adjustment to life in the living room, natural behaviors in companion parrots can change dramatically. With the concept of height dominance, there are some important considerations. When a parrot is encompassed from above and there is no route for escape, the instinct is for the parrot to submit or aggressively defend himself. People who approach their parrots towering over them in an overbearing, aggressive manner are responsible for any aggression they receive because they are forcing this behavior with their confrontational behavior. If aggressive height dominance is used consistently, some companion parrots become intimidated or frightened enough for it to damage the trusting bond they have with their caregivers.

Height dominance can be a significant factor in relating to many companion parrots but it is only part of many aspects of *Nurturing Guidance*. Height dominance is usually an accurate barometer of the relationship people have with their parrots. Those who have established a good sense of behavioral guidance generally do not have trouble with their parrot even if the bird is higher. For example, Paco and Rascal, acknowledge my "UP" command readily, whether they are on the ground or on the top of their ceiling swing. People who have not established *Nurturing Guidance* may have trouble with their high-up parrots, but they will most likely also have trouble with cage aggression, excessive screaming, biting, and other behavioral problems. I find that when people are having behavioral problems with their parrots, establishing non-threatening height dominance is only one of many ways people need to work with their birds.

The caregivers who have patterned their parrots to positive behaviors will rarely have trouble getting their avian companions to step on their hands or a branch no matter how far the parrots are above them.

Some young parrots become little tyrants when they are allowed to repeatedly hang out on the tops of their cages or even a tall playgym. They often become so focused on protecting their perceived territory that they may reach the point when nothing else seems to matter to them. They posture and strut, trying to scare away even the most benevolent person in their human flock. Unfortunately, these parrots rarely stay in their homes because they become too difficult for anyone to handle.

I remember one adorable six-month-old Double-yellow Head who was full of himself. He had his caregiver totally buffaloed. There was no doubt he was a very smart little bird — he already had a sizable vocabulary and he had quickly manipulated his new person into submission. The minute she opened the cage door, he ignored her attempts to pick him up and quickly climbed to the top and strutted around like a bantam rooster. The woman thought that getting a parrot had been a horrible mistake. All it took for her to regain control of her little tyrant was a step stool. Standing on it made her tall enough to win the power struggle almost immediately. Was it height dominance or simply that she had more confidence when she was higher than the parrot? — probably some of both. A little bluffing is helpful for the more timid owner. Sometimes all it takes is for the person to approach the parrot with confidence, and in an assertive enough manner that the parrot doesn't have the time or inclination to refuse his or her request. Several years ago, I was working in a home with two cockatoos. One was tame and would readily step onto the owner's hand, even off the top of his cage — the other was not tame and always tried to get a chunk of flesh first. In working with the 'toos, I became confused about which parrot was tame and which was normally difficult. I approached the wild one so decisively that he immediately stepped onto my hand off the top of his cage. At first, I couldn't figure out why my clients seemed so amazed. Holding a non-threatening "distraction object" in one hand and giving an assertive "UP" command will also often work in a situation where the parrot has patterned himself to ignore his caregiver's requests.

If a companion parrot continually becomes aggressive when he is above eye level, the obvious solution to this particular problem is to discontinue cage top time that allows a parrot to become king of all he surveys. A playgym that offers a lot of activity and/or multi-perch stand that does not place the parrot above the human flock's eye level, are far more appropriate places for him to hang out. Guiding a parrot's behavior and carefully watching body language are the two best ways to avoid problems with parrots that are higher than you are. ✦

Reading Body Language

Predictably Unpredictable

One of the most common questions I am asked is, "What does it mean when my parrot does _____?" I usually can provide the basics but often the same body language has a slightly different meaning for each individual parrot. Companion parrots often change their behavior and body language according to the responses they receive from their human flock. Consequently, over a period of time, what a parrot is trying to communicate with specific body language may not remain consistent. It is wise to observe the changes and additions to your parrot's body language repertoire. Careful observation and interpretation of can be of tremendous help to caregivers in understanding their avian companions. Although many parrot species have a reputation for unpredictable behavior, if we pay close attention to their body language, we can predict how they are going to act in most situations. While parrot body language varies some from species to species, and is not always consistently predictable in individual parrots, certain aspects of psittacine body language remain consistent. But the subtleties of body language can change.

As I examined many successful relationships that people have with their parrots, I modified some of my early theories of parrot behavior. One absolute statement I made was "Don't ever start anything you don't finish." To some degree, I still believe this but, like with most things in life, there are many variables to consider. I would change this maxim to read, "Don't start anything you can't be relatively assured of finishing successfully." In other words, don't reach into your parrot's cage and give him an "UP" command if he is napping, ripping a toy into shreds, or rabidly protecting a pistachio nut. Forcing a parrot to do what you want him to when he is not in the mood is asking for aggression. Often by cajoling an otherwise occupied parrot with a few flattering words and a smile will relax him and make him far more agreeable to your attention.

A comfortable parrot who wants to be with you will move towards you or puff up a little bit and shake his feathers to let you know he is relaxed and friendly. He may also flatten his body into a preflight posture and flutter his wings as an indication that he wants to fly to you. Comfortable, trusting companion parrots rarely exhibit the postures associated with the normal vigilance of prey animals. If they do, something is frightening them and we need to alleviate that situation so the parrot is no longer stressed. Usually when a parrot fluffs his feathers and seems just a bit pudgy, he is relaxed and comfortable. (Although, if there are indications of illness, continual fluffing accompanied by sluggishness is a reason to consult with your avian veterinarian immediately.) Often a parrot fluffs out his feathers and shakes his tail feathers as a way to express relaxation. A good fluff and shake is the way many parrots communicate they are through with whatever was happening and ready to move on to something else. Beak grinding before a nap or sleep is also a comfort behavior. A really happy parrot being indulged during a "skritching session" usually fluffs out the feathers in the areas he wants to be petted. Some birds, particularly cockatoos, seem to become *boneless* if they are really enjoying a good cuddle session. If, during these sessions, the parrot's body becomes less relaxed and more rigid, the cuddle session should be stopped. Either the parrot is no longer relaxed or he may be becoming sexually stimulated. Preening is a normal activity for a comfortable parrot, although there are some parrots who involve themselves with excessive preening as a displacement behavior when they become nervous or stressed.

Parrot aggression is shown with threat displays. The difference between fluffed, relaxed feathers and the erect feathers of aggression is noticeable. Fluffed feathers blend together, while erected feathers stand out individually or in groups. Specific feathers on the crest, nape, or other colorful parts of the body are erected as warning and to communicate excitement or aggression. Some parrots show aggression by standing very tall, trying to seem as large as possible. They spread their wings and raise their crest or nape feathers and sway back and forth. The beak is

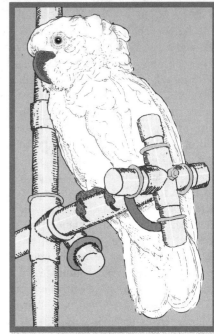

One of the most reliable indications that a cockatoo is relaxed is the fluff of feathers covering part of their beak. In fact, the species name for one of the black cockatoos is calyptorhynchus — this means "hidden beak." Relaxed cockatoos also look all fluffed and sometimes give the appearance of being somewhat boneless.

This is a dangerous situation to both the woman holding the parrot and the approaching person. The Amazon shows all the classic signs of aggressive posturing — eyes pinned and head feathers erect, with the wing and tail feathers flared. A parrot who is this excited could turn and take a chunk out of their best friend's face.

often open with the head forward. In some situations, aggressive posturing is shown by the bird flattening horizontally with wings slightly spread — often to show their color accents. In some parrots, the head is lowered with erected feathers on the nape. In others, the head is up with the beak thrust forward. Open beak lunging or lunge biting (when a parrot lunges forward to bite someone) is obviously aggressive behavior. Unless you understand and trust your parrot implicitly, don't *lead with your face.*

Excitement and aggression are two different behaviors, although they may have similar body postures and behavioral results — an overloaded, over-stimulated parrot may bite just as hard as an aggressive parrot. An excited parrot is more likely to be screaming than an aggressive parrot. If a parrot is either in overload or exhibiting aggressive behavior, it is best not to handle him without attempting to calm him down first. One of the most obvious signs of excitement in most parrots is eye pinning. The pupil expands and contracts as the parrot becomes more stimulated, often becoming just a bare pinpoint. This is not always an indication

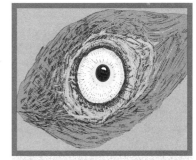

Eye pinning in parrots is not just a sign of aggression but is also an indication of excitement.

of aggression — it can simply mean the parrot is excited. This is easy to see in an Amazon or Macaw and not so easy in a cockatoo or other dark eyed parrot.

A companion parrot who is standing stiff and skinny with all his feathers flat against his body is usually stressed or frightened. His head may be held high and forward with his wings held slightly away from his body in a preflight position. In some situations, a stressed bird may jerk his head back and forth. Some parrots may sit motionless while with others the wings may quiver, and he may repeatedly raise one foot, sway, or shift his weight. Companion parrots are often confused about what to do when they are afraid because their normal fear behaviors of hiding, escape, or fighting do not usually work for them. It is important to pay attention to what causes stress or fear behavior and remove or prevent the causative factors. However, if stress is being caused by something that should be normal in a companion parrot's life, it is best to anticipate and gradually introduce these factors to the parrot in a gradual safe manner to prevent negative reactions. ✦

Leaning forward and fluttering his wings is usually an indication that your parrot wants you to come and pick him up. It is the posture of preflight and if the parrot could make the decision to fly to you, he would.

BEAKBITE TIP: Scared Stiff

I received a call from some people who lived with a Scarlet Macaw. The bird could be a bit nippy from time to time but was normally self-assured and playful. They called because her behavior had changed dramatically. She sat on one side of the cage in a tall, skinny posture with her feathers stiff against her body. Most of the time her wings were flat against her body but she would go into a preflight posture with them slightly out. Sometimes she would pace in that one area fluttering her wings. They were able to determine that she seemed hyper-alert and appeared to be afraid of everything. She had also stopped eating in her cage. The woman could coax the Scarlet onto her hand and out of the cage to take her into the kitchen. Once there, the bird would relax and eat. If the husband tried to take the Scarlet out, she would bite him viciously. While she often bit the man, it was usually a series of playful nips that could be painful but nothing like the bites she was giving him at this time. I encouraged them to take her to their avian veterinarian but her behavior seemed fine at the vet's office and she came back with a clean bill of health. The veterinarian recommended that they call me for an in-home consultation. I talked to them again on the phone for some time to try and get an idea of what was causing this unusual behavior. I asked them about changes in the bird's environment and the only thing they could think of was that they were gone for the weekend to an art show but they often left the bird for a day or two with their older son watching her. The problem hadn't started until they had been back a day or so. The minute I walked into their living room, I knew what the problem was. Hung on the wall about six feet from the macaw's cage was a large abstract painting with black and red slashes and shapes. I asked them when they had hung the painting. They had purchased the painting at the art show that weekend. They didn't think that hanging the painting would be a problem because its location wasn't right next to the cage. I asked them to move the painting and the minute it was out of the room, the Scarlet relaxed. She wasn't being an art critic. They had introduced the painting into the room too quickly for the macaw's comfort and to her, it must have seemed something like a window to hell.

Fear As A Cause Of Parrot Biting

Biting Out Of Insecurity

A great deal of biting behaviors that start in companion parrots are based on insecurity and fear rather than aggression. It is essential for the breeder/pet shop to teach their babies to be comfortable with several people and to readily step onto hands. If they have failed to teach this essential preparation for the parrot's new home, the novice caregiver will have to accept that responsibility. Unfortunately, very few new parrot owners really know how to handle parrots before they bring one home. Novices who buy babies who have not previously learned these simple skills will often have far more difficulty handling their young parrots from the beginning. Each time the person has to struggle with the bird to get him on his or her hand, the pet potential of the bird is challenged. Consequently people may immediately get into negative patterns that will often develop into biting problems. Parrots are highly empathic, picking up every nuance of their human flock's mood and energy. If a person is insecure picking up their new parrot, the bird senses it. In the world of parrot behavior, there are many valid ideas but one concept bears repeating because of its absolute truth: **Parrots are more comfortable with people who are comfortable with them.** The truth may simply be that a parrot who senses a person's discomfort, whether it be fear, aggression, or just insecurity may not want to step onto that person's hand. If the person is uncomfortable handling their parrot, the bird will quickly become uncomfortable being handled by him or her. Many new owners who have no idea how to handle their new parrot call me and some admit frankly that they are very afraid of the parrot's beak — even if their parrot is a handfed baby. For people who are having trouble handling their parrots, the best way to deal with this is practice and patterning. If there is a quality bird shop or aviary nearby, the novice should visit the parrots and ask to handle several of them with supervision. Of course, this is not always possible but a visit with friends who are comfortable handling their parrots could also be helpful. Even watching people handling their parrots with ease can be helpful to a person who is too insecure to handle his or her parrot successfully.

Fear is a frequent cause of aggressive behavior especially if parrots are approached too forcefully or too directly by strangers who are not an accepted part of the human flock. Some parrots, particularly rescue birds who have been mistreated, have learned to bite to get people to go away. They don't have a positive association with humans or their hands. Hands have too often been a source of mishandling and abuse and the association between hands and aggression is too strong to change quickly. Even though the intent of the new caregiver is positive, it will take time to win enough trust for the parrot to allow handling. People need to be patient and look for very small signs of progress. Although there may be exceptions, trying to just pick up one of these parrots with hands may further erode and trust they are developing.

Getting the Fearful or Aggressive Parrot Away From The Cage

A T-stand with a food bowl and food bribes can be very helpful. The first step is to figure out what is the parrot's absolute favorite food treat. Even if it is sunflower seed or peanuts that may not be that healthy, these foods can be used. Stop feeding these treats in the cage and only feed them if the parrot will accept them from your hand. In the meantime, gradually move a T-stand closer to the cage until the parrot is used to its presence. Once the parrot accepts the T-stand comfortably, then open the cage door and move the perch of the T-stand right into the door opening. Show him the favored treats and then start placing one or two in the food bowl on the stand. Then go away — as long as you stand over him watching, it is unlikely he will come out on the stand to get the treat. It may take awhile but let him get used to sneaking out on the stand to get the treats. Once he is used to being on the stand, place only one small treat item in the bowl. Gradually and calmly move closer to him without making direct eye contact and offer him more treats from your hand. Once he becomes used to this, start picking up the stand and moving it a little bit at a time until you can actually move it into a *neutral room* where it will be easier to handle the parrot.

Setting up a T-stand with a treat and placing the perch partly in the cage is one of the best ways to get an aggressive cage territorial parrot out of his cage. Once he comes out to get the treat, you can start picking up the stand and moving it to another room.

Truly Phobic Parrots

The true phobic parrot is a different matter entirely. These parrots are often too afraid to be aggressive; instead their response to attention is to thrash in the cage. This topic will be covered extensively in a future volume of this series. However, I need to caution that the only way to win the trust of truly phobic parrots is what I call "nurturing submission" which consists of very indirect attention with no strong eye contact or height dominance from caregivers. Often just sitting quietly in front of the open cage facing 3/4 away and reading without giving the parrot any attention is one of the best ways to patiently invite him into your human flock. Looking over at him with head bowed and eyes half shut and then lowering your head and looking away will help him be much more comfortable with you. Parrots are social animals and companion parrots will want the nurturing companionship of people. Using these indirect techniques, the sensitive parrot is invited to join the human flock rather than being forced into being handled in a fearful situation. Many parrots will initiate physical handling with this type of non-threatening attention. ƒ

Understanding Sexual Behavior

The Reality Of Sexual Maturity

Parrots can form strong sexual bonds with their favored person in their human flock. Whether your bird is a male or a female, he or she is reacting to strong biological urges towards you — his or her perceived mate. Since companion parrots often bond strongly to their human friends, these sexual behaviors are often directed towards them in the absence of a more natural mate (another parrot). Parrots raised with *Nurturing Guidance* usually do not form excessively strong sexual bonds with their caregivers. Understanding more about the factors that influence your parrot's sexual behavior as he or she matures will help you provide the guidance the bird needs to be content as a well-nurtured lifelong *celibate* companion.

Many of the people who keep companion parrots are just starting to deal with issues of sexual behavior in their pet birds. Caregivers with young parrots are often quite apprehensive that their birds will become some sort of raving, bloodthirsty monsters when they become sexually mature. Actually, if people have done a good job setting a foundation of positive interaction with their parrots, in the majority of companion parrots, sexual maturity should not present an unsolvable problem. In fact, I get calls from some people with five and six year old birds who wonder when their parrots will start this dreaded stage. They are not even aware that their parrots are actually remaining consistent and loving despite the fact they have already entered adulthood.

Young children "play house" as a way to practice being adults and young parrots may begin to "court" their caregivers long before they have the hormones to back it up. It is critical to realize that because a parrot exhibits sexual behavior does not mean he is mature enough to breed or even wants to breed. Sexual immaturity comes long before sexual maturity. Some young parrots may "act out" sexual roles before they are actually ready for that role. One of the most common behaviors that may eventually evolve into sexual behavior is regurgitation. It is natural for parrots to feed each other and the fact that your parrot wants to feed you simply means that he has a special bond with you — what a compliment!? Once parrots are sexually mature, they will be sexually mature for the rest of their lives. It is not something they get over. However, this certainly does not mean they can't remain exceptional companions. It simply means there may be a few times a year when a parrot may be more difficult to get along with. Parrots have complex personalities and are not just simply two-dimensional sexual animals and breeding behavior does NOT mean a companion parrot needs to breed.

Establish Guidelines

The key to having a lifelong well-behaved parrot is to establish guidelines and set rules from the very beginning. Although much of a parrot's behavior is instinctive, much of it is also learned. The more intelligent animals are, the more their behaviors are influenced by teaching and example. As I have stated many times, parrots, even domestically-raised bappies, have no idea how to adapt to life as a human companion. They do not come out of the egg being good pets — we have to teach and guide them with *Nurturing Guidance.* We need to be their surrogate parents or flock leaders. Parrots who have this type of guidance are less likely to have serious problems when they reach maturity and start being influenced by their hormones. By giving our companion parrots clear messages to guide their behaviors, we can actually override some of the natural behavior that creates problems for them as pets. Using the "UP" and "DOWN" command every time you pick up or put your parrot down, is one of the best ways to give parrots a clear message about what you expect from them.

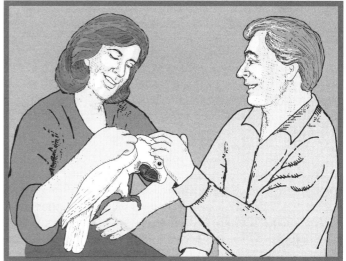

One of the best ways to keep a parrot from forming a strong bond (when he perceives the primary caregiver is his mate) is to make sure the bird gets attention from and therefore, has a bond of some kind with everyone in the human flock. Each person should spend individual time with the parrot and also time with the bird and other family members and friends.

Over-bonding

To keep a parrot from forming a strong sexual bond with one person, everyone who will be involved in the parrot's life needs to spend time with him and develop his or her own individual bond. A family spending consistent time with the parrot together and separately throughout his life will help prevent him from becoming a "one-person bird." If everyone sets rules and provides guidance, the parrot is less likely to form a mate bond with one person and exhibit sexual aggression towards others. A "neutral room" away from the cage and other family members, where the parrot is not used to being (and therefore does not have a territorial agenda) is a good place for each individual to spend a period of time each day developing his own special relationship with the parrot. People who live alone with their parrot should try to safely introduce as many trusted relatives and friends to their bird to keep him interacting with others.

Overdependent parrots who are allowed to over-bond with one person and are dominant in their relationship with that person are more likely to create serious problems for the people in their lives when they become sexually mature. It is not funny when a

Parrot breeding behavior can be influenced by many variables. If a companion parrot perceives something as a potential nest site, he or she may become more stimulated to protect the area. One of my clients returned home from work to find that her Blue-front Amazon had gotten out of his cage and climbed onto a bookcase. Obviously the bird had spent most of the day ripping up books to prepare a nest site.

mature parrot chases another family member around the house trying to do bodily harm. Nor is it amusing when they are sitting on their primary person's shoulder and bites his or her face when another person comes in the room. These are often the behaviors of an over-bonded parrot who perceives himself as his owner's sexual partner. In a positive relationship with a parrot, the primary person establishes himself or herself in a parental role or as either the dominant partner in the pair bond. Consequently, they rarely experience sexual aggressive behavior since the parrot defers to their dominance and is less likely to initiate sexual behavior.

External Influences

Sexual behavior in birds has several external influences including light, temperature, humidity, and food sources. In the wild, hormones stimulate birds to breed just prior to the time when food for babies is most plentiful. Food is more available during and after a rainy season. Companion parrots are also naturally stimulated by such factors, and sexual behavior in a mature parrot often starts at about the time the days start to get longer. However, artificial lighting, temperature and climate control in our homes creates stimuli for breeding that may be confusing to both our parrots and us. During the breeding "season," parrots can be visually stimulated by the presence of a nest cavity or something that resembles one, such as a box, paper bag, cupboard, bookcase, or other dark container with an opening. I know of one Scarlet Macaw who laid eggs when a carpet was rolled up next to her cage during home redecorating. The macaw saw the dark circle created by the rolled carpet as the entrance to a nest cavity. Another client came home to find her Amazon had escaped and was happily sitting on a "nest" of shredded books on the top shelf of a bookcase next to the cage. Paper shredding and increased wood chewing in a mature bird can be signs of nesting behavior, but can also be encouraged as a normal activity.

Dealing With Sexual Behavior

Without realizing it, people may actually be increasing the sexual behavior of their parrots with physical affection that may be misunderstood as sexual "foreplay" by the parrot. During the times hormones are exerting a strong influence on our feathered companions, interactions that would normally cause no problems, may create sexual arousal and serious confusion in our avian companions. During these periods, in many birds, it may he best to avoid petting under the wing, pulling on the tail, encompassing the body, putting hand pressure on the back or rump area, touching near the vent, and beak wrestling.

A hormonally influenced, strongly-bonded parrot may try to initiate copulation by rubbing his or her vent on the caregiver's hand, leg, etc. When this occurs I advise my clients to return their parrots to a T-stand or their cage for a time-out without making a fuss. This form of sexual behavior in companion parrots is a displacement substitute for natural biological behaviors and should not be punished. It should be ignored and neither encouraged or discouraged. It is best not to encourage sexual bonding from our companion parrots. Nest building, sexual seduction, masturbation, and even egg laying may be common behaviors in some celibate companion parrots. However, these are instinctive responses to internal and external stimuli and do not mean the parrot wants to breed and raise a family.

Many parrots masturbate — some frequently. This will come as no surprise to those who have lived with parrots for some time. After a fairly involved courtship and often-frenzied ritual "foreplay," parrot pairs consummate their sexual union by positioning their vents together. Many sexually mature single parrots derive pleasure by rubbing their vents against almost anything including, but not limited to, their toys, perches, and cage parts. People also receive this type of unwanted attention from their parrots. In some parrots, increased agitation and aggression are signs of sexual behavior. Watch for changes in body posture to know if you should be handling your parrot differently than normal. Parrots still need attention during these times, but you may have to relate to your bird less physically until he or she settles down. It is a good idea to train a young bird to step on a stick or branch. This way, if he or she becomes a problem during breeding season, you can still maintain hand control without being bitten. Not all parrots become aggressive or exhibit problem behaviors during breeding season. I have heard about several people who have reported that their beloved hens have laid eggs in their laps. Caregivers of well-nurtured parrots may not even notice sexual behavior.

The combination of sexually mature parrots, breeding season, and parrots on shoulders often means BIG trouble! Parrots relate to our faces. The shoulder situation is like this: the two of you are sitting together on a "moving tree branch." The parrot perceives you as his mate, and an "intruder" (your wife, husband, a kid, or even the dog) threatens the territory you are sharing (your body!). It is natural for parrots to strut and puff to defend the nesting territory. When you don't help, you become part of the problem rather than part of the solution. You get bitten, probably because your *mate* is trying to drive you away. He can't defend both you and the territory and wants you to come back later when everything is safe.

Overriding Natural Behavior

There are many variables that can influence and even override the natural tendencies in parrots. With handfed babies, early socialization can have a tremendous impact on whether a parrot will have quality pet potential. Socialization is not just the number of birds or people the young bird relates to in its early development. It is the process by which young animals learn their social and survival skills. Poorly socialized chicks raised in production type aviaries may not be able to form a trusting bond with anyone, parrot or human because they have not been exposed to nurturing. On the other hand, many young parrots will be able to bond with another parrot or a person if they have been properly socialized — whether the nurturing has come from their natural parrot parents or human surrogates. I believe that the reason so many domestically raised parrots do not transition to breeding situations has more to do with the fact they have received very little socialization rather than the fact that they have "imprinted" on humans instead of parrots. The concept of imprinting suggests that once a bond is formed, it will not change. However, it is clear to me from working with companion parrots over the last twenty-five years that their social bonding is not "engraved in stone." Parrots are clearly capable of bonding and re-bonding on many different levels throughout their lives. I believe that with the proper gradual transition, some companion parrots can become successful breeders. However, I feel this decision should only be a last resort but certainly not as a solution for behavioral problems. If a person chooses to keep their parrot as a lifetime pet, they should not be made to feel guilty for this decision.

Concerns For The Pet Owner

Companion parrot caregivers often seem to be at the low end of the power curve, pawns in a much larger game played by people with far more influence and money. We depend on aviculture to protect the interests of the people who keep parrots in captivity. However, aviculture sometimes seems to be "shooting itself in the foot" with companion parrot owners. People who are happy with their physically and psychologically healthy pet birds are the best advertising to sell more pet birds. For years, pet owners have been told that their parrots need to be put in breeding programs as a cure-all for almost any behavioral problem. I have talked to owners of parrots less then a year old who have been pressured into giving up their bird to a breeding situation because it "needed a mate." Although there are many reasons people do not keep their parrots, I doubt it is a coincidence that "ill-behaved" pets are now one of the major sources for breeding birds.

Without realizing it, this woman may be sexually stimulating her Cockatoo by continually putting pressure on his or her back when she handles the bird. Although this type of handling might not be always create a problem, it certainly will intensify sexual behavior during breeding season.

I have talked with many people with young parrots who have been told to put their bird in a breeding program because the bird has developed behavior problems. This misconception of turning parrots into breeders to solve their behavior problems is so common and the advice is often given in total contradiction to the reality of the situation. Don't even consider putting a bird in a breeding program until he or she is actually sexually mature and physically ready to breed. A bird that exhibits courting behavior is not necessarily sexually mature. Just as children develop some sexual behaviors before they have the hormones to back up their behavior so do parrots practice being adults before they are actually ready to breed. Placing a young hen that is not yet ready to breed with a mature male may result in serious aggression or even death in several species.

Are birds really happier as breeders than they are as human companions? Not necessarily. It depends on the quality of the pet home and the quality of the breeding situation. With both, there are ranges from excellent to atrocious. There is nothing wrong in keeping parrots as human companions as long as they are cared for properly and are content in their situation. A well-nurtured companion parrot may be very traumatized by suddenly being ripped from his home and placed in a breeding program. Most parrots are in far better lifelong situations with knowledgable caregivers than in many breeding programs.

Parrots make wonderful lifelong companions, but only if people understand and pay close attention to both their physical and emotional needs. Feeding a varied, nutritious diet is essential. Providing a roomy, secure, clean cage environment allows parrots to feel confident and safe. Toys and a playgym are necessary for exercise and activity. Frequent bathing or misting is a must. Proper veterinary care should be provided. But the most important consideration of all is that parrots are highly social animals who need consistent handling, attention, and affection. Understanding the environmental and emotional influences on a companion parrot and developing nurturing strategies to deal with them successfully is essential to their well-being. Provide them the excellent care they deserve — the rewards are substantial. ✒

Changes in the Environment

Change is Inevitable

There will always be changes the lives of companion parrots because there will always be changes in the lives of the people who care for them. Some parrots have little, if any, trouble with change in their lives while change can create serious behavioral changes in the lives of more sensitive parrots. It is not so much change that some parrots have trouble with, it is the way the changes are made that can create problems. Most companion parrots like routine but establishing too rigid a routine can create serious problems. The parrot can become so rigid he will accept very little change in his life. Whenever possible, new situations should be introduced gradually. If the change is something that has to occur quickly, the caregivers should understand that their parrots might need time to adjust to the changes.

Because of their well-developed senses of sight and hearing, companion parrots are very aware of what goes on in their environment. The sight of parrots is more developed than ours and they visually perceive ultraviolet light. Basically this means that they are aware of our emotions because of the colors we project. Different energy has varying colors depending on whether it reflects or absorbs ultraviolet light. We can make what we consider to be subtle changes in our appearance and mood and our parrots will be very aware of these changes. If we make more noticeable changes, our parrots may have a strong response. Even though, they recognize us, the change may cause a dramatic and even negative reaction to us until they adjust to the change in our appearance. It is critical to be aware of the fact that this change in behavior starts out as an incident and not an established pattern in the parrot's life. We can't take it personally because if we change our behavior too drastically it may seriously upset the trust our parrots have established in us.

I received a call from a man whose African Grey had suddenly "turned on" him. One morning he took the Grey out of his cage and the bird bit him viciously. This was totally unexpected and not at all a behavior the parrot had ever exhibited before. From then on every time the man tried to take him out of his cage, the Grey lunged at him to bite him. As with all of my consultations, I spent the first hour asking him questions to try and find out how much he knew about his parrot. He was knowledgable enough to provide his Grey with good care but he was at a loss about why the bird was acting the way he was. The parrot's early socialization was better than that of many young birds with whom I had worked, but he still was sensitive with new situations in his life. My client couldn't think of any changes in the parrot's environ-

One morning this previously tame African Grey lunged at his caregiver and bit him viciously. He couldn't think of any changes that could have caused such a dramatic change in his parrot but there was a reason ...

ment. He hadn't been gone any length of time and he certainly had not been aggressive with the parrot. We talked several times and each time I asked him, "What has changed in you Grey's environment?" It was important to try and figure out why the Grey's behavior had changed so abruptly so that he could undo whatever happened if it still was causing a problem for the parrot and make sure that type of situation would not be repeated again without special considerations. My advice to him was to calm down and not push the bird and to be indirect and somewhat submissive when he approached the parrot. Within a week or so, the Grey had settled down and was pretty much back to his normal behavior. Case closed? No. About a month later, the man called to ask me something. He remembered that he had shaved off his moustache the morning that the bird became so upset — could that have caused the problem? Absolutely yes!

In another situation, a woman had a young Meyer's Parrot who had become very phobic after she had treated herself to a manicure for the first time since she got the parrot. When she approached her parrot with her newly long, red nails, the Meyer's threw himself on the cage of the floor and responded as if she was a predator looking for lunch. Similar reports have come from people who have made other changes in their appearance including a new hair color, hairstyle, or even unusual clothing.

Changes in the cage environment may also create fear responses in companion parrots. On page 55, I discuss a Scarlet Macaw who had a very

A new manicure with long bright red nails was enough to set this Meyer's parrot into an aggressive reaction. Sudden changes can create serious problems for some sensitive parrots. When a parrot has this type of reaction, it is best to let him calm down and not try to force him to be your friend again.

negative reaction to a new painting that was hung a few feet away from his cage. If the people had tried to slowly acclimate the Macaw to the painting by first placing it across the room and then gradually moving it closer, the bird's reaction may not have been so negative. In another situation, a couple moved a large piece of furniture into the living room. Although it was placed across the room from their African Grey, the bird still had a strong fear response. A new cage location may also cause fear responses, especially if there is something in the location that the parrot is not used to. For example, it may take a parrot time to adjust to being next to a window if this is a new experience for him. Night thrashing can be caused by car headlight reflections on the wall near the parrot's cage.

New people in the household may also cause a fear response in parrots if those people are not introduced properly. One call I received was from a woman whose teenage son had brought his friends in to see her Grey. They were trying to feed him French fries and although the parrot loved these as a treat, the fact that they were being offered by high-energy strangers caused the parrot severe apprehension. The woman knew something was wrong when she came in the room later and her loving parrot bit her severely when she tried to take him out of his cage.

Almost any change in the environment can threaten a companion parrot in such a way that it will create alarm and cause him to bite defensively. This is especially true with sensitive parrots and those who have been poorly socialized and do not have a positive sense of exploration or curiosity. Well-socialized parrots who have been introduced safely to many changes when they were young, will rarely have profound reactions to change in their lives. If they do, these birds will usually shake themselves out and settle down in a short time rather than responding with a serious change in behavior. When a sensitive parrot has a negative reaction, his caregivers often rush over to reassure him. In some cases, this is the worst thing to do especially if the person is upset about what is happening. A classic example of this occurs during an earthquake. Because they have encapsulated nerve bundles in their joints, parrots feel vibrations sooner and more intensely than we do. In an earthquake, most companion parrots have a problem because they can't take to the air to avoid the vibration. They still try to fly and usually end up thrashing about in their cages. If the concerned and also frightened caregiver rushes over to check on the parrot, their intense energy can exacerbate the stress the parrot is already feeling making the situation much more volatile.

Change happens on a daily basis. If caregivers pay attention and know what changes are likely to cause problems for their parrots, these changes can be made gradually. If the change has to be immediate, caregivers can monitor their parrots' reactions. Before anyone tries to soothe a traumatized parrot, it is important them to first calm down their own energy. Since a traumatized parrot is likely to be in "prey mode" the person should approach the parrot indirectly and submissively to avoid alarming him more. He will settle down more quickly if he is not approached with high-energy concern.

BEAKBITE TIP: Returning Home

I have often said that I have learned much of what I know from working with parrots by trial and error. In other words, I tried it and it didn't work so I try not to do it again. But sometimes I forget. I was gone to Tucson for 6 days and had a great time. My assistant, Gayle Reece, went with me, and Pascal, my DYH Amazon adores her. I have to add (somewhat defensively) that she adores me too. When we got back from the airport before Gayle left for home, she brought the extremely excited Pascal out of her cage and placed her onto the playgym on top.

Some readers may remember that I stated that the word bite was not in Pascal's vocabulary. Even though she does have some health problems, she has her moments of overload exuberance. On several occasions, in articles and in my books, I have written about this topic. If I had followed my own advice, I would never have run over to Pascal and with enthusiastic verbal greetings and great gusto swooped her off of her perch to give her a big hug. I only realized it was too much, too soon as she chomped down on that tender, fleshy area between the thumb and forefinger. I have to admit that my feelings were hurt and I immediately felt betrayed by my precious little grand-bappy. Of course, Gayle was there to remind me that I had broken a few of my very own behavioral tenants — duh!

1) Don't pick up a parrot who is in overload.
2) When you come home after being gone for a period of time, give your parrot a chance to adjust to you being back before you try to handle him. When you do approach him, move slowly speaking in a calm voice and watch him for his reactions..
3) Even though you are excited to see him, check out his mood and don't try to handle him if he is too excited by your return.

While some parrots are fine with immediate greetings, others need time to readjust and/or get over the excitement. Parrots are creatures of habit and if we are gone for any length of time, they tend to get into new routines while we are gone. If we move too fast with them, they may become threatened. It is obvious that parrots remember their people for a long time so we do not become strangers — they seem to just get out of the habit of us being around. Are they aggressive in this type of situation to punish us — because they are mad at us for leaving them? Perhaps, but I think it probably has more to do with getting used to us again and changing their routine. Whatever the reasons, as I sit here with my throbbing bite, I know I learned my lesson again. I went more slowly and Pascal and I are great friends again.

Using Common Sense

Over the years I have learned that there are some times when it simply does not make sense to try and handle a parrot. While many situations can create aggressive behavior in most parrots, some birds have their own triggers. An aggressive reaction could have to do with territory, mate protection, defense of a food item, overload and over-stimulation. When caregivers get to know their parrots, they can usually figure out what situations will most likely bring out aggressive behavior in their otherwise delightful parrots. Once these situations have been identified, it would certainly show a lack of common sense to try and pick up the parrot when the variables triggering the aggression occur.

Two parrots may get along just fine on a playgym. However, if they are both strongly bonded to their caregiver, there are situations that can bring out aggression in one or both parrots. While some parrots may behave on their caregiver's shoulder, two parrots on the shoulders greatly increase the potential of aggressive behavior — especially if they have ever shown any jealousy toward each other. One on each shoulder could turn the person's face into a battleground if one of the parrots decides to defend his caregiver or if the birds decide to fight over his or her attention.

Different situations create different behaviors in various species and individual parrots. Some parrots become somewhat threatened when they are on the floor and this makes them easier to pick up. Others become aggressive on the ground and will stalk people and even chase them around the room. While not all Cockatoos become ground stalkers, they are the ones most known for this aggressive behavior. Being on the floor can put some 'toos into immediate overload especially if the person they are stalking jumps around giving the bird a drama reward. Picking up a parrot who is in overload is one of the best ways to get bitten. Let him settle down first!

Know when, where, and why your parrots will become difficult to trust ... and avoid these situations!

Two Examples

I am extending an invitation for Spikey to bite me if I reach for him when he is eating a favorite treat — especially a pistachio nut. All I have to do is look at his pinned eyes and that should be enough warning for me to leave him alone. At a conference, Spike was being held by one of his fans while she waited in a buffet line. I had asked her to watch him so I could get my notes ready for my program. Everything was fine until she gave Spike a food treat. He immediately became a possessive little tyrant and bit her because she brought her hand too close to his food. Spike's defensiveness around food is very predictable and if I have to handle him, it is critical for me to snap my fingers and/or call his name to distract him first so he won't bite the person he is with or me.

TOOLS FOR WORKING WITH PARROT AGGRESSION

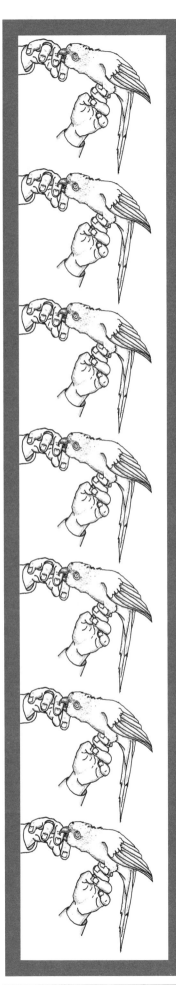

Yabbit, I've Tried Everything!

When I talk with people about their problem parrots one of the most common statements I hear is, "YabbitBut I've tried everything." I believe that they think this is true. The truth is that they have tried the wrong things and if they have tried the right things, they have not tried them for long enough. Unfortunately most people will fall prey to quick fixes that are not only ineffective but they cause even more damage to the bond between the parrot and his human caregivers.

I have been working with companion parrots for well over a quarter of a century and during that time I have seen the rise and fall of many people who have sought credibility in this field. Many are tireless self-promoters who seem to suddenly be everywhere. They are given media coverage because most people in the media have little experience with companion parrot keeping. They become more famous (or infamous, as the case may be) on the Internet because everyone writes about them. Before long they have invitations to speak at bird clubs and seminars all over the country because the people who invite them have no clue about the nature of their theories and/or have not taken the time to really analyze their information. They stand up in front of the audience and tame a (previously?) tame parrot. It seems like a miracle to the audience who may not realize that it is so much easier to work with a parrot in an unfamiliar situation than in a home routine. I have worked the same "miracle" in front of a group but I know that if I can't leave my audience with a sense of long-term rededication to their parrots, I have done nothing more than put on a good show. These so-called "bird trainers" are often charismatic and entertaining but are they really helping people with their companion parrots? ... rarely, if ever.

It is my belief that most of these people are incredibly harmful to the relationship between people and their companion parrots. Like the classic snake oil salesman and the medical quack, these people offer the attractive quick fix. This often keeps people from seeking out information that will make a positive change in their parrots' behavior. These entertainers stand in front of an audience and work "miracles" with demonstration parrots and people think that what they see is the answer to all of their problems.

Quick-fixes may seem to work. After all, they can stop the parrot from biting (screaming, feather picking, etc.) *each and every* time the parrot does it. What some people don't realize is that the parrot is still acting *each and every* time in a negative manner. The parrot's behavior is still unacceptable. In other words, the quick fix may treat the symptoms of the problem but it is not dealing with the problem itself. The long-term fix for the problem itself can be relatively simple such as providing more focused attention or not responding to negative behavior but it always requires a change in the way caregivers interact with their parrots on a long-term basis. The caregiver needs to establish *Nurturing Guidance* with his or her parrot. Most of all, *Nurturing Guidance* requires understanding and patience. Long-term changes cannot be made without patience. When a quick-fix charlatan decries the "patience method," he is not aware of what it truly takes to have a long-term positive relationship with a companion parrot.

The serious problem is that the people who follow quick-fix advice are using the wrong tools for a positive lifelong relationship with their parrots. They try several quick-fixes and when they are unsuccessful in changing their parrots' permanent behaviors, they believe they have tried everything. They have tried the snake oil salesman's cures and quick-fixes and they have not worked. They can't duplicate the success of someone who has worked "miracles." Then they do the worst thing they can do — they give up. Parrot rescue, rehab, and adoption centers and sanctuaries are overloaded with parrots that people have given up on. Many of these parrots have come from homes where the people tried "everything." **Unfortunately they did not use the right tools for long enough.**

Basic Skills To Keep A Parrot Tame

Positive Patterning

The best relationships with companion parrots are those where people have taken the time to teach their birds a few basic skills that will improve the quality of the parrot/human experience for both of you. Teaching and maintaining these skills will make interactions with your parrot safer and more enjoyable over your lifetime together.

◷ **BASIC VERBAL COMMANDS** • Using consistent verbal commands (cues) from the beginning of your life with your new parrot will help you handle him throughout his life. Teach him to step on your hand with a friendly and clearly stated "UP" command, and to step off using the word "DOWN." As you develop confidence with your parrot, you may find a need for other verbal commands. Using verbal commands and cues consistently will help both of you to avoid mixed messages and the confusion they cause.

◷ **FULL BODY HANDLING** • While some parrot species are not usually comfortable with full-body handling, others delight in being held. Even parrots who don't seem to enjoy being stroked or skritched may enjoy some limited physical affection. A well-socialized bappy should enjoy being handled, but as he gets older, he may balk at full-body handling. This does not necessarily mean he doesn't ever want to be handled again. It may just mean he is being more particular about when he will accept handling. Without forcing him to accept your affection, continue to gently handle him from the top of his head to the tips of his toes as much as possible on a daily basis. If he complains, stop for the time being and try again when he is more relaxed.

◷ **WING & TOE EXAMS** • Grooming is far less traumatic for a parrot who is used to having his toes and wings touched. While your young parrot is perched on his T-stand or playing in the towel, play "this little piggy" with his toes while you touch and handle each one with your fingers. Encourage him to play 'Eagle Boy' (or Girl) by gently lifting each wing with your fingers. When he is comfortable with both wings spread, touch each flight feather individually, smile, and say "Eagle Boy" (or whatever does the trick for you) so that he knows to spread his wings and let you touch his flight feathers.

◷ **TOWEL HANDLING** • Getting a parrot used to being handled in a towel will make a major difference in his life. Even parrots who are afraid of towels can be introduced to them in such a way that they accept them without fear. The neutral room is very helpful in teaching a parrot to accept a towel. Prepare the neutral room first by laying the towel flat on the bed and then bring the parrot in and place him on the towel. It may help if you place some familiar toys or treats on the towel first to keep him occupied. Gradually pick the corners up and play peek-a-boo. Once he is used to that, gently and playfully wrap him in the towel to pick him up and cuddle him. Make a practice of handling him in the towel on a regular basis to keep him used to it. Parrots who enjoy towel cuddling often stay tamer and getting him used to being in the towel will help tremendously to make his trips to the vet easier. To avoid the stress of his being approached by a person he may not know, you can gently towel him and then hand him to his veterinarian for examination. The less stress he has, the more accurate his medical test results will be.

◷ **STICK TRAINING** • Trying to get a parrot to step on a stick the first time by poking it on can be quite threatening for many parrots. Lay a branch or dowel (appropriately-sized for your parrot so he can wrap his toes around it) on the bed or couch while you are playing with your parrot. Let the bird get used to it and, without poking it at him, encourage him to step on it while it is flat on the bed. As he steps on it, gradually lift the branch. Once he is used to it, ask him to step on it with the "UP" command. Pick him up with the stick from time to time to keep him used to it. This way, if you have any trouble handling him in the future and become afraid of reaching for him with your hand, you will feel safe asking him to step on the stick. You and others can maintain hand control of a stick-trained parrot even when he is a bit "frisky."

◷ **T-STAND TRAINING** • Getting a parrot to stay on his perch can be difficult but young parrots can be patterned to sit on a T-stand next to their caregivers. Each time he tries to come to you, hold up your hand in the stop position and say "Stay." When you want him to come to him, give him verbal permission. Parrots communicate verbally with each other and are as easy as (if not easier than) dogs to teach behaviors using verbal commands (cues).

◷ **SELF CALMING** • If a parrot is able to soothe himself in a uncomfortable or threatening situation, there will be a lot less stress in his life. By calming yourself down when you are with him and using words or sounds (such as humming) to label the change in your energy, he can learn to use the same sounds to reassure himself. If used consistently, these same sounds can be used to calm down an agitated parrot when he is with you. ⨍

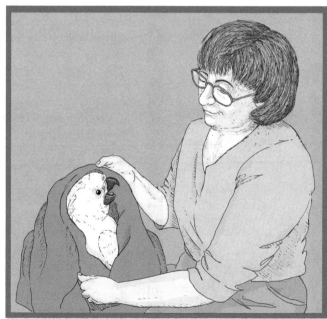

There are several advantages to getting your parrot used to being handled in a towel. He will become less stressed when he has to be toweled for examination or grooming. Towel games like Peek-a-boo and towel wrestling can also be great fun and some parrots love to be cuddled in a towel.

Picking Up A Parrot

Hands Should Bring Pleasure

The number one reason that people lose control of their parrots' behavior is the loss of hand control. They have not been consistent or they get sloppy about approaching their parrots. Inconsistent handling can be very confusing to a companion parrot and the more confusion people create for the parrot, the less likely he will want to be handled. Caregivers should not create situations where companion parrots view hands in a negative manner. Hands should bring pleasure to parrots in many ways so handling a parrot should be a positive interaction. If your parrot has a negative reaction to your hands, you need to work to win him over again. Finger-feeding treats and gentle head skritching are two of the best ways to get a hand shy parrot used to being approached by hands.

If your parrot is afraid of hands, move slowly and try not to approach him from above. Parrots bond to our faces and holding your hands near your face is one way to let a hand shy bird know that your hands are part of you. Be sure and check a parrot's mood and activity before attempting to pick him up. If he is busy eating or excitedly playing, it may not be a good time to pick him up. It is best to greet him first by saying something like "Hey, what are you doing?" before you attempt to pick him up. Sometimes you will need to pick a parrot up and he will be uncooperative, either because he is playing a game with you about coming out of his cage, he is in overload behavior, or he is busy playing or eating. Some parrots are very possessive about food and play objects. Rather than just reaching in and trying to get him to step up at that time, you can distract him by holding a non-threatening object like a magazine or a potholder in the other hand and then use the "UP" command to ask him to step on your hand.

The ability to ask a parrot to step onto your hand and have him do so in response is critical for keeping a positive mutual relationship. The purpose is not to be "the boss" or force the parrot to comply, but to make handling a rewarding experience for both the parrot and his human flock. Make sure before you approach your parrot to ask him to step onto your hand that he is not involved in something that will keep him from complying when you use the up command.

Parrots can be incredible game players and it doesn't take too many inappropriate responses from people for a parrot to set his own rules for a new game. If your parrot reaches out with his beak and you pull back, this routine may become your bird's favorite game to let you know he is in control. Using the "UP" command properly changes the rules of this game and turns both of you into winners with the prize being a positive relationship.

Once they are on your hand, many parrots will try to run up your arm to your shoulder. If a parrot gets into this habit it can be difficult to change. The best way to prevent this behavior is not to let it happen. When my Caique, Spikey Le Bec, first came to live with me, whenever I got him on my hand, he was up my arm, onto my shoulder, and then up to the top of my head. Before I could stop him, he was hair surfing. It took me a few weeks of constantly putting my other hand in front of him as he darted up my arm and using the "UP" command to get him to step off of my arm onto my hand. But then, of course, he would try to run up to my shoulder on the other arm. I repeated the same process with the other hand. We did that dozens of times before he finally realized that he was not allowed on my shoulder unless I put him there. To reinforce the "UP" command, make a friendly game out of laddering your parrot. Slowly transfer him deliberately from one hand to the other, saying "UP" each time. Go slowly and take time to praise him often — the purpose is not to wear his little legs off. Using laddering as punishment defeats the purpose of getting your parrot to see hands as a friendly interaction. Therefore, I do not recommend laddering a parrot as a discipline or punishment. Many parrots interpret this as confrontation or may become over-stimulated by aggressive laddering.

Many people lose their parrots' hand tameness because they take it for granted. I have had dozens of people tell me that they thought the "UP" command was only for training and once their birds learned it, they didn't use it anymore. You are only as good as your last successful "UP" command. Being consistent is essential to maintain a lifelong relationship because it helps you to approach your parrot in the same manner and it gives your parrot a clear message about what you want from him. Always bring your parrot out of his cage with the "UP" command instead of just letting him come out by himself. To establish guidance, make it your choice instead of his. Always use the "UP" command to ask him to step onto your hand. Keep it friendly and clear. Don't let him run up your arm to your shoulder. If you want him there, place him there with the "DOWN" command. Do not force him to go from hand to hand in an aggressive manner. Always keep your commands decisive and friendly. →

Some Basics of Hand Control

Being able to have your companion parrot step on your hand is an essential part of a successful relationship with him. The loss of hand control is often the first step in the development of behavioral problems. Being able to handle your parrot makes it much easier to prevent problems from developing. Following are important concepts in keeping him tame:

➤ Parrots communicate verbally and are easily trained to respond to verbal cues or commands.

➤ Being clear and decisive, but not aggressive, is the key to maintaining hand control of your companion parrot.

➤ Parrots need to be given a clear message to step onto your hand. This avoids giving him mixed messages causing the parrot to be confused and non-compliant. Biting is often the result of confusion from the parrot.

➤ Using consistent commands or cues to pick up your parrot patterns both of you to consistent behavior.

➤ Using direct but friendly eye contact along with the verbal "UP" command will establish a consistent nurturing authority with your parrot. Focus on what you are doing instead of doing something else at the same time.

➤ Say "UP" once with a friendly but firm and clear voice in the same way you might give a dog a "SIT" command. Be clear and assertive but not aggressive. If the bird does not respond, say it again as a new command.

➤ Don't say "uuuuuuuuuupppppppp" too softly or "???up?" as if you are asking a question. The motorboat command, "upupupupup" is also confusing and ineffective. Neither is the 5-syllable word "uuu-uuu-uuu-uuu-uup." Saying "!!!!UP!!!!" too loudly or aggressively will have an undesired effect because aggression is often met with aggression.

➤ Placing the command in the middle of a sentence is also not a clear message. "Hi Spikey, how are ya doin'- up- here we go."

➤ Using the "UP" command at the wrong time, for example, before you present your finger to your parrot or after he has already stepped on your hand, gives a confusing message.

➤ Many people make the mistake of trying to pick up a parrot by just placing their hand in front of him and expecting him to automatically step on — some parrots will but many won't. Just as they always say in a perfect golf swing — follow through.

➤ Push your fingers gently into his lower belly, say a clear "UP" and follow through by getting your parrot on your hand. Don't push him or move too fast, but make a continuous motion.

➤ Just wiggling your fingers around in front of a parrot does not give him a clear message. Expecting him to step onto your moving hand is unrealistic. The parrot may become confused or agitated, and that wiggling finger can be too tempting. Just as a fish can't resist a wiggling worm, your parrot may not be able to resist biting your wiggling finger. If you do it often enough, fish bait biting may become a patterned game your parrot plays with you.

➤ Watch to see which foot your parrot uses to hold food and toys. A left-footed parrot will generally be more comfortable stepping onto your right hand and a right-footed parrot is more likely to step on your left hand without hesitation.

➤ Some parrots are far more comfortable stepping back onto your hand. If you consistently have trouble picking up your parrot from the front, try approaching him from the back. Use the same decisive techniques and the "UP" command. Giving a "back-stepper" the opportunity to step on your hand in this manner may give him less opportunity to be a "beak-stabber."

➤ Always check out your parrot's body language and mood before you try to pick him up. Picking up an overexcited parrot is asking for a bite. A non-threatening distraction, such as snapping your fingers, may be needed to get his attention first.

BEAKBITE TIP: A Self-fulfilling Prophecy

Over the years, several parrot species have become defined as being aggressive. Although these generalizations may occasionally have some factual basis, all birds within that species will not fit the stereotypical description. Unfortunately, these generalizations have become so established that people often avoid these species as companion parrots. In some situations, the parrot species they avoid may actually be the perfect companion for them. Sometimes people are so sure certain parrots will become aggressive, that it becomes a self-fulfilling prophecy. Once their parrots show even the slightest aggressive behavior, they are told over and over that this is what they should expect. Often because of the assumption that their avian companions belong to an aggressive species, the people do not work with their parrots to avoid, prevent or solve problems with aggression.

Amazon parrots are often dismissed as being aggressive. However, they have been successful human companions for centuries and there has to be a reason for this. For many years, Amazons were the most popular companion parrots in this country. Then because of rampant generalizations, all Amazons developed a reputation for being aggressive and people started avoiding them as companions. In my opinion, these people have missed out on one of the most remarkable companion parrots. I know Amazons who are every bit as cuddly as any Cockatoo or other parrot-family bird with the reputation for being cuddly. Although the generalizations say that they are unpredictable, the truth is that Amazons are usually predictable for the caregiver who pays attention to their body language and learns to understand their behaviors. Amazons are the "what you see is what you get parrot" and most are loyal, affectionate, entertaining and great fun and most of all, many rarely, if ever, show any severe aggression.

The Parrot/Human Bond

No Two Are Exactly the Same

One of the reasons that quick-fix advice rarely works is that each situation is different. If caregivers don't have some basic idea of the dynamics of their relationship with their parrots and why their avian companions act the way they do, it will be difficult, if not impossible, for them to change the negative behaviors. When people with parrot experience stand up in front of a group of people, they may make parrot handling look very easy. But it is rarely that easy for the people in the audience because they have not developed the same skills. When they get home and try the same techniques, they rarely work — often because it is too much too soon for the parrot. Just as no two friendships are the same, the mutual bonds between parrots and their caregivers are also unique. There are so many variables that influence this bond but the personalities of each are the major factors. While companion parrots are still instinctively wild animals, the people in their lives have a tremendous effect on their personality development. Quality early socialization is imperative for the pet potential of companion parrots. A well-socialized parrot who has been nurtured, allowed to mature at his own pace, weaned gradually, and fed abundantly, learns to trust the people in his life. Once he learns to trust people, he will readily transfer his bond with them to new people in his life — as long as those people deserve that trust. Parrots are capable of bonding on different levels to different people throughout their lives. Companion parrots can have multiple relationships with several people in a household and behave differently with each person. I am familiar with many families where the parrot has some level of tameness to every person in the home and to good friends of family members — it might surprise some people to know that one is an adult male Yellow-nape. He was domestically raised and from the very beginning each person in the family established their own special relationship with him. Most of the year every one can handle him when they are all together, but during breeding season, he is more strongly bonded to the mother. During this time, the other family members know not to approach when he is with her. However, in their own rooms away from her, they can handle him without any problems. He is an "if-you-can't-be-with-the one-you-love, love-the-one-you're-with" type parrot.

While their ability to develop strong bonds with people is one of the traits that make parrots such wonderful companions, there is a flip side. Many parrots who live with families and are allowed to develop a strong bond to just one person in that family can become aggressive to the other people in the household. This is especially true when the parrot perceives the favored person as his or her mate. When this happens, the bird may direct sexual behavior towards the person and this can include aggressive protection from the other people in the human flock. Some people think this protective aggression is funny but encouraging this type of behavior will result in a parrot who becomes more aggressive as he matures. The best way for a parrot to stay tame to the entire family is for everyone to establish their separate relationship and also for everyone to handle the parrot together. I recommend playing a game that I call "warm potato." This involves everyone who wants to be part of the parrot's life getting comfortable together in the living room or any room where they can all be together. Everyone should be calm and relatively distraction free. Each person gets the parrot on their hand and provides some special treat, abundant compliments or praise, or a good head skritch. Then the parrot is passed on to the next family member. Of course if one member of the family is very afraid, he or she should not try to handle the parrot until they can become comfortable doing so but that person can sit in and observe the others.

BEAKBITE TIP: Rekindling the Bond

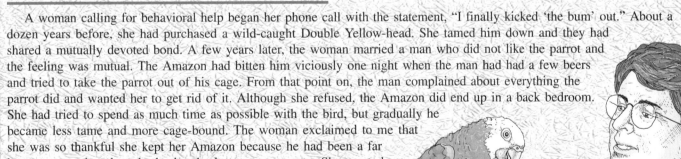

A woman calling for behavioral help began her phone call with the statement, "I finally kicked 'the bum' out." About a dozen years before, she had purchased a wild-caught Double Yellow-head. She tamed him down and they had shared a mutually devoted bond. A few years later, the woman married a man who did not like the parrot and the feeling was mutual. The Amazon had bitten him viciously one night when the man had had a few beers and tried to take the parrot out of his cage. From that point on, the man complained about everything the parrot did and wanted her to get rid of it. Although she refused, the Amazon did end up in a back bedroom. She had tried to spend as much time as possible with the bird, but gradually he became less tame and more cage-bound. The woman exclaimed to me that she was so thankful she kept her Amazon because he had been a far better companion than the husband who was now gone. She wanted her parrot back in her life the way he had been. She had moved his cage back into the living room. She could easily skritch his head through the cage bars since she had been doing this all along but she was afraid to handle him. When I visited her for the consultation, I observed the Amazon carefully. He watched her every move and, even though she had not handled him for a few years, it was clear that his strong bond with her was still there. She just needed the courage and the proper techniques to handle him. It took less than a week of trust-renewing work with him for the friendship to be rekindled.

The Neutral Room

A Distraction-free Comfortable Place

Many companion parrots become territorial around their cage. This means that they may defend the area from perceived intruders. It also means that many parrots are generally more threatened by new situations or objects in their cage or in the area around their cage. Because of this people who have had little or no success working with their aggressive parrots around their cages, often find it much easier to work with their birds in a neutral room. This usually is the best place to interact with any biting parrot. It is an area that is not familiar to the parrot and therefore, he has not established any territorial imperatives. The parrot's cage, or playgym should not be visible from the neutral room. There should be no distractions, such as the television, other people, or pets in the room. If the bird is strongly bonded to one person and a less favored person is trying to work with him, only that person should be in the room. Even the sound of the preferred person's voice should be excluded from the scenario. In this area, the bird has no agenda to defend anyone or anything. Consequently, the person in the room with the parrot becomes the most familiar person/thing in an unfamiliar area. Since this is most often true, the less favored person can also provide a sense of security for the parrot in an unfamiliar place. Your

The "neutral room" should be an area of the house where both the parrot and the caregiver can relax and be comfortable. It should not be a threatening area or one where the parrot feels intimidated but it should be an unfamiliar area where the parrot can't see his cage or has not established a sense of territorial defense.

presence may provide the parrot with a familiar face and added security but the parrot shouldn't feel as if he needs to be rescued. Most importantly, it critical that the neutral room should be a mutually comfortable place and not a place where the parrot feels intimidated or threatened.

Working with a parrot who is in, on, or near his cage often results in aggression, however the same bird can become quite docile with being in an unfamiliar area. It is important for people who have been apprehensive about handling their parrot to trust the fact that their bird will be far less likely to be aggressive in the neutral room. If people can't relax enough to present a fearless and non-aggressive confidence with their parrots, the same patterns established in the cage territory can become established in the neutral room. Just as human beings are, parrots are creatures of habit. Behaviors that are repeated over and over become patterned and once they become a pattern, these behaviors are repeated in an automatic manner without much thought directing them. A neutral room with minimal distractions is an excellent place to start patterning positive behaviors.

The neutral room should be a place where both the person and the parrot will be comfortable and relaxed. I recommend a bedroom or den with a couch rather than the cold floor of a bathroom or hall. Plan ahead and set up the "tools" you need before your bring your parrot into the neutral room. These include a T-stand, special behavioral reward treats, a few favorite toys, a big fluffy light-colored towel, a dowel or stick for stick training. Prepare the room by setting the T-stand near where you can sit, spreading the towel on the bed or couch and placing the items on the towel.

Approaching the bird with decisive confidence is essential for the neutral room to work. Smile, talk softly and make friendly eye contact. Parrots generally do not bite if you are looking at them. Place the bird on the back of a chair or a T-stand at just below eye level and start by gently pushing the back of your fingers into his lower belly and say "UP." If he doesn't step on your finger, gently pick up his toes one at a time until he is sitting on your hand. Slowly transfer him to the other hand saying "UP" again. Do this 3 or 4 times and then say "DOWN" and put him back on the stand. Smile and praise him — *"What a good bird!"* Repeat the process several times until he accepts and obeys the command. Stay friendly and if he starts to become antsy after a few short sessions, put him back on the stand with the "Down" command, praise him and give him a treat before he gets too grouchy. Once he is patterned to step on your hand, start handling him in the same decisive manner out of the neutral room.

Once two people are comfortable handling their parrot separately in the neutral room, they should work together there to accustom the parrot to being handled by both of them together. Playing the game of "warm potato" by slowly passing him from person to person will pattern him to go one to the other. It is critical to not set up a biting situation whereby one person rescues the other after the parrot has bitten him or her. Each person should hold the parrot for a minute or so, praise him, skritch him, sing to him, give him a treat, or whatever helps him be comfortable and then the other person can reach for him using the "UP" command and share a few enjoyable minutes with him. The neutral room is also a very helpful place to introduce your parrot to new people in his life. It is also important to remember that if your normally well-behaved parrot begins to forget his good manners and patterning, the neutral room can always be used for re-patterning him to behave in a more positive manner.

Calm Focused Attention

The Best Way to Control Aggression

In the vast majority of the consultations I have done with parrots who are exhibiting aggression, the first step was to have the caregivers slow down their own energy. Calm focused attention is the best way to say everything is OK. It is obvious that companion parrots are highly empathic and quickly pick up the energy of those around them. If people approach parrots in a fearful or aggressive way or in a sudden, haphazard, or unfocused manner, the parrot is bound to reflect that negative energy. This is particularly true with sensitive parrots, those that do not yet trust their caregivers, and those parrots who have not yet adapted to the capriciousness of their human flock.

During one of my early San Francisco Bay Area consultations, I worked with a young woman with a semi-tame imported White-front Amazon. Within an hour, the Amazon was putty in my hands. I had gently wrapped him in a towel and started skritching his head. His response was so positive that I could handle him without the towel almost immediately. The caregiver saw how easily I handled her parrot but could not duplicate my success no matter how much I tried to explain and demonstrate. To this day, I clearly remember my thoughts on my drive home. I was driving across the San Francisco Bay Bridge wondering how I could transfer this wonderful parrot handling ability to the people I worked with. It became clear to me that I had to teach the people how to effectively calm themselves down before they even tried to handle their parrots during the consultation.

Prejudice or Unfamiliarity

Several years ago I did a consultation with a very uptight African-American doctor and his new Blue and Gold Macaw. The doctor was clearly used to being in control but his macaw was not cooperating at all. The macaw was biting him every time his he tried to handle him and a local avian veterinarian recommended my services. The man was convinced that the bird didn't like him because of his skin color. Of course, the concept of a young macaw exhibiting prejudice has little validity. However, the bird had been raised and handfed by white women so, in actuality, the man's appearance was very different than the people the bird had known, but the same concept would be valid if a Caucasian man with a moustache and beard had purchased the macaw. After the short time it would take for the macaw to become accustomed the man's appearance, there would be no reason that the young bird couldn't form a trusting bond with him. Parrots, particularly bappies, are often reticent in new situations so, at least a small portion of the bird's negative reaction to the man could have been based on his physical differences. As long as the man believed this to be true, he would not examine the real reasons the Blue and Gold wasn't comfortable with him — the doctor was totally uncomfortable handling the macaw. This was very obvious as I watched him stiffly holding the macaw at arm's length using the other hand as a shield. The man kept turning his head away as if the bird was about to rip off his nose. **An absolute rule of parrot behavior is that parrots are more comfortable with people who are comfortable with them** and this man was certainly not comfortable with the macaw. Even though he was just a bappy, the macaw's beak was big enough to cause some trepidation but the doctor was not willing to admit that this was a problem for him.

My job was to help the doctor become comfortable handling his new avian companion. It wasn't going to be easy because he disagreed or disputed almost everything I said. "Well, I just don't understand why THAT would make a difference," and "You think I am going to do that!" were just two of his statements as I talked to him. He had a great sense of humor so I thought that would be the best way to win him over. With my own determination and some humorous cajoling, I was able to get past the man's stubbornness and in time we were both sitting on the floor with the macaw. First, I showed the doctor how easy it was for me to handle the very tame and sweet bird. I showed him a few important handling techniques and then I tried to teach the doctor something that seemed very alien to him — I showed him how to relax. I had him shut his eyes, let his head droop, and take a few slow deep breaths. At first, it was obvious that the doctor thought this was all very silly but after a few tries, he realized that I was not going to leave until he at least tried to relax. After about a half an hour, the man had actually calmed himself down and at that point I put the macaw on his hand. Then I had him skritch and hug the big bird. As he was successfully handling the macaw, a little boy smile came over his face. When his wife came home, she was amazed to see her husband sitting on the floor having so much fun with their new companion macaw. I knew I had done my job. ✒

Parrots are more comfortable with people who are comfortable with them. While the macaw, who had been raised by white women, found the black doctor's appearance different than what he was used to, this was not the reason the bird was uncomfortable with his new caregiver. The reason was that the man had not yet learned to be comfortable with the macaw. Once he could relax, the macaw could too.

Using Distraction and Redirection

Interrupting Negative Behaviors

Most parrots have a lot of energy. In the wild, they expend that energy in their daily search for food. Just about everything is provided for our companion parrots, so unless we provide them with a tremendous amount of exercise and stimulation they will still have a good deal of pent up energy. Sometimes it is this energy that gets them into trouble. Parrots are also creatures of habit and without positive intervention can easily be patterned to negative behavior. One of the best ways for us to stop that negative behavior is provide them with positive distractions that interrupt the negative behaviors and provide them with something positive to do. For example one of the first things I taught my Caique, Spikey LeBec to do was a somersault in my hand. When he gets willful and nippy, I put him in the position and have him do a somersault. Then I make a big deal with verbal praise. Spikey's demeanor changes immediately because he know that the somersault will get him positive attention. If I am near a table or a flat surface, I can also get him to hop or shoot him with my finger and get him to roll on his back. I didn't just teach him these behaviors to get him to show off. I also taught them so I could use them to alter his mood from negative to positive. I can also put a knotted rope and leather toy in his face for him to chew on instead of me. I try to vary what I use as a distraction so I don't pattern him to misbehave in order to get to do tricks. This same concept works very well with Bosco, my high-energy Blue-front Amazon friend who lives with my assistant, Gayle Reece. He visits the CPQ office frequently and he will stop almost anything he is doing and put his foot up to the verbal cue "Gimme Four."

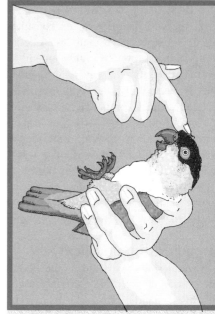

When Spike gets excited and nippy with me, I usually have him do one of his somersaults in my hand and then give him verbal praise for the positive change in his behavior.

Companion parrots tend to become patterned to whatever behaviors are repeated over and over. Just as we can pattern them to positive behaviors, without realizing it, we can also pattern them to negative behaviors and if we just let them do what they want to, they can pattern themselves to negative behaviors. Say a parrot starts refusing to come out of his cage. Each time you reach in and retreat, he becomes more willful and stubborn until you can't get him out at all without being bitten. The longer you keep doing the same thing, the longer he will keep doing the same thing. Changing your role in the negative behavior will distract the parrot from his normal patterned behavior. While he is distracted, it is usually much easier to get him to step on your hand. If I try to get a parrot out of his cage and his refusal has become a pattern, I check several aspects. First I ask myself, did I approach him a sloppy manner that gave him a mixed message? Was he busy doing something else like eating a treat or playing with a toy? If I determine that he is not in a good enough mood to come out or if he doesn't seem like he wants to have anything to do with me, I don't force him. However, if this has simply become a patterned game he is playing with me, I use a distraction to change the pattern he has established. For example, I hold some routine item that is not threatening like a magazine, TV remote, etc. in my other hand to

Teaching a companion parrot a friendly trick using a verbal cue is one way to distract him from negative behaviors. Bosco loves to raise his foot to the words "Gimme four." Saying this to him will distract from just about anything he is busy doing.

interrupt his patterning and get him to come out more easily. The purpose of this technique is not to threaten him, but to get him to stop his patterned behavior long enough to wonder why you are doing something differently. While he is wondering why you are holding that potholder, you can use the "UP" command to get him back to his old pattern of stepping on your other hand.

When I need to pick Spike up and I know he doesn't want me to, I use an object to distract him from biting me. Usually this is when he has found some prize that he is protecting with great possessiveness. In some cases, it is something I do not want destroyed while other times it is something that could be harmful to him. I also need to distract him from situations where he has become aggressive towards someone else. I usually do this by snapping my fingers right above his head and/or saying his name in a relatively loud voice. It usually works but sometimes he has to be pried off of his victim.

Distractions and redirection should lead the bird from negative to positive behaviors in a trust building manner and should not perceived by the parrot as aggression or punishment. Threatening or scaring the parrot is trust-destroying and, while it may stop the specific negative behavior, it will create serious problems in the relationship between the parrot and his caregivers.

Cause and Effect Logic

For years, childcare experts have been writing about the ineffectiveness of punishment — especially for small children who have not yet developed a sense of cause and effect logic. I have been writing the same basic information about parrots for about as many years. Like small children, parrots don't have a cause and effect sense of logic. It is unlikely that there is a clear understanding that one event will always lead to another in the parrot's mind. Parrots do not have the ability to associate misbe-havior with a particular punishment in the sense that they will not stop misbehaving simply because they want to avoid the conse-quence. For example, this logic would suggest that if they know they will have their toys taken away if they bite and if they want to keep their toys, they would not bite anymore. Studies have clearly shown that young children do not have a sense of cause and effect that is developed enough to understand these concepts of punishment. Likewise, a child told to stand in the corner for ten minutes for misbehaving may have some idea that he was bad when he was sent there but quickly loses ant perception of being punished over the ten minutes. He does not understand he is

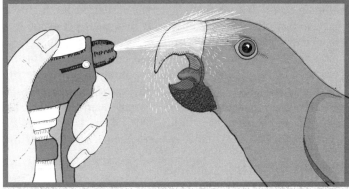

We want our parrots to love water — frequent bathing and showering is essential to their well-being and feather condition. Water should NOT be used as punishment. Putting the spray bottle or water pistol on stun and shooting a parrot in the face with water is trust-destroying. A quick-fix such as this may stop the negative behavior when it happens but it won't stop the parrot from doing the same thing again and again because he can't relate his punishment with his "crime."

standing in the corner because he had been acting in a negative manner. Consequently he will not associate the misbehavior with the punishment so the future behavior will not be changed to avoid the punishment. Whether it is accurate or not, we often hear that parrots have the intelligence of a two-to-three-year-old child, yet we often expect our companion parrots to understand they are being put in their cage and having their toys taken away because they were biting. They don't understand this and we can't be upset or disappointed because they can't make the association between their behavior and its consequence. There is actually more of a chance that if the response to the misbehavior occurs in a timely and dramatic manner, the parrot may actually learn to bite to get to go back to his cage. I had a client who watched the late news with his Amazon. When the man nodded off, the parrot bit his ear so the many got up and put the parrot in his cage. What influenced what?

While immediate, non-aggressive disapproval or correction may sometimes be effective in changing a parrot's behavior, complex punishment rarely works. Complex punishment suggests several concepts that make it ineffective with parrots.

Immediate Calm Corrections

Most parrots can understand an immediate cause and effect correction to misbehavior. A calm but firm "No" and a quick (no more than a second or two) "evil eye" is effective feedback for a parrot. Much more and the person's response is ineffective and may even reinforce the negative behavior by becoming a drama reward, or causing a parrot to become alarmed and afraid.   →

BEAKBITE TIP: The BIG DON'Ts

STOP THE INSANITY!

The key to having a positive relationship with a companion parrot is mutual trust. They need to trust that we will take care of them, provide properly for their social needs, and keep them safe from harm. We need to earn that trust. The more they trust us to be consistent and nurturing the more we can predict and trust their behavior. With trust being so important, why do so many people expect that trust-destroying quick-fixes and punishments will work with their companion parrots? It beats me! Over the years I have heard about people recommending and using so many abusive, traumatizing, trust-destroying quick fixes, deprivations, and punishments. These include, but are not limited to; squirt him with a water pistol or a spray bottle, *thunk* his beak, put him in a "naughty box" or a plastic container, pinch his toes, pull out a feather, wrap him in a towel and hold him tight until his spirit "breaks," notch his beak, mutilate his lower beak, throw something at the cage, ladder him, deprive him of attention and affection for two months, keep his cage covered, confine him in a back room, make him afraid so you can rescue him, show him you are the boss, put him in a dark closet, put him under running water, don't feed him, take away his toys, hit the cage with a shoe, drop cans on his cage, grab his beak and shake it, pull his tail, scream at him, drop him on the floor, put him in the bathtub ... It is no wonder that there are so many unhappy, and even dysfunctional parrots losing their homes when so many people think these and other trust-destroying methods will be successful in changing their parrots negative behaviors. Stop this insanity!

Parrots can become excited by a dramatic response to their negative behavior. If we continually give them immediate dramatic attention for negative behavior, the parrot may find the immediate attention so rewarding he will learn to misbehave just for the attention. Parrots are flock animals and we should be their *flock leaders*. Companion parrots look to their flock leaders to define their boundaries and the safety of their world. If the caregiver's response is greatly excited, the parrot may interpret this as a communication that the flock is in danger. Parrots are highly empathic and respond almost immediately to a threat (real or perceived) by fleeing the situation. If they can't get away, it is nature for them to respond with aggression. Since parrots are instinctively prey animals, if we express alarm by yelling, being aggressive, or being too dramatic, the parrot may respond with alarm and become afraid enough to go into prey mode (the strong aversion and fear response shown by prey animals when a predator is nearby). Repeated fear responses do not create positive behavioral patterns. Confrontation is often met with confrontation. Aggression is usually met with aggression, and excessive aggression will be met with fear, which may result in an aggressive response, or in some parrots, extreme fear. Continued aggressive punishment may create a phobic parrot who becomes afraid of almost everything in his environment. Deprivation of attention or affection as punishment quickly destroys the trust and security necessary for a positive parrot/human bond and will create a whole new set of behavioral problems.

Distractions — Not Solutions

Quick-fixes such as those mentioned on the previous page do not work to change behavioral problems on a long-term basis because they are simply a distraction from the symptoms — biting, screaming, and so on. They do not treat the underlying cause of behavioral problems such as fear and confusion, realistic needs not being met, and/or a *parrot in control of his own life doing a bad job of it*. At the worst they are confusing, trust-destroying and can severely exacerbate problems, and at best, they do not address the variables in the complex relationship between human and parrot.

I have talked with dozens of people who tell me that they have tried everything and they have given up. All they have tried is a series of quick-fixes. Their comment usually involves the statement that what they tried only worked for a while. The quick-fix may distract a parrot from each incident of misbehavior but some people seem to miss the point completely. Using a quick-fix never solves the problem. It only stops each incident. These people had not been dealing with the problem, but only with the symptoms. While they seem easy, in the long run quick-fixes makes life more difficult because the reason the parrot is biting is never addressed in a way that could actually change the behavior. Even after stopping each biting situation, the parrot is still a biting parrot, and the more he bit, the more it became a patterned behavior making it even more difficult to change. Perhaps eventually, these people's parrots would become aggressive enough for them to decide to *get rid of* them. That happens way too often in situations in which there are actually positive methods that could be used to diminish the biting or other misbehavior. These caregivers needed to work with the cause of the biting and, most likely, change their way of interacting with their parrots to make a positive, permanent change in their behavior.

Not Just Ineffective

Working with the underlying cause of the behavior — finding out why the parrot bites and working to change that — is far more productive than punishment. Most often it is not the parrot's behavior that needs changing first — it is the human flock's interaction with a problem parrot that changes the parrot's behavior. The more permanent the changes are in the people, the more the parrot can be re-patterned to behave in positive ways. While some of the quick-fixes I hear recommended are simply ineffective ways of dealing with a problem behavior, most will confuse a parrot. Other quick-fixes are severely trust-destroying and some are abusive. Many quick-fix behavioral *solutions* sound too good to be true and they are. Real solutions to behavioral problems take understanding, time, and patience. These intelligent companions deserve people who are willing to work to change the cause of the behavioral problems — not just the symptoms! ✒

BEAKBITE TIP: The Real Purpose of Time-outs

I have always believed in time-outs for parrots. This should be the cage or another quiet place where the wound up parrot can calm down or where a parrot can go while his caregiver's anger or frustration subsides. Placing a misbehaving parrot back in his cage should NEVER be viewed as punishment and/or done in an aggressive or threatening manner. The parrot's cage should always be a comfortable place where the parrot likes to be when his caregivers are not available to give him attention. Too many people think of a cage as a prison for their birds instead of as his room where he keeps his stuff and hangs out. There should always be enough stimulation in the cage for a parrot to enjoy keeping himself entertained. Cages should be in a location where the parrot can get ambient attention while the caregivers are busy doing other things nearby. Anything that happens to a parrot while he is in his cage is extremely threatening so the idea of hitting the cage or throwing something at it is not only ineffective but also very trust-destroying. When my Caique, Spike, gets too wound up, I usually put him back in his cage to let him calm down. In a very calm manner with no anger or hysteria in my voice, I say, "OK Spike, back you go." Sometimes he beats up a toy but he often settles down and I can usually handle him within five or ten minutes.

Lack of Cooperation in the Human Flock

Do not to force your parrot on an unwilling participant. Over time, with information, patience and the right techniques, people can learn to tolerate and even enjoy parrots!

⊃What if Someone Doesn't Care about the Parrot?

Over the years, I have talked with many people where there is a member of the family who does not like their parrots. Sometimes there is a valid reason such as the parrot continually showing aggression towards them but more often than not the problem can be managed. Sometimes one of the family members is immature enough to be sabotaging any attempt to teach the parrots new behaviors. In some consultations I have done, my inclination was to recommend a human therapist or a marriage counselor. Unfortunately the people who love their parrots are often forced to make decisions that they regret later. People love their parrots but what happens if not everyone in the household is committed to resolving the parrot's problem behavior? What happens if a family member sabotages your positive efforts? What if a member of the household simply wants the problem, or the parrot, to go away? In these situations, it is important to realize that not all people feel the same about parrots. You may enjoy a loving relationship with your bird, he loves you and you both benefit from this bond. However, if the other person (the non-participant) doesn't share that closeness and doesn't have the desire to develop a relationship of his or her own with the bird, the motivation just won't be there. There may be some jealousy involved. The non-participant may be jealous of your relationship with the messy, loud, obnoxious, "mean" bird or the parrot may be jealous of the "difficult-to-understand" person. You may be dealing with both. This makes the dynamics of the flock even trickier. The bird will act differently when the non-bird person is in the same room or nearby mostly to protect the favored person. The situation may be hopeless in some ways without a modicum of cooperation from the person who does not like the bird. Knowing how much the parrot means to you, more reasonable family members will try to do their best to either tolerate the parrot or establish a lesser relationship with him. Attempt to instill in these people just how important a few minutes a day can be to both you and your parrot. The following are some ideas on how the non-bird favored person can establish a positive relationship with your parrot.

⊃ Indirect Attention

When you are not around, ideally, it would be nice if the non-participant would sit next to the bird's cage in a chair and read, pay bills or watch TV and occasionally glance at the bird, say hello, and look down. This submissive form of interaction would allow a special kind of relationship to form that would improve the flock scenario. Not everyone needs to have a "hands-on" kind of friendship with the parrot. Try having some very special treat that only this person hands the bird (or puts in his dish).

If you're dealing with a non-participant that absolutely *hates* the bird and reacts in a way to alienate or antagonize the bird, you have to get that person to STOP. Explain the merits of establishing a "live and let live" relationship. Ask that this person try the above indirect ten-minute exercise for just ten minutes a day over a three-week period. It will make a difference.

⊃ Neutral Room Training

If the parrot is not openly aggressive to the non-participant, neutral room training may help to establish a more positive relationship. Parrots are less likely to be aggressive to another person when they are in a room where they have not established a sense of territory. Set up a guest bedroom with a T-stand, a towel, a few toys, and some special treats. Take your bird in there and let him get comfortable. Then leave the room and have the less-favored person come in. They don't have to do anything active with the parrot. The idea is for the non-participant to have some positive time with the parrot without the favored person there. They can just relax and read and only have positive interactions with the parrot by giving him special treats.

Until the parrot is comfortable being handled by more than one person, don't try to handle him together. This can be a setup for more problems. Too often the parrot bites the less favored person and the person with which the bird has the strongest bond quickly comes to the rescue. They grab the bird away and admonish him for biting the other person. If this is done enough times, it quickly teaches the parrot to bite the less favored person to get to go to the person they like best.

⊃ Anticipate and Prevent — Don't Rescue

Try to anticipate and avoid problem behavior. Just before the difficult person comes home, shower the bird, put some warm cooked foods in his cage, add a new toy or some enrichments and put him away. Don't wait until that person walks in and make his or her arrival necessitate the bird going to the cage. Take this time to give the non-participant a little one on one attention!

If the non-bird person gets home first and cannot deal with the parrot, instruct him or her on how to calmly insert some food treats and, if necessary, partially cover the bird's cage until you get home. This is better than forcing the parrot and the non-participant to endure a session of "I hate you," no "I hate you more!" from the two sides of the cage. Then, when you get home, you can calmly bring out your parrot for a cuddle session or some playtime.   →

➲ Set Up Your Parrot's Life for Success

It helps a great deal in homes like these to have more than one cage. Having a cage in the opposite part of the house is great for a change of scenery for the bird and some peace of mind for the family. This should not be construed as a "punishment cage." Some people call it a "sleeping cage" but mainly it is just another place for your bird to play or rest safely. Of course, it should be well equipped with toys, food, and water. Having multiple playstands throughout the house will allow you to easily have the bird near you wherever you need to be. Always try to "anticipate" rather that "rescue" the needs of the bird. Parrots need to learn how to be happy with simple ambient attention. From the beginning of the parrot's life with you, it is a good idea to have each family member establish their own separate relationship with the bird and also for everyone to gently handle the parrot together slowly passing him from person to person. I call this exercise "warm potato" and it will make a big difference in your parrot's ability to accept many people in his life.

➲ Let's Talk

Have a calm talk with the non-bird person. After all, you live under the same roof and you at least try to work it out. Make it clear that you care about how the person feels but you are going to keep the bird. Reiterate that you will work diligently to resolve the problem behavior but it takes time and patience. Request cooperation and suggest a trial period of the "ten minutes a day" exercise. Don't promise any results. Explain that even without their active participation, you need that person to not react to the bird's negative behavior. They cannot tease, shout, punish, slam doors, or otherwise act tense when the bird upsets them. They need to calmly walk away and let you handle things. You must be careful to not get into the mode of running to the bird to remedy the situation. If you get into the practice of hurrying to "make it okay" the bird will pick up on this and will act out to get you to perform. If you weren't successful in anticipating the commotion… wait a while, then, casually walk indirectly to the bird and, without fanfare, cover or move him.

➲ The Unexpected

Instruct the non-bird person what to do if he/she enters the room and the bird is out. Depending on how the bird relates to this person, there can either be an immediate retreat until you have the bird confined, or there can be a submissive hello and acknowledgment of the bird, or perhaps even a treat. Because of mate protection, remember that the bird is likely to bite you and not the "intruder" to get you to leave this bad situation.

➲ Sabotage

Be on the lookout for sabotage. If you think the non-bird person is teasing, taunting, or otherwise torturing your parrot when you aren't around, he/she may be trying to make the situation *so bad* that you'll give in and get rid of him. You'll have to use your own judgment as to whom to get rid of…

➲ Peace Maker

You must become a family therapist when you have a parrot. Not only to interpret the bird's behavior and interactions with the "flock" but also with the human members of the household as well. You cannot dismiss their dislike of the situation and you cannot cave in to their demands for an immediate resolution. You will have to work diligently to insure the safety and sanity of your parrot and the overall peace in the home. ⨍

BEAKBITE TIP: Respect Me — Respect My Parrot

Chances are not everyone you know is going to love your parrots as much as you do. That shouldn't be a big problem if the people in your life cooperate on some level and accept the fact that your parrot is very important to you and may love you best, even showing some aggression towards them from time to time. Through the years I have been an observer in the households of many people with parrots. Four college level courses in psychology related subjects didn't prepare me for some of the human dynamics I have seen. While most people have been mutually concerned about providing their parrots with the best they can, some couples and families are creating serious problems for the parrots and the human flock. We all know that children often become pawns in their family's disagreements and dysfunctions and, unfortunately, this seems to be equally true in similar situations with parrots. I have left more than one consultation knowing that the only way I could have helped the parrot was to recommend a visit to a therapist, marriage or family counselor. Many people seem to compete for their parrot's affection. Triumph seems to come when the parrot bites the other person or tries to chase him or her out of the house. I did a consultation where a man complained bitterly about his wife's screaming parrot yet every time her back was turned, he would do something to make the bird scream. She would rush in to fix everything by trying to quiet both the parrot and her husband. In other situations, people have tried to force their parrots on their spouses only to have the bird dislike them to the point of severe aggression. In a "love me love my bird" situation one must have enough patience and knowledge to do a positive gradual introduction to be effective. Purposefully sabotaging the mutual bond between parrot and human is a no win situation for people and their parrots and cannot be tolerated. Although it is the ideal situation, not everyone needs to love the parrot and the parrot doesn't need to love everyone. Mutual respect and toleration of the imperfections of both parrots and people goes a long way in creating a benevolent environment in a parrot household.

Pascal

Twiggy

Whodee

Spike

Rascal

Paco

No Parrot is Perfect

Most of us have had other pets at one time or another — dogs, cats, and small furry little animals, maybe even a budgie or a cockatiel. We grew up with domesticated animals and somehow their adequate care *seemed* instinctive to us. Unfortunately, most of us didn't take the time to get a lot of education about them. I remember my Budgie and Cockatiels all came with little guidebooks — most of the information was actually pretty bad or an attempt to sell some product. This really hasn't changed much in the pet industry. Budgies and 'tiels are relatively easy to keep — that is, if you don't expect anything special from them. Yes, they bite but although it hurts, their potential to do serious damage is negligible. However, if you want an exceptional Budgie or 'tiel, you either have to have a lot of intuition or you have to seek out quality information. With parrots there are very few people who have enough intuition or self-knowledge to do right by them. Education is essential and the person who wants to have a positive lifelong relationship with a companion parrot never stops learning. When we bring parrots into our lives, we all usually start out with the idea that we will do the right things so that they will be wonderful companions. With good intentions and high expectations, we start life with a very unique pet — different than what we are accustomed to. Some of us start out with overwhelming obstacles if we do not buy our parrot from a source that is concerned about both the physical and emotional welfare of the birds they sell. Sometimes the parrots are sick or misrepresented as being younger or tamer than they actually are. Others choose a sympathy purchase and buy parrots with a sad story in the hopes of making a better life for them.

I think the biggest problems come when people don't realize that parrots are not easy pets. If we are to have a rewarding relationship with a parrot, we have to work for it. The work doesn't have to be hard. It can actually be fun to establish a positive, consistent, nurturing interaction with a parrot. The people who are not up to the challenge never reap the rewards of the relationship. No parrot is all bad and no parrot is all good. Those of us who are able to keep the balance tipped even slightly to the good side know how much fun life with parrots can be.

Don't give up on your parrot. There are too many birds without good homes and too few good homes available for them. If you care at all, the best place for your parrot is with you. I have lived with parrots for almost thirty years and there have been a lot of changes in my life during that time. There were times when I thought I had no business having parrots, and other times when I knew I could not give them what they needed. But we worked it out and got past it together and my parrots continue to add an incredible dimension to my life (some people who don't have parrots may think I mean *dementia* rather than *dimension*). Despite the fact that none of my parrots are perfect and everyone one of them can be a total pain from time to time, I love them and can't imagine my life without them. I have always known that their actions are my responsibility and I can't blame them for their negative behavior. When one of them really starts to act up, I know he or she needs more focused attention so I slow down my energy and give my avian companion the time he or she needs. Sometimes it is that simple. Try it, it is amazing what a difference it can make.

BEAKBITE TIP: Know Your Own Parrot

Each parrot is unique with his or her own personality, preferences, and abilities. Stay open to the possibilities of your parrot's special characteristics rather than trying to fit him into a mold by making him try to fit the species generalizations. For example, every African Grey I have ever met is unique. About the only thing they have in common is that they all have grey feathers. They come in different sizes, shades of grey, and different temperaments. Some are laid back and some are hyper — some are very acrobatic and some are perch potatoes — some are curious and adventurous while others prefer their own boundaries — some are playfully nippy while others are far too dainty to bother with this kind of nonsense — some love to be cuddled while some do not like such close interaction — some bond strongly to one person while others accept almost everyone — some become excellent talkers and other only utter a few words. When someone tells you their experience with Greys, they are telling you about their Greys — not yours. Learn what you can from others but learn to know your own parrot. Pay attention to his behavior, his body language, his moods, his likes and dislikes. Don't expect him to be exactly like another grey you know. Accept him for his potentials and work in a nurturing manner to develop them.

Basic First Aid for Parrot Bites

By Ellen Selden Schreiber, M.D. • Anesthesiologist • Prosser, Washington and
Brad Selden, M.D. • Attending Staff Physician Department of Emergency Medicine •
Maricopa Medical Center Phoenix, Arizona

WHEN TO SEEK EMERGENCY MEDICAL CARE:

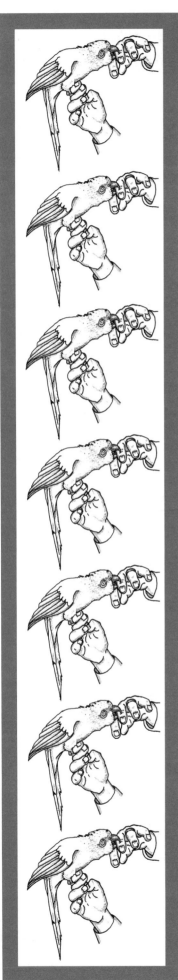

⮑ <u>Any Eye or Eyelid Injury</u>
  ➤**Any injury to the eye** and area around the eye needs to be seen by a physician.
  ➤**A scratch on the cornea** (the clear part of the eye) causes pain, sensitivity to light, and persistent blinking and watering of the eye. All corneal abrasions or scratches to the eyeball should be evaluated and treated by a physician as these injuries can lead to permanent impairment of vision. An ophthalmologist should be consulted to provide care and follow-up until the injury has healed.

⮑ <u>Other Facial Bites</u>
  ➤**Any Significant Nasal Laceration** (bigger than a scratch) — needs to be evaluated by a physician for possible cartilage damage. Professional treatment will provide the best cosmetic result.
  ➤**Any Significant Ear Laceration** — the same considerations as an injury to the nose apply. Both ear and nose wounds are at a high risk for infection if the cartilage is involved and this cannot be evaluated at home.
  ➤**Any Bite Involving the Vermilion Border of the Lip** (the border between the lip and the facial skin) or
  ➤**Any Bite Perforating Completely through the Lip or Cheek —** needs to be evaluated by a physician and will most likely need stitches for best cosmetic results.

⮑ <u>Hand/Finger/Foot/Toe injuries</u>
  ➤**Deep Finger Lacerations** — need to be evaluated in the E.D. (Emergency Department) or joint, nerve and tendon injury. This cannot be done at home.
  ➤**Severe Bites to the Hands, Feet, Fingers, and Toes** — these are at a high risk for infection due to the relatively decreased blood supply to these body areas. These bites must be seen in the E.D.
  ➤**Significant Laceration to the Fingernail Bed** — should be evaluated in the E.D. for repair.
  ➤**Bites Involving a Joint** — these can rapidly lead to a severe infection requiring hospitalization for surgery and intravenous antibiotics.
  ➤**Bites Causing Numbness of the Fingers or Hands —** may suggest a significant nerve injury and need to be seen by a physician.

⮑ **Bites to the Bone** — may cause chronic bone infection (osteomyelitis) and may lead to finger or toe amputation, especially in diabetics.

⮑ **A Bite with Severe Crushing of the Finger** — typically from a large cockatoo or macaw, must be X-rayed for possible fracture. Subsequent swelling can also compromise nerves and blood supply. Any prolonged loss of sensation or development of numbness or increasing pain may be a sign of nerve compression or ischemia (lack of blood flow) and should be evaluated by a physician.

⮑ **Amputation of Any Part of the Finger or Toe** (or any body part) — should be seen in the Emergency Department for repair or reattachment. Bring any torn-off skin or flesh parts in to the E.D. with you in a damp, but not soaking, cloth placed in a plastic bag. Do NOT add ice to the bag. (Because of the grinding action of the beak, it would be very difficult, if not impossible, for a parrot to bite a finger off.)

⮑ **Soft Tissue Injuries**... may include nipple injuries. Be cautious when bathing or showering with your parrot.

⮑ **Grossly contaminated wounds** ... with feces, hairs, feathers, dirt or foreign bodies (beaks are keratinous structures and small parts of them regularly shed) should be seen by a physician for meticulous decontamination, antibiotics and possible surgical intervention.

⮑ **Bleeding wounds**.
APPLY FIRM DIRECT PRESSURE to the bleeding wound with a clean cloth for at least 10 minutes by the clock. DON'T dab at the wound. Do NOT apply any kind of tourniquet. Inability to stop bleeding requires a visit to the E.D. not only to stop the bleeding but also to repair what is probably a major laceration with the potential for significant scarring.

⮑ **Diabetics and Immune Problems**
If the person bitten has DIABETES, any IMMUNE SYSTEM PROBLEMS or has a PROSTHETIC HEART VALVE, they should be treated in the Emergency Department.

Most of the Above Injuries will warrant systemic antibiotics, specifically prescribed by a physician.

TREATMENT AT HOME:

⮑   The person with the bite injury should strongly consider being seen in the E.D. for evaluation and/or laceration repair that may lead to a better outcome.

⮑ Stop bleeding... by applying direct pressure to the bleeding wound as described above. Do NOT apply a tourniquet.

⮑ Thoroughly rinse... the wound under plenty of running water. Clean the wound with soap and water. DON'T use peroxide as it kills cells and slows healing.

⮑ For minor cuts... Applying bacitracin ointment regularly to a wound has been shown to improve cosmetic outcome by decreasing the associated inflammation and scarring. Apply at least twice a day to healing wounds. "Triple antibiotic" ointments carry a higher risk of allergic reactions.

⮑ For major skin tears ... without excessive bleeding: bring the edges together with "Steri-strips," "butterflies" or other medical tape strips and apply bacitracin ointment twice a day. A small drop of "Super-glue" applied under the ends of the tape strips will safely keep them on much longer.

⮑ Keep the wound cleansed ... remove crusting with gentle washing daily.

⮑ Check the wound daily ... and go to the E.D. or your family doctor if you observe any of these signs:
➢Increasing redness around the wound
➢Any yellow or greenish discharge from the wound
➢A bad smell from the wound
➢Any red streaks leading up the arm or leg from the wound
➢Worsening of pain or increase in swelling

⮑ A tetanus booster is required if it has been over ten years since your last shot. There is no risk of rabies from a bird bite since rabies is only carried by mammals.

⮑ Antibiotics:
Improper use of oral antibiotics such as using "leftovers" from the medicine cabinet may lead to one of a number of problems:
➢Incorrect therapy and untreated infection
➢Antibiotic-resistant bacteria and use of increasingly toxic drugs to treat the infection
➢Incomplete treatment and recurrence of infection
➢Side effects or allergies to medicines prescribed for other family members
There has been a recent decrease in antibiotic use for many wounds including bites. However, antibiotics ARE indicated for many of the severe bites described above.

⮑ Gram-positive bacteria normally found in the oropharynx of companion parrots that can cause wound infections include staphylococci, streptococci and Bacillus species. [B.W. Ritchie, et al, Avian Medicine: Principles and Application, abridged edition (Wingers Publishing, Inc., 1997), p. 254.]

⮑ Don't forget that old adage: An ounce of prevention is worth a pound of cure!

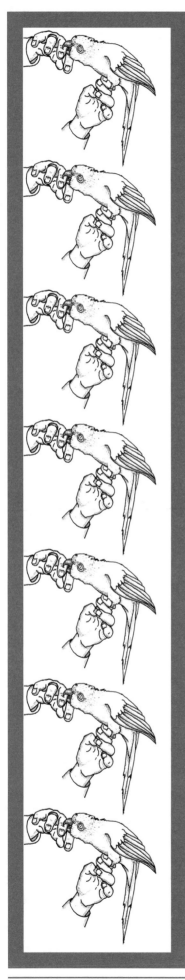

BITING & AGGRESSION
QUESTION & ANSWER

I have been giving programs and/or writing articles about companion parrot behavior since 1980. In 1988, I started writing articles for Bird Talk and in 1991 started writing their monthly Parrot Psychology Column. Many of my ideas have changed since my first columns but I have updated the following columns about biting and aggression to reflect more current thinking on these questions and answers about biting and aggressive behavior in companion parrots.

Q. BEAK AFFECTION

Dear Sally,

We have read a lot of confusing information from people on the Internet. In one discussion, several people who seem to be quite knowledgeable vehemently stated that we should never, under any circumstances, ever allow our parrots to touch their beaks to our skin. We have two young parrots — a Green-winged Macaw and a Moluccan Cockatoo. We have tried to follow your advice to raise them with rules and so far we have not had any trouble with them biting us although the Macaws sometimes gets a little nippy when he plays with us for too long. He is almost three years old and is a hands-on bird who likes to play wrestle with my husband and I. He never bites us from aggression. He only nibbles on us a bit too hard if he becomes excited. It took us a while but we have now figured out how long we can play with him before he gets too excited. You can just see the devil come into his eyes and we put him back on his stand to let him calm down. When he is calm, he is so gentle and we let him explore us with his beak. It often seems as if he is giving us little kisses and caresses.

At 20 months, the Cockatoo is younger and so far, she has never bitten either of us or for that matter, shown any aggressive behavior at all. She does become very expressive in the late afternoon but we know just to leave her to her dancing and not pick her up then. She gives us wonderful beak kisses when we ask for them (of course, our mouths are closed) and loves to gently preen the hair on my husband's hands and arms and it has never turned to aggression. Several people have warned us that if he continues to let her do that when she gets older it will turn into biting behavior. Just when we think things are going well with our parrots, we read or are told something that frightens us and makes us wonder what horrible problems are in store for us. Is it true that we are making a horrible mistake by allowing our parrots to touch us and express their affection for us with their beaks?

- A -

An absolute rule such as this one has no place in the world of parrot behavior. In reading your letter, I am reminded of the statement 'a little knowledge is a dangerous thing.' However, I think that many people with parrots can become very confused by all of the conflicting information on the Internet. The computer discussion groups are one of the most wonderful advances in parrot information, but because there are so many opinions and it is so difficult to know who is really knowledgeable and who is not, the Internet can be one of the most confusing information sources. The Internet has actually created a different level of behavioral work for me. I can almost always tell when I start a consultation whether the person has been receiving information from the computer boards. One woman I talked with had become totally confused by the conflicting and, sometimes, rigidly authoritarian advice she had received about feeding her 5-month-old African Grey. She had become so desperate about this critical developmental period that the bird was becoming traumatized by her negative energy about his food independence. It is extremely important for everyone reading this source of information to carefully evaluate every piece of advice to determine if it is actually a logical positive step to building trust and forming a nurturing bond with a companion parrot. I think one good test to determine the accuracy of information is to stop and think if it is based on 'black and white," or "all or none" concepts. I would not accept this type of rigid information as valid. Another is to carefully think about whether the information will have a trust building or trust destroying effect on the parrot/human bond.

If you have read my column and articles for very long, you know that I try not to deal in absolutes. I think there is way too much black and white thinking about parrots. Each parrot species and each individual has its own special characteristics and each companion parrot home situation presents its own unique situation. There are very few rules in parrot behavior that absolutely apply to every bird. One is that parrots are more comfortable with people who are comfortable with them. Parrots know immediately if a person is uncomfortable with them and they are apprehensive being handled by these people. Another absolute in parrot behavior is that the best way to establish a trusting relationship with a parrot is to work with them in a nurturing, patient, and consistent manner to earn their trust. This is especially true with handfed, domestically raised baby parrots.

While there are most likely some parrots that should never be trusted to touch their beak to our skin, I think that when people set this kind of rule for their handfed babies they are missing some of the most wonderful aspects of having companion parrots. Parrots are highly physical animals in their relationships with each other and, therefore, will strive to have this type of interaction with the people in their lives. The parrot beak is not innately a weapon simply used to bite intruders. Parrots use their very sensitive beaks much as we use our mouth, lips, hands and fingers – to explore, to touch, to sense, to manipulate, to preen, and as you suggest with your parrots, to give affection with gentle kisses and caresses. If we set absolute rules that say a parrot can never touch us with their beaks, we are essentially denying them the natural inclination to explore us and give us affection. We can warn them if they are going beyond what is comfortable to us with the words "gentle" or "no bite."

I personally can't imagine never allowing my Black-headed Caique, Spike, to touch my hands or face with his beak. I pay close attention to his body language and there are certainly times when I am smart enough to keep him away from my face. There are also times when he is so wound-up; I don't even want him chewing on my fingers. But when he is calm and loving, I welcome and completely trust his soft kisses and gentle preening of my hands and face. He also trusts me to completely encompass his body with my hands and kiss him on the top of the head. Our friendship for the last eight years has been based on this mutual trust and he knows this as well as I do. My Grey, Bongo Marie, is more reserved about physical handling than Spike but when she is in a mellow mood, she trusts me to hug and pet her. I also pay close attention to her mood and know when it is appropriate to allow her to give me kisses and preen me with her beak.

There is another misconception that is perpetuated by this absolute rule of not letting a parrot ever touch a person's skin. Beak exploration does not lead to biting. The exploration a parrot does with its beak, even if it occasionally may be a bit painful to the human flesh, is a totally separate behavior from aggressive biting. There is no logical cause and effect progression from allowing a parrot to touch your skin with his beak and aggressive biting behavior. Aggressive biting behavior most often comes from a parrot that has received little or no behavioral guidance and learns to bite as a reaction to fear and/or aggression, or as a way to manipulate or control the people in its environment. If explorative beaking of fingers becomes too painful, the best idea is to find a textured 'foot toy' to stick in the bird's beak instead of your fingers. But when a parrot is in a calm, loving mood, allowing physical affection from gentle beak touching is an important part of the parrot/human bond.

It is obvious from your letter that you are the kind of person who can separate the helpful information on the Internet from the rigid rules that simply do not apply to your relationship with your Macaw and Cockatoo. Your idea of paying close attention to your Macaws to determine whether he is too excited to be allowed to chew on your fingers is excellent. It is this sort of common sense observation that is extremely important in creating the best pet potential in companion parrots. From your letter, there is no doubt in my mind, that allowing your Macaws and Cockatoo to touch you with their beaks is abso-

lutely necessary to the good relationship you have with them. Denying this type of affection and interaction would be a big mistake. I think you are sensitive enough to their body language and moods that you will know the particular times when this type of close interaction is inappropriate.

Q. CHEWING ON FINGERS

Dear Sally,

We have a new baby Macaws who is now 6 months old. Rainbow is a wonderful bird and has never tried to bite us even when he gets a little cranky. My one concern is that he wants to chew on our fingers all of the time. We take hold of his beak and gently shake it when he does this to let him know we disapprove. We also tell him he shouldn't be chewing on us but he just seems to want to do it more and more. Sometimes it hurts and I am worried that he will eventually start biting hard instead of just playing. What can we do to stop this from becoming a serious problem?

- A -

There is a difference between chewing or play biting and actual aggressive or fear biting behavior. They have different behavioral causes. Chewing is one of the ways a young bird explores his environment including the people in his life. It can even be a way for the young bird to show affection. Beaking and tonguing is essentially the same to a parrot as touching objects with fingers is to a person. Your attempt to discipline Rainbow by grabbing his beak and shaking it is most likely more of a reward since parrots often "beak wrestle" as a form of play and even affection. It is natural for a parrot to want to chew on or play bite their caregiver's fingers. It is probably not a good idea to encourage the behavior because, as you are beginning to realize, as the bird gets older or more excited about finger chewing, it can become painful. However, if you wiggle your fingers and carry on about wanting him to stop, your behavior can easily be interpreted by the bird as an invitation to play. The finger chewing becomes a game and is more and more difficult to stop.

Without realizing it, you are playing a game with your Macaws and he is setting the rules. Reacting to his misbehavior by fiddling with him instead of giving him a clear decisive message of disapproval sets up a game that will reward the chewing. The more verbal the reprimand is, the more it is a "drama reward" for your Macaws.

The best way to handle finger chewing from the beginning is to provide Rainbow with some sort of textured foot toy he can chew on instead of you. Wiggle the toy in his face every time he starts chewing on you. If he continues to try and chew on you, give him a basic disapproving "evil eye" and say a firm "NO."

Q. HEIGHT DOMINANCE?

Dear Sally,

The practical advice of keeping pet parrots below eye level in order to stop aggressive behavior really works. But the reason people give as to why it works bothers me. All sources I have read or heard say the same: keeping parrots below eye level establishes our dominance over them. They become tame and submissive once they recognize our dominance. If they are held above eye level they will try to establish their dominance over us and therefore become aggressive. Is this reason based upon scientific evidence or cultural bias?

Reasonable, evidence based support of this height/dominance concept would be if wild parrots were observed to have hierarchies of dominance where the most dominant bird consistently perches on the highest branch, defending its position from competitors within the flock. This behavior would have to be evident in all species of parrots observed in the wild, since the advice of lowering a pet parrot's perch level seems to apply to all species. I have found no sources that say this is so.

The height/dominance concept is given too quickly, too universally accepted, as an easy to understand explanation, which makes me suspect it to be based upon cultural bias. When I was explaining parrot behavior to a friend of mine who is not a bird owner, he was offended by the height/dominance concept. He is Caucasian American and his height is 5'5" — he is considered 'short' by American standards. He is very sensitive about his height. I have often heard from 'short' Americans one of the attractions for going to Asia was they would feel 'tall' there. The assumption being Asians are on average shorter than Americans are. This view that short is subordinate and tall is dominant seems subconsciously entrenched in American society. Also, the corporate concept that those who hold high positions have authority and control over those who work for them is entrenched in our society as well. I wonder if these biases are hastily and conveniently applied to our relationship with pet parrots.

If there is no solid observational evidence to support the height/dominance hypothesis then I would like to offer an explanation of my own: My hand tamed cockatiels, if they are not calling me over to them to handle them, will always react, initially, in fear of my hand. Their first automatic response is to escape. This makes sense among parrots, since they have not had their 'wild' instincts bred out of them — any foreign, moving object is a possible danger. Their most effective protection is to fly upward out of reach from even tree climbing predators. Establishing itself as higher than any other living organism gives the bird a sense of safety. The pet parrot becomes aggressive because it knows it cannot go further than the ceiling so it protects itself with its beak. It becomes less aggressive when kept at a lower height because it 'knows' escape via height is not an option, and has resigned itself to, and tries to make the best of its situation. It is a sensible and self-preserving line of reasoning within the parrot.

If the exhibition of dominance and submission is often viewed as pathetic stupidity in human interaction, why do we readily accept it as the nature of our relationship with parrots — an animal viewed as intelligent?

- A -

When I first started working with parrots, I handled them in ways that were quite different than the popular philosophies of parrot training at the time. I was able to tame many wild-caught parrots by working in a patient, methodical manner to win their trust rather than to establish control through fear or aggression. After working with a number of parrots, I realized it was important to be able to define what I was doing in a way that people would understand. This was particularly true as I began to write articles about my theories of working with parrots. Although as time changed, many people began to purchase handfed babies, I found that my concepts of winning and main-

taining trust were valid whether the parrots were imported or domestically raised. I chose to call my theory "Nurturing Dominance" which according to the definition I researched means "Teaching with Influence." Unfortunately, after awhile I realized the word "dominance" is one of those loaded words that seems to many people to have a definition that implies "aggression" or, as you state, the opposite of "submission." In many cases, dominance is viewed as negative and consequently, to many, the concept as it applies to the human/parrot bond is viewed as aggression and excessive control. The reality is that a companion parrot is not able to be in control of its own life. Parrots who are allowed to be in control of their lives without guidance from their human companions will continually rely on natural behaviors, which will be blocked causing frustration and confusion. Often, they will "make up" substitute behaviors when they can't complete natural responses. Called displacement behavior, these are often the cause of many of the problems we have with parrots living in our environment. We need to teach parrots to adapt to living in our world. Consequently, they are dependent on us for their guidance and in order to teach them properly we must establish authority and leadership (or dominance) similar to that of properly parenting a child. There is not really such a thing as a submissive leader and parrots will not follow our guidance unless we present it with authority. In this sense, "dominance" is certainly a positive concept that also takes into consideration the intelligence of parrots. A well-taught (or well-nurtured) parrot will be a good learner because parrots are capable of learning throughout their lives. In no way, have I ever recommended dominating a parrot to the point that he becomes so submissive that he loses his sense of security. In fact, I believe that part of being a good teacher is helping to develop the student's individuality and sense of well-being.

Although the concept of "height dominance" is a significant factor in relating to many pet parrots, it is only part of many aspects of what I refer to as "Nurturing Guidance." Actually I believe that height dominance can be a barometer of the relationship people have with their parrots. Some people who have established a good sense of behavioral guidance generally do not have that much trouble with their parrots even if they are higher. For example, my Amazons Paco and Rascal obey my "UP" command readily whether they are on the ground or on the top of their ceiling swing. People who have not established a nurturing guidance will have trouble with height dominance but they will most likely also have trouble with cage aggression, excessive screaming, biting, and other behavioral problems. I find that when people are having behavioral problems with their parrots, establishing height dominance is only one way an owner needs to work with their birds.

I have to admit that it never occurred to me that "height dominance" in parrots could be viewed as cultural bias against being short. Certainly parrots are much shorter than we are and we tower over them most of the time so we must be careful not to become so dominant in an aggressive manner that they will fear us or perceive us as being a predator. As to whether the "height dominance" theory is based on "scientific evidence" or cultural bias, most companion parrot behavioral information is based on observation rather than scientific evidence. I do not believe from all of my observations and readings that most parrots exhibit an aggressive hierarchy in nature. I think a better concept would be "flock leader." We know very little about the actual structure of most parrot flocks. Clearly in most flock species, there are family groups. Some groups and individuals have better nesting sites but there may be many different situations that warrant certain birds getting the most desired mates and territories. In many cases, it is probably the genetically more colorful or flashy birds who are dominant rather than the more aggressive ones. I have read and heard from several reliable ornithological sources that many species of parrots have sentinel birds who sit high in a tree guarding against danger while the rest of the flock forages. These parrots may be "flock leaders" and/or the more dominant birds but I have never read any reports of these birds establishing this position through aggression. Many parrot flocks seem to base much of their survival on mutual cooperation. It is my understanding that genuine aggression in wild parrots is probably only used as a defense of family and/or territory from predators and not within the flock.

The longer a person has been working with parrots and the more parrots they have worked with, the more valid their theories are. Of course, observational skills and common sense are also important factors. Over a period of time, one learns from those who follow their advice whether it is effective or not. Your statement that "the practical advice of keeping pet parrots below eye level in order to stop aggressive behavior really works" is most likely the reason this advice is given by so many parrot behavioral consultants. Over many years with many, many parrots, this advice has proven to be helpful over and over. Of course, it is important to think about why this is true. It may involve many variables, one of which may be the hypothesis you present. Certainly when a parrot is encompassed from above, there is no route for escape and the parrot must submit or aggressively defend himself. However, this is one of the major reasons why I have always encouraged my readers and clients not to approach their birds in an overbearing, aggressive manner. Trust is the most important factor in a quality parrot/human bond and trust is lost when the owner acts aggressively towards their bird. I appreciate your letter as it has given me the opportunity to think of an established protocol from another perspective.

Q. ONLY AN INCIDENT

Dear Sally,

Although he has been a well-behaved pet for the six months or so he has lived with me, my African Grey, Echo bit me yesterday. It was not a hard bite and he was not really being nasty but I am afraid that he will become that way now that he has started biting. I purchased him as a handfed baby shortly after he was weaned and he has always been a gentle bird. Why would he change and suddenly start biting? I want him to continue to like me. What can I do to keep biting from being a problem?

- A -

Many of us (not excluding parrot owners) seem to jump to the conclusion that when one bad thing happens, it is an omen of a future full of disaster. Following these prophecies of doom, many a parrot owner goes off the deep end the first time their parrot bites them. Often the owner's first reaction, which is totally illogical, is "my parrot doesn't love me anymore!" The first bite rarely has anything to do with whether or not a parrot 'loves' its owner or not. The parrot may simply be exploring a bit too hard with his beak or it may be an expression of confusion, over-stimulation, or even a testing of limits as the parrot reaches an independence stage. Responding to the first (and consequent) bites in a gentle, instructive manner will usually keep the behavior from becoming a pattern. Removing your hand slowly and softly saying, "no, gentle" can go a long way to teach a young bird to use his beak gently. If the biting seems to be more aggression than exploration, using a quick 'evil eye' (dirty look) with a firm 'no' will express your disapproval. Beyond that, too much response can become a 'drama reward'. Punishing him by putting him in his cage for biting usually has little significance because by the time he is placed in the cage, the association between the biting and the 'punishment' is usually lost on the bird. Acting aggressive toward the bird will either frighten him or cause him to return the aggression increasing the biting behaviors.

I often write about parrots being "addicted to drama." Certainly many of their behaviors (both wild and domestic) can seem quite flashy. However, it is also important to realize we are dealing with a prey animal (one who can become another's lunch at the slightest misstep) who also clearly exhibits the importance of the understatement. There are certainly times when it is best for a parrot to be as quiet and unobtrusive as possible. I would like to make the equally accurate observation that we humans also tend to be drama addicts. And our parrots thoroughly enjoy this aspect of our behavior. In fact, it is our dramatic responses to their behavior that are most likely to turn a onetime action into a habituated pattern. Our parrots love our drama whether we are attempting to be positive or negative. Providing them with a dramatic response reinforces the behavior we are responding to and these are often the very ones we would rather not have repeated.

So in actuality, we are the ones who so often turn our parrot's initial misbehaviors into habituated patterns because we do not deal with them correctly. It is doubtful to me that Echo will ever become a biting bird unless you reward his behavior with drama or returned aggression in the form of punishment. If the single bite is dealt with as a single bite and not as if Echo has suddenly turned into a blood-lusting vampire, the single incident will not become a habit. Be careful about mistaken interpretation of Echo's biting incident. It appears to me there are people who actually seem to have an investment in their parrot's misbehavior. Perhaps they also love the drama it brings into their lives. Others seem unable, no matter how important it is, to set rules and provide guidance for their parrots. These parrots usually end up with some serious behavioral problems.

Use caution if you hear the advice, "Oh, don't worry it is just a stage he is going through, he'll be fine when he gets through it." While biting, screaming and other negative behaviors may be part of a stage a parrot is going through and he will indeed get through this stage, it is important to realize we will be the ones who make the difference whether he gets through it just fine with his pet potential intact. I strongly advise parrot owners to take each behavioral misadventure as an event by itself, work with it at the time, and not go off the deep end about it. However, it is also important to do your homework so that you know how to deal with these incidents so they won't become repetitive patterned behaviors.

Q. TOO MANY AGGRESSIVE QUICK-FIXES

Dear Sally,

We have a "mostly" well-behaved Umbrella Cockatoo. By that I mean to say that Kokomo is as well behaved as any umbrella can be expected to be. However, lately he's been biting. Kokomo is a 2-year-old male who we got when he was exactly 3 months old. We've read all the books and have tried to bring him up according to what the experts say, although we're certainly not perfect. The problem is that when Kokomo wants something and we retrieve him from his effort or attempt to get out, he bites.

Kokomo has his wings clipped and comes out on his stand every time we are home, but he's acting really spoiled about this. How can I discourage him from biting when all the tail-feather plucking, tub-staying and toy withholding has failed?

- A -

It is your last sentence that gives me a clue as to why you have been unable to effectively set rules for your Cockatoo. If I understand correctly you have most likely been using ineffective quick-fix punishments to try and let Kokomo know he is not behaving properly. Actions like pulling a tail feather, placing a parrot in the bathtub, and withholding attention or toys are not successful in dealing with parrot behavioral problems. Often they just confuse the bird more and worst of all, damage the trust necessary to maintaining a positive parrot/human bond.

Much of the biting I hear about from companion parrots is actually developed from interaction with their owners. It is a misconception to presume that most biting in parrots is a result of aggressive behavior. Many people who call me remark that their parrot has become mean. Parrots are not mean because they bite — biting behaviors normally start because a bird is confused. The vast majority of biting I see in pet parrots develops because the parrot is given confusing mixed messages and is then rewarded in one way or another for biting in their interactions with people.

Once a parrot is in his new home, he either develops his own behaviors or learns from his owners how to behave. A pet parrot will not naturally develop the traits that will make him a good pet. It is up to the new owner to show their pet how to behave in acceptable ways. The problem is that many parrot owners do not realize that they are teaching their parrots the traits that make them a "bad" pet bird. The parrot that bites often does so because his owner has reinforced or rewarded the bird for biting. Without realizing it, many owners are actually teaching their parrots to bite. If every time Kokomo bites you, you grab him up and with dramatic conversation and gestures, "punish" him or take him somewhere to be punished, it will be the drama he associates with the biting, not the punishment which in some cases (particularly that of pulling a tail feather) borders on abuse.

Working with Kokomo by setting rules and providing guidance to prevent biting will be far more effective than trying to punish him for biting. Start by always using the "UP" and "DOWN" commands when Kokomo steps on or off your hand. Take him out of his cage with the "UP" command instead of just letting him come out by himself. Don't

become aggressive in your guidance but it is important to gradually start taking better control of Kokomo's behaviors. Once you have established yourself as the "flock leader," Kokomo will be much more likely to understand the discipline of the "evil eye" (a quick disapproving look) combined with a firm "NO."

Q. A "One-Person" Timneh

Dear Sally,

I am having a small problem with my Timneh Grey and I would like some help. Her name is Timiah and I have had this wonderful bird for about 1½ years. The problem is with anyone other than myself who tries to approach or touch her. She growls and will try to bite them. I would love to have others enjoy her as much as I do, but I am so afraid she will take a chunk out of them. What can I do to make her feel more comfortable and enjoy the company of others, and have others not so afraid of her?

- A -

Unfortunately, many people start out by allowing strangers to approach their young parrots in a threatening manner. Once a parrot becomes defensive around strangers, they often stay that way unless his or her caregivers work with the problem. First we have to realize that parrots are prey animals. This, of course, means that they have to be very observant or they will become another animal's meal. Our companion parrots may not be in danger of being a Harpy Eagle's lunch, but they are still innately wary of strangers, especially in their flock territory. When we allow a stranger to come into our homes and just let them try to establish their own relationship with our parrots, the relationship is often doomed. Parrots often become defensive of their cage area. It is pretty natural behavior for them to defend not only their territory but also the other members of their flock. When parrots are bonded to us as their caregivers, we become part of their flock. While it may be arguable that there is a specific leader in a wild parrot flock, I believe that it is critical for us to become the flock leader for our parrots. Parrots simply do not know how to become good pets and living in our homes is a very unnatural situation for them. We need to establish a positive and *Nurturing Guidance* to help our companion parrots adjust to life in our homes. Part of that trust-building guidance involves successfully introducing them to new situations and people in their lives. We can make a big difference as to whether or not our parrots accept new people or not.

I discovered many important things about the behavior of parrots over the years when I did in-home consultations. One was that if I assertively walked right up to a parrot in his cage, he would usually be threatened by my presence in the room. If I tried to pick him up, he would invariably try to bite me. Once I learned this, if I made the mistake of being too direct with a parrot, I deserved to be bitten. After all, I was not a flock member — I was an intruder. However, if I walked in and glanced at the parrot and then lowered my head and eyes, the parrot was much more relaxed with me as a stranger. I would generally sit with people and talk to them about their parrots for at least a half an hour before I ever approached the parrot. If the caregiver could handle his or her parrot, I would usually ask them to bring the parrot over to where we were sitting rather than going over to the cage myself. Often, I would have them introduce the parrot to me in a "neutral room" or an area of the home where the parrot could not see his cage. Parrots are usually more threatened by new situations and people around their cage, so it is usually much better to do introductions in another room where the parrot is not used to being. He is much more likely to follow the guidance of his "flock leader" in the neutral room. I had the caregiver introduce the parrot to me in a calm, friendly manner. It was important for me to be calm and approach the parrot in a comfortable manner as if I had known him for years. I had a great deal of success handling parrots because they were introduced to me as if I was a new and acceptable member of the home flock.

If someone comes into your home and wants to become friends with Timiah, you need to plan the situation and choreograph it so that it is optimal for them to win her trust. Since she is tame to you, it should not be too difficult if you work with her in the right way. First prepare a comfortable place where Timiah has not established a territory to defend. Most parrots who are aggressive around their cages, are not aggressive in the neutral room. Whether it is a dining room, den, or spare bedroom it should be an area where she can't see her cage. If there is no comfortable place in your home where she can't see her cage, it might help to place her on a stand and then cover her cage with a sheet. Before you make any introductions, have the new person watch you handle Timiah so he knows how tame your parrot can be. Explain the techniques you use and why they work for you.

Even in a neutral room, your parrot may have trouble adjusting to three types of people. If your friend is really afraid, Timiah will know. People who are afraid tend to approach parrots in a very indecisive manner. They give a very push-pull message that can confuse the parrot. Parrots do not want to be handled by people who project fear or indecision and they quickly learn that the best way to make these people go away is to bite them. Often the first bite is not an aggressive bite. It is what I call the clamp bite. The parrot clamps his beak around a finger with some pressure as a warning. It may hurt a little but it rarely breaks the skin. If people can learn to be comfortable and non-reactive to a clamp bite, then the beak pressure usually goes no farther. However, if a person reacts with fear or drama and pulls back, the clamp bite can turn nasty. Many people are afraid of parrots simply because they have never handled one before. If you have a friend who really wants to be a part of Timiah's life but is uncomfortable trying to handle her, patience is essential. If you have a quality local bird shop that has tame handfed babies, it can really make a difference if he or she visits there to handle the parrots. The more birds he becomes comfortable handling, the more comfortable he will be with Timiah.

The second type that will create problems is the person who can't lower their energy to win Timiah's trust. It is unlikely that she will allow this person to handle her if they can't calm down. It may seem silly, but ask the person to shut his eyes, let his head and arms droop, and take deliberate slow deep breaths to try and relax. Once he is relaxed, it is likely that Timiah will also be comfortable. Another very important rule of parrot behavior is that parrots are more comfortable with people who are comfortable with them.

The third and perhaps, most troublesome, type is the overly aggressive person who simply will not listen to you and insists on handling Timiah in an overtly decisive or aggressive manner. This type of person can create such mistrust that a parrot may have a difficult time trusting anyone new after being approached so aggressively. If your friend or relative who wants to be a part of your Grey's life is like this, Timiah should be hands-off for that person.

Once you have decided everything is optimal for success and the neutral room is set up, have your friend go in and sit down. Then bring Timiah in to the room. If Timiah has a strong trusting bond with you, what you do will make a big difference in what happens next. Move slowly and smile. Let Timiah know that this is a positive situation where everyone is relaxed and having fun. Bonded parrots quickly pick up our energy so being happy about the situation will help set the mood for Timiah. If you are afraid and convinced that Timiah will bite your friend, then chances are she will. Sit down or kneel down near the new person, and talk to him about what a wonderful parrot Timiah is. Tell your parrot what a wonderful person your friend is. If everything is going well, the person can reach over and use the "UP" command to have Timiah step up. If this doesn't work, place her on the person's knee or a nearby stand. Take your time. Cajole Timiah by telling her what a wonderful bird she is. Make sure that the new person is somewhat submissive with you so that Timiah does not feel like she has to defend you from an "intruder."

It may take awhile or more than one session, but when the two are comfortable with each other, tell Timiah what a good bird she is and slowly leave the room. Let them interact and remain ready to come in if there is any problem but don't rush in to rescue either. If the situation is becoming tense, just have the person place Timiah on a T-stand or the back of a chair, leave the room and then go in to take her back to her cage with lots of verbal praise. Be patient and try again later or another day. Let the person work with your Grey with you but make sure that he develops his own special relationship with her. In most cases, this positive patterning situation will result in Timiah becoming comfortable with the new person. The eventual goal is that, after several sessions, Timiah should perceive the new person as a member of her human flock.

Q. SHE'S BITING ME BUT NOT MY WIFE

Dear Sally,

We have a very lively and fun 3-year-old Senegal. She loves my wife, and loves to roughhouse, cuddle, play, etc. with her. Kelly allows my wife to scratch her all over even lying on her back so my wife can scratch her stomach. The problem is as she has become more loving and open to my wife, she has gradually gotten worse with me. I used to be able to hold, pet, play etc., but not anymore, and the problems seem to be getting gradually worse. I have never been mean to the bird in any way. I do work out of my home and she sits beside my desk all day and plays on her jungle gym and seems content and happy with that. She will still climb onto my finger, but is not happy about it and continues to dance around looking to get off

as soon as possible. She seems to be frightened of me, and I assure you, I have never treated her (or any other animal) poorly.

I have read the article "The Relationship between Focus and Trust" on your web site and tried the suggestions there, although I do not feel that his situation was the same as mine. I do have plenty of time to devote to Kelly and before she started pulling away from me, I used to get her on my finger to talk to her and play with her several times a day as we worked together in my office. She went through a three-month period where she bit me pretty hard every time she was upset about something or was not happy with any situation, but that (thankfully) has totally stopped and now she just seems afraid. Having racked my brain as to the problems, there are only two or three situations I can think of that may have started this down slide. She got spooked at something several months ago and jumped off my finger, and due to her wings being clipped, she of course started toward the ground. I instinctively reached out to catch her, missed, and she bumped into the wall ... not hard enough to physically hurt her, but it scared her. Secondly, they are building a house outside my office window and she seems to be frightened of the workers for the past 6 months. The only other thing I can think of is that I used to play catch with her, where I would throw a piece of wadded up paper on her jungle gym and she would run to it, grab it, and throw it on the floor. She seemed to be having fun, but certainly in a rough, frenzy-like manner. I know I am grasping in the wind, but I am stumped and would most certainly appreciate any help you could give me.

Our pet storeowner has told us that single parrots do pick a "mate" and that is normal. Kelly has definitely picked my wife. This is great, but I do wish that I could at least hold her and scratch her a little like I used to be able to do. I would certainly appreciate any help/insight you could provide for me.

- A -

This is a topic I have dealt with frequently but since it seems to be such a serious problem for some people, I believe it needs to be addressed on a frequent basis. Several species of parrots seem to exhibit the behavioral problem of sudden fearful behavior. Often they become afraid of the very person they were the most bonded to. In extreme cases they become extremely phobic about what were normal situations before. These fearful birds often seem to quickly transfer their bond to another person — often a person who did not pay that much attention to them before. I have been working with parrots for twenty-five years but did not start to see what I consider "phobic" behavior until I started working extensively with domestically raised parrots about 15 years ago.

One of the very first parrots I worked with who had exhibited this sudden onset of fear was a young Meyer's parrot. His owner had a friend who the bird liked very much. One day the friend came over right after she had been to the beauty parlor. She had her hair done in a new way and normally she did not wear nail polish but the woman was very excited because her nails were now bright red with sparkles on them. She decided to show them off to her parrot friend and when she reached for him, the bird became terrified throwing himself all over his cage. To the Meyer's, she was a different person — not the friend he knew and trusted. She looked different and had these brightly colored fingers flashing at him. Because she didn't know to take the time to introduce her new look to him slowly and her energy

was too high and she moved too quickly, the bird became very frightened. Parrots are prey animals and to the Meyer's, it seemed as if this person he had trusted had suddenly become a predator. With no way to escape, he thrashed in his cage. After the situation was over and the friend went home, the Meyer's transferred his fear to his very confused owner who had never had trouble with him before.

I think that most poorly socialized parrots are accidents waiting to happen. They have not developed enough sense of security to get them past a traumatic situation. I do not know if the Meyer's mentioned above was poorly socialized, just a more sensitive bird, or if this is a potentially normal trait of Meyer's parrots. I do know that there are species of parrots that seem to become excessively threatened by traumatic situations in their lives. Often situations like a drastic change in the owners appearance, overly aggressive handling by a groomer or veterinarian, a significant threat to their environment, or the changed energy of their human flock seem to create long lasting fearful behavior. This seems to be more likely to happen in Senegals and their close relatives including Red-bellied parrots, Brown-headed parrots and, sometimes but perhaps not as commonly, Meyer's parrots. This behavior also seems to affect African Greys and some Cockatoos, but can occur in almost any species if the perceived threat is great enough.

I do not believe that Kelly's situation is simply a matter of her choosing your wife as her "mate." While many species of companion parrots have the reputation of becoming one-person birds, I think this is often poor behavioral management and a self-fulfilling prophecy. If people absolutely believe their parrot is naturally a one-person bird, they will usually not work to keep the bird tame to everyone in the family.

It is my guess that several things have created an excessive alertness in Kelly making her fearful of certain aspects of her life. The way you played with Kelly sounds fine for most parrots, and the wadded up paper game is something I do with my Caique Spike, however, the combination of events and the fact that you roughhoused with her may be one of the reasons she became wary of you in her more vigilant state. If your wife has always played with her more calmly, there would be less of a reason for Kelly to perceive her as a threat, or even as a predator.

After the earthquake in the San Francisco Bay Area in 1989, I worked with many parrots who became excessively fearful and even phobic about almost everything in their environment. Many started feather picking for the first time. While the earthquake was enough to frighten everyone, including their birds, the problems many people had with their parrots seemed to start later. Certainly, the great number of aftershocks that kept everyone on edge didn't help the problem for people or their parrots, but it became evident the parrots that had the most problem with fearful behavior were those who lived in areas where there had been a great deal of destruction. Consequently, there was a tremendous amount of rebuilding in the area with the constant sounds of construction — jackhammers, big trucks, hammering, drilling, yelling, etc. It was not just the sounds that caused problems. Parrots are also highly tuned into vibrations in their environment and I believe this was a major factor in keeping these parrots on guard and wary of their environment. The construction going on near your office window may be a serious threat to your Senegal and may be the trigger for many of the problems you are having. If her cage and the main place she lives is near a window or against the wall on the side where the construction is going on, I would recommend moving her to the other side of your house until the house next door is finished.

Patience and a calm demeanor are the keys to winning her trust again. Choose the time of day when she is the mellowest — not necessarily ready to go to sleep — but quiet and relaxed. This should also be a quiet time of day when you can also relax. The approach I have advised with fearful or phobic parrots has worked many times. I call this a "Nurturing Submission" approach. First have your wife leave the room where Kelly's cage is so the Senegal will not look to her for security. Calmly place a chair in front of her open cage and sit down with your side or back to her. You are not facing her or even paying any attention to her. In fact, you are being somewhat submissive and essentially ignoring her. Have some kind of special treat with you that she really likes. Just let her see the treat and make it accessible for her if she comes out to get it but don't try to give it to her. Read a book or magazine and from time to time look at her for a second or so without making direct eye contact and then lower your head and look away. The concept is one of indirectly asking her to join you. Since most parrots are highly social animals they normally want to be a part of their human flock if they trust what is happening. This exercise should last from 10-15 minutes or longer if you have a good book. When she approaches you, remain calm and stay indirect with her until she is genuinely comfortable coming out on you again. It is amazing the number of parrots who become friendly again within only a few days when this indirect nurturing approach is used.

Q. AGGRESSIVE WELCOME HOME

Dear Sally,

We are the owners of a wonderfully social Greater Sulphur-crested Cockatoo who is about four or five years old. Teddy is normally an affectionate clown who loves a good laugh, considers himself a key family member, and seems to enjoy all the other members of our family equally. He is particularly attached to my husband and me and carries on with each of us in a most undiscriminating fashion.

However, this lovable fellow exhibits a dramatic personality change when I return home from a trip. My job takes me overseas quite frequently for two or four weeks at a time. When I return, Ted spends the first day or two trying to kill me — literally. His hostility seems to last in direct proportion to the length of time I have been away. Typically, he attempts to attack me and targets my face (particularly my eyes). He is, however, usually satisfied with great bites to any part of my body. The attacks are ferocious and very disturbing. We can't figure out how to stop them. It seems to make no difference if I "greet" him in his room, in the kitchen, or in our bedroom (where he loves to come for a late day cuddle). As you can appreciate, there is nothing remotely funny about this behavior and I would like some advice on how to prevent it. I should add that after a day or so of nastiness, he settles down to his old self and we are once again great pals. Any help with this Dr. Jekyll/Mr. Hyde behavior would be most welcome.

Through my years of working with parrots I have heard similar stories of how parrots "abuse" their caregivers when they come home from a trip. Although I believe that on some level parrots do miss and remember their owners, I do not believe that the basis for this aggressive behavior is the parrot trying to "punish" the owner. The key lies in the fact that parrots are creatures of habit and patterning. Although, they do adjust well to gradual changes in their routine, it may take some time for them to adjust to these changes. When you are home, you are part of the usual daily routine.

Once you leave, the routine abruptly changes forcing your Cockatoo to adjust to your not being a part of his life pattern. People certainly have a far better grasp of life pattern changes and when you come home, you remember the way the relationship was before you left and expect it to be exactly the way that it was when you come back. However, after a few days of your absence, Teddy has become patterned to a routine that doesn't include you and has, so to speak, "gotten on with his life".

This doesn't mean he doesn't like you or enjoy you as a part of his "flock," it just simply means that you are not a part of his present pattern. When you return, you want him to immediately be your friend like he was when you left. Unfortunately, he perceives it differently. Much of a companion parrot's existence (no matter how tame) is based on his perception of protecting his territory and defending his "flock." This is a strong natural behavior that is often confused in a pet parrot because the natural behavior related to territory becomes distorted by the adaptation to the unnatural environment. While you have been gone, you have not been a member of Teddy's flock and when you return he perceives you as an intruder until he becomes re-patterned to accept you as a member of his flock again. For some people, their birds re-pattern and relate to them almost immediately. With others, it may take a few days. I am not sure why. It may depend on several things including the number of people in the family and their relationship with the birds, whether the parrot was at home or with a bird sitter, the care the bird received while the person was gone and/or the length of time the person was absent. Certainly the longer you are gone, the more patterned Teddy has become to your absence.

I would recommend that when you come home that you don't try to handle Teddy right away. Talk to him and relate to him from a distance but don't pick him up and give him a chance to attack you. Pushing yourself on him as soon as you come home does not give him a chance to re-pattern and forces him to go into a defensive mode. Give him time to accept you as a member of the flock again by letting him re-pattern to your presence over a few days. You write that he is aggressive whether you are in his room, the kitchen or your bedroom. Because he has most likely spent a great deal of time in each of these rooms, he perceives them as his territory. If there is a "neutral" room in your house, one that he is not used to being in and therefore has not established as his territory, it would be best to have your husband take him in there and place him on a T-stand. Your husband should then leave the room and you can go in and reestablish your relationship with Teddy gradually.

Although it sounds like Teddy is a wonderful companion, many problems, such as this one, also have a basis in a lack of guidance from the caregivers. Make sure that you are constant in using the "up" and "DOWN" commands to maintain your authority as the "flock leader". If you can work to establish yourself in a higher position in the "pecking order" with consistent Nurturing Guidance, re-winning his affections after you have been gone will most likely take less time.

Q. FEAR BITING AND PHOBIC BEHAVIOR

Dear Sally,

I recently learned about the Pet Bird Report (CPQ) and bought a copy of your Companion Parrot Handbook. It is wonderful and has helped me understand my African Grey's behavior more than anything else I have read. It also helps me to understand what I have done wrong and to try and help him with his problems. I think that my local pet shop where I purchased Riley does a good job with the birds they raise but after reading your information, I think they could do a much better job. This is why I am sending you the money for a subscription for the store. Hopefully they will find the time to read some of the wonderful articles in the Pet Bird Report.

Although I have read several of your articles about African Grey parrots and I am following the advice in them, I still have more questions about my African Grey. Mostly I am looking for more specific information about how much time it will take to get him past his fear of me.

Riley is 15 months old. He always seemed a little anxious about new toys and new situations but I presumed he would just grow out of this. I didn't understand that I needed to work with him to get him past this fearful behavior. Instead of getting better, he got worse. One morning when I got him up, he acted like I was going to kill him. He was viciously biting at me and thrashing around in his cage. I honestly can't think of any reason or anything that I did to frighten him that much.

The pet shop recommended a person to work with Riley. He came to my home and worked with Riley in what I now consider to be an aggressive manner forcing him out of his cage and making him step from one hand to another. Once he saw how frightened Riley was, he told me that taking Riley with him for training would be the best thing to help him. He kept him for over a month and when I called him, he told me my Grey was doing great but when Riley came home, he was even worse. I couldn't even go into the room without him thrashing around in his cage. I wish I knew what I know now. I never would have let that man take Riley away and mess him up even more.

It was at that stage that I traveled over an hour to take Riley to a veterinarian who is an avian specialist. She is the one who told me about the Pet Bird Report and insisted that I buy your Companion Parrot Handbook. She ran several tests on Riley and found that he had some health problems. I am grateful for the fact that Riley is a good eater since we are giving him medication in his food so I don't have to handle him. I can't even imagine how he could have survived me toweling him to give him medicine. She said that his health could have something to do with his fearful behavior but didn't think medicating him would be the only solution to his behavior problem.

After reading your book, I can identify with the part where Riley thinks of me as a predator instead of his friend but I don't know why it happened. I am trying to follow your advice and have started working with Riley by quietly sitting in the room next to his cage and reading. I am not quite sure what that is supposed to accomplish but as long as I am quiet, he seems to accept my presence near him. I approach him quietly with my head bowed and don't make eye contact with him as you suggest. As long as I move slowly and don't look at him from above, he doesn't throw himself around the cage. If I don't think and enter the room too quickly, he still seems so afraid. He does appear to be more relaxed with me but it is difficult to remain patient because it really doesn't seem like I am making much progress. Isn't there something else that I could do that would make this all work more quickly? I feel like I have to walk on eggshells to keep him from hurting himself. It's been almost two weeks and he still doesn't seem to want anything to do with me. I wonder if he would be happier in a new home.

Can I really make a difference with him? How do I know I am doing the right thing? How much longer will it take for Riley to like me again? Will he ever be happy again?

- A -

From your e-mail, it is clear to me that you understand the basic principles of winning back the trust of a phobic bird. You are doing the right things by lowering your energy, being submissive with Riley, and spending non-threatening calm time with him. I know it can be difficult to maintain a positive attitude when the task seems so hopeless at times. The techniques you are using now have helped many parrots to trust their caregivers again and renewed trust is what you are striving for.

The purpose of sitting next to his cage and reading only makes sense when you begin to think about the social nature of most parrots. It is important for Riley to be a part of a flock — as a companion parrot, the people in his life form his human flock. He wants to be a part of your life but he has become afraid of you because of something we may never completely understand. The more time you spend with him in an indirect, calm manner, the more likely he will be to reflect your energy and relax enough to get past his fear. In a sense, by spending indirect, quiet time with him, you are inviting him to rejoin your flock. Once he trusts that he is safe with you, he will most likely make a step towards you. As long as you stay patient with his progress and do not expect too much too fast, the progress should continue — one step forward, one step back, two steps forward, and so on.

There is one very significant statement that you have made in your letter that you need to focus on in working with Riley — "*He does appear to be more relaxed with me but it is difficult to remain patient because it really doesn't seem like I am making much progress. Isn't there something else that I could do that would make this all work more quickly?*" The three most important considerations for success with Riley are:

1. PROGRESS — recognize progress as small steps. Progress in working with serious behavioral problems is rarely an overnight phenomenon, especially with parrots who have become phobic. In all the successful consultations I have done with phobic parrots, there seems to be a common aspect — the people only recognized the progress they made with their parrots in hindsight. They were not always able to recognize the small steps they made every day. If they got bogged down in the daily routine, the situation seemed pretty hopeless. Progress with serious behavioral problems rarely goes from start to finish without any side trips. It may not seem significant now but the fact that you recognize that Riley seems more relaxed is critical to his recovery because it will motivate you to continue.

2. PATIENCE — remain patient, particularly around Riley. Patience is a key factor with any behavioral work but this is particularly true with a phobic Grey. Parrots — especially Greys — are so empathic that impatience during the work process can become trust destroying.

3. PERSEVERANCE — keep on doing the right things and don't fall prey to the concept of quick fixes. Many people do not succeed in their work with phobic parrots because they give up to soon and try a series of unsuccessful quick fixes. If someone promises an overnight solution to the problem, they don't understand anything about what motivates such a serious fear response in companion parrots. Keep up your good work!

AN IMPORTANT PIECE OF ADVICE!

I talked to an agitated woman who said her previously *wonderful* Moluccan had suddenly gone on a rampage — biting, screaming, and chasing everyone around the house. It occurred to me again that the MAJOR mistake people make when *a good parrot goes bad* is to immediately become agitated and even terrified of their parrot. How could the Moluccan go back to being the good parrot he was supposed to have been when his caregivers had become so agitated any time they were near him? Her husband's response was to get rid of the Cockatoo even though he supposedly had really *loved* the bird.

An important piece of advice — if (out of nowhere) your parrot turns into a biting, screaming monster, ask yourself what he is responding to. It could be your bad mood. Then, most of all, slow down your energy so he doesn't feed off of your agitation and become even worse. Don't overreact. Treat the incident as an incident and not as a portent of a good bird turning bad..

Q. BITING AND OUR ENERGY

Dear Sally,

I have a handfed 6½-year-old Timneh Grey. Recently she has embarked on a biting spree. She was biting me often and I was mulling it over when something dawned on me. Each time she bit me, I had just finished exercising. After each workout, I would let her perch in the bathroom while I showered. There is obviously a change in my body chemistry after I'm done working out, what with a more distinct body odor and a higher level of heat radiation. My bird is apparently not used to seeing me in this condition and senses some type of "trauma." I think it frightens her, therefore, when I try to pick her up, she bites me. After I shower and cool down, she acts as if nothing has happened and is back to normal. From now on, after the workout, I'm going straight to the shower before taking her out of her cage.

- A -

You have figured out one of the most important principles of maintaining a good relationship with a parrot. One of the reasons that parrots have the potential to be such marvelous pets is because, in

good relationships with humans, they are incredibly empathic and closely match our moods. If we are excited, they're excited. If we're calm, they're calm. When taming and training, it is essential that people lower their energy level so that birds will trust them. People who don't do this will have a much more difficult time maintaining harmonious relationship with their pets.

A few months ago, I was visiting a friend who has a Blue and gold Macaws. We were late for a meeting and my friend was upset. She was having trouble getting her Macaws back into his cage. He would try to bite her every time she reached for him. The proverbial "vicious circle" resulted — the more she insisted, the more excited he became, causing the bird to resist even more. I suggested that she walk away from the cage, go into another room, shut her eyes and take a few deep breaths to slow herself down. She did, and when she came back into the room and reached for the Macaws, he stepped right onto her hand. Through the years I've had several clients who have had serious family problems that have created behavioral difficulties with their companion parrots. Stress at home causes stress for everyone, including our parrots.

Q. YOU DON'T HAVE TO BE THE "BOSS"

Dear Sally,

We purchased a baby African Grey 4 months ago. I have read every book in my local library about parrots and have read most all of my back issues of Bird Talk. About a month after Waldo came to live with us, he started biting me. The first bite really hurt but I was firm with him and made him step up immediately. I moved him several times from one hand to another to let him know that he was not supposed to bite me again. I always make sure that he knows I am the boss but he is very nervous and flighty around me. I have never had any problem with my cockatiels but this has been going on for over a year. Waldo likes my husband and my son and he doesn't bite them but they let him get away with murder with no rules at all. I have tried to do everything like the books and articles told me to but nothing is getting better with him. I take him out of his cage and work with him everyday for at least a half hour. He knows he is supposed to do what I say but he just won't do it. He seems to hate me. Please help me nothing I have tried works. I can't imagine spending much more time with this bird not liking me so much. What can I do with Waldo to stop him from biting me?

- A -

You don't have to be the "Boss" to provide guidance and set rules for Waldo. This is one of the major misunderstandings about parrot behavior. Much of the early literature about parrot behavior stresses the importance of being dominant and in control at all times. When I first started writing about parrot behavior, I wrote about dominance, control, and other words that were easily misunderstood as aggressive. Over the last decade, I have learned to choose my words much more carefully. We need to establish ourselves as a sort of "flock leader" so that we have some sort of authority but that authority should be that of a benevolent teacher or a nurturing parent — not that of an aggressive dictator. Parrots are highly empathic flock animals whose survival depends on their ability to pick up the behavioral cues and the energy of their fellow flock members. Humans are the flock of companion parrots and they reflect our energy. If we are aggressive to them, they become aggressive to us.

From moments before the very first time Waldo bit you, your relationship has been on the wrong track. Waldo bit you for a reason. You may never know what that specific reason was. It is probably that by always trying to be the "Boss", you were behaving in a manner that seemed aggressive to him. He may have responded positively to your behavior before, but the first time he bit you, he probably just wasn't in the mood to be messed with. Once he bit you, you escalated your aggressive behavior by laddering him from hand to hand. Parrots don't really understand this type of punishing behavior and since parrots so easily match our energy, Waldo's aggression escalated towards you. He might have responded with aggression, excitability, or fear. All three responses could result in a bite.

Relax and stop trying so hard with him. One of the few absolute rules of parrot behavior is that **parrots are more comfortable with people who are comfortable with them**. Working with a companion parrot does not have to be work. People can have fun with their parrots and teach them positive behaviors at the same time. If you are uptight and rigid with Waldo, he will be uptight, rigid, and unresponsive to you. The only way you will stop Waldo's biting, is to interact with him in a different manner. **Stop thinking of yourself as Waldo's boss — think of yourself as his teacher.** If he has been biting you when you try to force him out of his cage, then you need to start by letting your husband or son take him out of the cage. Choose a location in your home where Waldo isn't used to being and you can be comfortable. Your husband or son should take Waldo into this "neutral room" and place him on a T-stand or the back of a chair. He should leave the room as you enter. Calm yourself down as much as possible before you enter the room. Move slowly and speak very quietly without making intense eye contact. Since Waldo knows the "UP" command, say it but say it softly without any aggression in your voice. Push your hand very gently against his lower belly to get him to step on your hand. In a situation like this, Waldo will most likely step on your hand readily because you have changed most of the variables that have patterned him to bite you. Once he steps on your hand, praise him verbally and then slowly ladder him to the other hand. Repeat this a few times and then place him back on his stand. Smile and praise him for being so good. Laddering should never be used as discipline or punishment because it is such a valuable tool to pattern a parrot to consistently step on your hand. It is also a wonderful way to pattern people to approach their parrots in a consistent manner.

Stop taking Waldo's behavior personally. He didn't start biting you because he hates you. He most likely started biting you because he was uncomfortable with the way you approached him and this caused him conflict or confusion. As you begin to change your attitude towards Waldo and become gentler with him, he will gradually change his attitude towards you. Parrots are capable of learning new behaviors throughout their lifetime — especially if they have patient teachers.

Ask yourself what it is about your husband and son that Waldo likes. Why is he so comfortable with them? Although Waldo may seem like he dislikes you and likes other family members instead, the truth is that, for some reason, he is more comfortable with them. How do they act with him? You wrote that they let him get away with murder and that they don't set any rules for him. They probably also have a relaxed relationship with him — one where nothing is expected of him much of the time. He gets to just hang out with them. While we do need to provide guidance for parrots, we are not trying to turn them into little soldiers. Most African Greys really do love to just spend time with their human flock. They like to be a part of what is going on without expectations placed on them all the time.

Keep looking for better advice. Few libraries have current books that deal with companion parrot behavior in a positive manner. Not all parrot behavioral advice is good and even good advice does not necessarily apply to every companion parrot. All behavioral advice, no matter where it comes from, should be evaluated by one basic criteria — is the advice trust-building or trust-destroying? There are so many variables in a relationship between parrots and people. Each home situation is very different and the individuality of every parrot shines through, even beyond the basic species characteristics. Each companion parrot caregiver has to analyze every bit of information to see if it applies to their situation. What serves as a quick correction for one parrot, may be too aggressive for another one. Although I do not believe there is any reason to be aggressive with any companion parrot, some of the methods you have used with Waldo might be effective on a short-term basis for a secure, stubborn parrot but they will rarely, if ever, be effective with an African Grey. Gentleness, patience, praise, and nurturing guidance are the most effective behavioral tools for Greys and other parrots. With the Greys in my life, I have always found that I can create a much happier relationship with gentle sweet talk than I ever did with being the "Boss."

Q. WILL HE STAY TAME?

Dear Sally,

We are getting a baby African Grey from an excellent breeder who breeds only a few birds at a time. He will come home with us in a few weeks as soon as he is weaned. Right now he is very cuddly and sweet to both of us. I have talked to the breeder and she says that he will stay that way if we follow all the principles in your <u>Companion Parrot Handbook</u>. Although your book has a lot about this topic, it doesn't specifically cover keeping African Greys tame. Are they so different from other parrots? We have a great little cockatiel who likes us both and I know that getting a larger parrot is a lot more responsibility. I have read a great deal of confusing information. Some people on the Internet say they are only cuddly as babies and don't stay that way. Other people say that they only bond to one person and usually transfer their bond to another person when they are a couple of years old so there is not much point in counting on them to stay bonded to you. I have also read that as they get older, they reach the point where they do not want to be touched and trying to touch them will result in a nasty bite. All of this information frightens me because we so much want to do everything right so we don't have problems with him as he gets older.

- A -

When I first got my parrots, there was hardly any information about species behavioral characteristics. Now many people tell me that they are confused by an overload of information. This is particularly true on the Internet where anyone can sound like an expert. I have read many articles by people who had a limited and sometimes negative experience with one parrot and write as if they had extensive knowledge. My first piece of advice is to carefully filter the information you read.

I have worked with many Greys over the years and talked with hundreds of Grey caregivers. Each one has his or her individual personality. They are certainly not all alike and most generalizations are just that. Although you can probably tell a lot about the personality of your baby Grey in the first few weeks he is home, you probably won't really know who he is until a year or so passes. I think this is truer of Greys than most other parrot species. Greys grow on you, or perhaps it is actually that you grow on them. They are so empathic to the favorite people in their human flock that their personality becomes closer and closer to that of their caregivers as they mature.

When my Grey, Bongo Marie, came to live with me, she was a frightened older, imported Grey. She lived with me for 25 years. She was totally wild when she came to live with me but each year she seemed to add a new dimension in her personality increasing both her trust in me and her bond with me. I was very patient with her mostly because I had no idea of any other way to develop a better relationship with her. It took over five years for her to reach the point where I could pet her and hug her. I learned to recognize her body language that told me that she wanted to cuddle and that kind of handling was always on her terms. I never tried to handle her closely unless I could tell she wanted to be touched and cuddled. About ten years into our relationship, she would let me initiate close contact if I would quietly ask her, "can I cuddle with you Bongo Marie?" Towards the end of her life, she would just sort of fall against my chest and shut her eyes for cuddling almost every time I picked her up. Looking back, it seems as if the friendship developed with a steady increase in her trust and affection for me. While this was essentially true, there were many detours and side trips along the way. This was true mostly because of the changes in my behavior towards her during difficult times. I would have to work with exceptional dedication to win her trust back if I had become too unpredictable.

My new Grey, Whodee, came from the Gabriel Foundation. The person who owned him had decided he was an aggressive biter and evidently did not want to get the information or take the time to work with his problems. He lived in a foster home for a while before coming to live with me and was not a biter there. Knowing his history when I got him, I was very careful not to establish any kind of a negative situation with him. I did not want to start our relationship with him biting me. I let him adjust to his new home for a day without trying to handle him. During this time, I calmly approached him in a somewhat submissive manner. The next afternoon, I placed my hand into his cage and gently pushed my hand against his belly as I said "UP." He immediately reached down with his beak and clamped his beak on my finger. I quietly said, "No, gentle" without moving my hand. He was testing me and I knew I had to pass the test so I kept my hand there. He immediately loosened his beak. From that time on, a very positive progression of trust started. In the beginning, he did not want me touching him. Each day, we would have our quiet time where I would calmly and slowly touch a little bit more of his body. While I was handling him, I would always quietly compliment him, "Oh Whodee, you are so handsome, it just takes my breath away." Now anytime I compliment him in this manner, he fluffs up his head in response to my gentle manner. It is during these times that I could handle him a bit closer each time. He has now lived with me for almost two years and if I present myself in a calm enough manner, I can do almost anything with him. He loves for me to lift up his wings and give him a raspberry on his side. I can roll him over on his back and cradle him in my arm against my chest. I can rest him gently on his back on the top of my head. I can pet, kiss, and stroke him almost anywhere and he loves it. When I walk past his cage, he sticks his foot out and says, "Kiss toes." This is why it frustrates me so much when I read or hear the massive generalization that Greys do NOT like to be cuddled. I am afraid that it becomes a self-fulfilling prophecy and many people simply do not make the patient effort to win enough

trust for their parrot to love this kind of handling.

Years ago a woman brought me her Congo Grey for a wing and nail trim. Her first statement to me was that her Grey hated all women except her and that he did not like to be touched. I've heard statements like this so many times — I simply don't believe them. I think it often has more to do with the attitude (often misguided) beliefs of the caregivers in regards to what their parrots will accept. In working with the Grey, I slowed down my energy and then picked him up in a non-threatening indirect manner. I placed him on a towel on the table and then wrapped him from the front with the towel. I reached into an opening in the towel and started gently rubbing the skin around his beak and then the back of his head. Within a few minutes he was very relaxed. Once he was calm, I trimmed his wings and then his toenails. He didn't struggle at all and afterwards, we had quite a cuddle session. The woman was both surprised and shocked that her bird accepted this type of handling. Of course, she had never tried this kind of calm, patient technique to get her bird to accept touching and cuddling because she had accepted the "fact" that Greys are one-person birds who don't like to be cuddled.

I have not observed that Greys automatically transfer their bonds at any given time to another person. I think that some go through a difficult time when they are a year old or so and may get just a bit independent or even aggressive. If the person the bird has bonded to becomes impatient and does not know how to get past this stage, the bird may transfer his bond to someone who is more comfortable handling him. One of the few absolute rules of companion parrot behavior is that parrots are more comfortable with people who are comfortable with them. When a person is no longer comfortable handling their parrot, the parrot will not be comfortable with them. The parrot may show this discomfort by biting, refusing to step on that person's hand, going more readily to another human flock member, or even becoming afraid of that person. The way to quickly regain the comfort level is to slow things down and start over again. Increased calm and focused attention in a neutral room is the best way to rebuild that bond. A neutral room is a place where the parrot is not used to being where he can't see his cage. This way the person is the most familiar aspect in the room.

I think that any bappy who is well-socialized and affectionate when he or she is young has the potential to stay that way. However, I strongly believe it is up to his human flock to treat him with nurturing affection and provide the kind of guidance that continues to establish and maintain the gentleness in his personality. This is particularly true for Greys who look to us so strongly for their behavioral cues. If you believe your Grey will stay cuddly and work to achieve that knowing that you have to evaluate his mood first, I would bet that he will allow you to handle him closely throughout his life.

Q. AMAZON GENERALIZATIONS

We are in the process of adopting a 15 plus year old Blue-front Amazon from a rescue organization. We have been told that he came from a very neglectful situation and hadn't been out of his cage for years. He may have been a breeding bird in an aviary before that but no one knows for sure. They are pretty sure he is an imported bird but he has no band. He lets us handle him at the facility and one or two of the women there can also handle him. He has been there for almost a year because he was very sick and they wanted to make sure he was healthy before they let someone adopt him. He now has a clean bill of health and will be coming home with us within the next month. He was on a seed only diet but will now eat some fresh food, but they are still trying to get him to eat pellets. Since he has become healthier, he has become a little bit more aggressive. We have two other parrots (a 7-year-old African Grey and a 3-year-old Illiger's Macaw) and have no real problem with them but I am a little bit concerned about how to deal with male Amazon hormones. I have read many places that male Amazons do not make good pets. We will keep him and do our best to take good care of him even if he becomes aggressive with us. Do you know of male Amazons that have stayed tame and, if so, how did their owners keep them that way? How long will it take for him to become a good pet? Thank you.

- A -

Yes, I personally know or have been told about many male Amazons who have stayed very tame. A good number of these are Blue-front Amazons. Double-yellow Heads and Yellow-napes also have this aggressive reputation but there are individuals who simply do not deserve these negative generalizations. Many of these parrots love to be handled and form strong bonds to the people in their lives. Few parrots of any species never cause their caregivers any problems and, certainly, Amazons are not as problematic as any other kind of parrot. The thing that makes most Amazons easier to work with is their predictability. They are very honest parrots and once they have exhibited their full range of body language, any observant person will know when these parrots do not want to be handled. Some Amazons remain leery of hands but can be stick-trained to come out and spend time with people. Generally speaking, Amazon parrots are easier to food bribe than most other parrots and this can always be used to an advantage by the people in their lives.

Amazons are generally very resilient. I have known of many who have suffered unspeakable neglect, abuse, and trauma but yet, with patient, knowledgeable caregivers, these parrots have blossomed and provided great emotional rewards to their new human flocks. It sounds as if you have done a good job with your other parrots so I would guess that you have "the right stuff" to work with an Amazon. When people adopt them who are dedicated to their long-term success, many "second-chance" Amazons do very well in their new homes.

Most of the time, a "second-chance" parrot comes with little background information. The new caregiver may not know how old the bird is, its gender, whether it was wild-caught or imported, or what kind of behaviors (positive or negative) he was taught along the way. Many of these parrots have totally lost any trust in human beings if they ever had any before. It is important to note that some of these parrots have been in multiple living situations before they even reach a rescue organization. Not too long ago, I talked with a woman who had adopted an imported Blue-front Amazon. According to the information she had been given (which she believed was accurate), the parrot had been in a dozen homes in the twenty plus years he had been in captivity.

A good number of "second-chance" parrots were never very tame or trained to follow basic behavior commands or cues. It has always amazed me how many people purchase parrots who were somewhat tame and perhaps even understood basic verbal commands or cues, but at the first sign of aggression, they stopped handling them. As someone working with parrot behavior for a long time, I can guarantee that the first step in a companion parrot losing his home is when the owner loses hand control and can no longer successfully or safely pick up their parrots. At the Companion Parrot Quarterly, we have

been conducting an in-depth questionnaire with thousands of people responding. One of the most telltale aspects of this survey is the number of people who report serious behavior problems with their parrots based on biting and aggression. Yet, very few of these people have consulted with a behavioral consultant about these problems. Many do not even read literature about parrots, while some rely on the Internet for all their parrot information. Most of us know that information on the Internet is a mixed blessing with a vast range of opinions. Some Internet "experts" provide excellent advice but other information is based on quick fixes and potentially trust destroying advice that has no place in the benevolent treatment of parrots. If people sought good advice before a problem occurred or when it first becomes evident, most behavioral problems have fairly simple solutions. If and when many people look for advice, the situation has gone on so long that the aggressive behavior has become patterned. Not only has the parrot been allowed to establish a pattern of aggression, but the person has an ingrained pattern of fear that either causes them to not handle their parrot at all or causes their handling to be so indecisive, it escalates confusion and, therefore, more aggression from the parrot. Sadly, some people keep these parrots for many years despite the fact that the bird is never handled or given any attention. This is a typical scenario for many previously tame Amazon parrots who end up needing new homes. Often these parrots are the easiest to work with because they do not really need to be tamed — they simply need to be reminded that they are already tame.

Some rescued Amazons are older birds who may have spent much of their captive life in breeding situations. A good number of parrot breeders feel some obligation to these parrots who have provided them with chicks over the years, while others don't give a damn what happens when the parrots are no longer productive. Some of these retired breeders are sold to brokers, at swap meets, bird shows, etc. Many are misrepresented and are purchased as part of a viable pair often over and over and over ... Some of these parrots can become successful human companions while others can't. Their greatest need is a stable permanent situation whether it is in a home as a companion, a home as a well-cared for aviary bird (hopefully with a parrot buddy), or a caring sanctuary situation with another parrot.

The first step to working with your Blue-front is to determine if you have what it takes to adopt a "second-chance" parrot. Four basic qualities are extremely important:

Dedication: Many "second-chance" parrots will require a great deal of work to become successful human companions. Most abused and neglected parrots will take time to learn to trust people. Cage-bound parrots usually take time to be comfortable away from the security that their cages provide. Even those parrots who have come from homes where they received love and good care will need help in adjusting to the many changes in their new situation. Parrots who have lost a beloved caregiver will need a period of gentle understanding to get beyond their grief. Some parrots will exhibit signs of depression and others may become aggressive. Parrots are creatures of habit and although their routine shouldn't be too rigid, extreme change can be both disruptive and disturbing to a parrot who loses his home.
Patience: One of your questions is frequently asked; "How long will this take?" Some people have been frustrated when I tell them I don't know. There are so many variables in working with previously owned parrots, it is impossible to predict how long it will take to earn a particular bird's trust. It depends on the parrot, the environment he came from, the people involved, and a myriad of other influences. Because of this, my answer is usually, "It will take as long as it takes, be patient." Most people expect results immediately and unfortunately give up too soon when they don't see progress within a few

days. People don't tend to see how much progress they are making until a big enough step occurs that they can look back and remember what it was like when they started. Make a promise to keep trying, be patient and to notice very small steps. This can make a tremendous difference in the parrot's life. Progress is rarely linear with one triumph following another until the bird is "cured." Progress is usually two steps forward, one step back, three steps forward, nothing happening, two steps back, nothing happening, two steps back, one step forward, one step forward, nothing happening, and so on. A classic example is trying to get a cage bound parrot to step out on a T-stand to get a treat. It may take over a week for him to gingerly step on the perch. If nothing happens to threaten him, he may go for the treat. If he becomes insecure for any reason, he may go back into his cage without the treat and it may be another week or more before he tries again. I have always thought of it in this way; you and the bird both have your whole life ahead of you. What's the hurry?

Determination: Remaining determined to help your Amazon accept his new life despite setbacks, inconsistencies, and lack of progress is essential. Don't let yourself give up too soon. Even if all you can do is give the Blue-front quality care and attention without handling him, he will still be receiving better care than he had. I have worked with several caregivers who never gave up even though they could not handle their parrot. They did not try to force their bird to do anything but gently cajoled him by offering treats on a T-stand placed up against the open cage door. It took some time, but once the parrot came out on the T-stand, the person was able to move the stand away from the cage and then into a neutral room. This is an unfamiliar room to the parrot and therefore, he has no reason to defend his territory there. Again over a period of time, the person was able to give treats by hand to the parrot and then, eventually, start to gently handle him. Stick training was also possible by simply picking up the parrot and holding the stick for him to climb up and then, moving the stick so the bird could climb up to the other hand. Even though a parrot can be handled most of the time, it is still important to stick train him so he can be handled during times if and/or when he is more aggressive. This keeps the person from being bitten and maintains trust. Don't try to stick train a parrot by poking a stick at him in the cage — this is the best way to accomplish the exact opposite of what you are trying to do. Parrots who have sticks poked at them in their cages, often become afraid and/or much more aggressive when they see someone holding it.

One person I talked to always spoke quietly to her Amazon but was never able to handle him. After about two years of this, he actually climbed down off of his cage and walked across the room and climbed up on the couch to be with her. Once this happened, it took another six months for the parrot to allow her to skritch his head. Now they are good friends. It took time for the parrot to take the initiative and let her know how important she was to him. If she had given up or tried to force herself on him, it would not have happened.

One of the keys to working with your rescued Blue-front is to lower your expectations about what he needs to be for you and raise them about what you need to do for him. Let go of any time frame you have. Look for and be rewarded by small improvements rather than expecting big immediate changes. In everything you do with him, remember that you are working to win his trust. That is really what a tame parrot is — one who trusts you.

Q. TAMING A HANDFED BABY

A month or so ago, we purchased a baby African Grey from a source who came highly recommended to us. However, it appears that our parrot received little socialization and she is now very afraid of us. We have never been abusive to her in any way whatsoever. From the very beginning, she didn't seem to know how to step up on to our hands. We doubt now that she received any handling except when she was being fed. We have talked to several people about what we should do and their advice has been to find her another home. We were even told that she should be placed with a rescue organization. Even though she is not tame to us at this time, we have developed a great amount of affection for her and are willing to do whatever it takes to turn her around. So far most of the advice we have received has not helped and has just seemed to make her more afraid of us. Now when we approach her cage to take her out with the "UP" command, she throws herself around the cage. If we try to force the issue, she bites us. We have been told to go ahead and take her

out of the cage despite her fear and that when she sees that nothing bad has happened, she will get used to it and accept our attention. Now we can't even look at her without her getting upset. Is this situation hopeless or, since we are so willing to work with her, can we really work out all the problems we have with her?

- A -

First of all, there are more than enough birds in rescue situations without adding one that has dedicated caregivers willing to work with the parrot's problems. Clearly at this point in her life, your Grey's best hope is with you. I cannot guarantee that you will be able to work out all the problems you have with your Grey but I can assure you that if you give up now, you have not given her a fair chance at all. Winning the trust of a parrot like yours will take much longer than a few weeks and the more you try to demand progress from her, the harder it will be to make any progress with her. Give up any schedule you have and work with her in a manner that is guided by her level of acceptance to new experiences. You will never accomplish anything by being too direct with her — in fact, you may even set her back more. If your Grey is stressed and fearful every time you try to take her out nothing else bad has to happen to her for her to associate fear with coming out of her cage or stepping on your hand. Forcing her to come out in the hopes that she will get used to it will not win trust and one of the most important rules of companion parrot behavior is "all work should be trust-building and not trust-destroying." It is important to realize that your Grey may be on the edge of becoming a "phobic parrot" and being too direct with her could push her over that edge.

Over the years, I have worked with many Greys who have been either hyper-vigilant or excessively fearful. There can be many reasons why these birds become afraid of almost everything and everyone. Many parrots are uncomfortable with change or new objects in and around their cages but this is not considered true phobic behavior. Phobic behavior is not unusual with Greys although not all Greys are in danger of developing excessive fears. While many parrots who exhibit phobic behavior do not do so until they have reached the age when they would normally start being independent of their parents, some seem extra sensitive from the very beginning. With some, the quick slide into phobic behavior seems way out of proportion to the triggering trauma or event. The immediate cause is probably some situation where, consciously or subconsciously, the parrot senses that he is simply not prepared to deal with what is happening. Being prey animals, these types of situations can create trauma. A parrot who is constantly traumatized by daily situations in her life can become very apprehensive. Change becomes an ordeal because they have not developed any resiliency to bounce back after a threatening or traumatic situation. With many poorly socialized parrots almost any traumatic event, no matter how small, can push them into excessive fearful behavior. Parrots are prey animals and, in the wild, a predator can kill an ill-prepared parrot quickly. Fear puts the parrot into a hyper-vigilant mode where normal activities and even the favored people can easily be viewed as a threat.

With people who are sensitive to the needs of their parrots, the tendency is to protect their overly sensitive birds from any change and situations that may create problems. This is just as big a mistake as being oblivious to the parrot's fears. The positive middle ground is to present sensitive parrots with small changes in a consistently nurturing manner so that they are not overwhelmed but also learn to accept new experiences. Teaching a parrot to accept new adventures should involve gradual trust-building patterning — one step at a time — building with each step.

I believe that many overly sensitive parrots are "accidents waiting to happen." Some people feel that there is a genetic component that causes some parrots to be much more sensitive than others and this leads to phobic behavior. This certainly must be a factor but I am also convinced that production-raised parrots are poorly socialized and unprepared for life as a human companion. They often lack the resiliency to bounce back after a threatening situation. If no one has taught your Grey the social and survival skills she needs to be a parrot and/or adapt to life as a human companion, her difficulty with you is understandable. It is clear that there are specific skills that are best learned at specific times. Does this mean that a parrot will not learn a particular social or survival lesson if they miss the optimal time to learn it? It may be more difficult but over the years it is certainly evident to me that parrots ARE capable of learning throughout their lives.

This brings me back to your African Grey. While your Grey may always be somewhat sensitive, I believe it is possible to build up her resiliency and win her trust so that she will be happy in your household. It will take time and a good amount of gentle persuasion to convince your Grey that you are trusted members of her flock. Patience and consistency are your two best tools. In the beginning, indirect attention is less threatening than direct attention. Any behavior perceived by your parrot as being too assertive may seem aggressive to her. It is best to approach her is a submissive manner — keep your head lowered and do not make direct sustained eye contact. If she won't come out of her cage and you don't want to threaten her by forcing her to come out, there is another way but it may take a few weeks to work. If you do not have one, purchase a basic T-perch with a food bowl on it. Place it near her cage and if she doesn't have

any problem with its presence, move it a little closer until it is right up against the door. Most Greys can be food bribed with great success. Pick out her absolute favorite food whether it is a nut, a grape or a biscuit and stop feeding this to her for a day or so. Without approaching her and making eye contact with her, open her cage door and put the stand up against the open door. Show her the special treats and make it very obvious you are placing them in the food cup. Once the treats have been placed, walk away and busy yourself with something else. Don't act as if you have any interest in what she is doing but watch with your peripheral vision. She will probably not come out until she is patterned to accept this new situation. After a few times, she may come part of the way out but run back in if something else gets her attention or startles her. This will be particularly true if you show too much interest in what she is doing. Let her get used to coming out on to the stand until she does it almost immediately when you place the treat in the bowl. The next step is for her to come out on the stand with you there. After that start lifting the stand and moving it a little bit at a time. Pay close attention to her comfort level but try not to stare at her or give her too much direct attention. The plan is to eventually move her into a neutral room where you become the most familiar aspect of her environment. Most parrots are much easier to work with away from their cages. It should be much easier to get her to step on your hand. Plan ahead and make sure there are a few special bribe treats ready in the neutral room. Always be calm and go slow at her pace. After you have spent a little bit of time in the neutral room calmly interacting with her, you can take her back to her cage on your hand. Get her used to being on your hand for a short time before you place her back inside.

Stop and think before you do anything with her — will she perceive your approach as being too threatening? Learn to approach her in a calm manner that shows her you are a friend instead of a threat. Measure your success in small steps rather than looking for some sort of miraculous major breakthrough. Many people do not see progress until they look back and then it seems amazing. When my Grey, Bongo Marie, came to live with me over twenty-five years ago, she was sick and terrified of almost everything. Six months later she was much better but two years later, she was very sociable and totally full of herself and no one would have ever guessed she was the kind of Grey who threw herself on her back screaming whenever anyone looked at her. With patience and consistency, I think, in time, you will also look back with surprise that your Grey was ever so threatened to be a part of your life.

A Few More Reasons for Aggression

As I was preparing the Index, I realized there were a couple of important concepts that I wanted to include.

⮑ Aggressive behavior and biting can evolve from physical problems, pain, and discomfort rather than behavioral problems. Several years ago a woman called me because her baby African Grey was becoming exceedingly aggressive and lunging at her whenever she approached the cage. She had only had the parrot a few weeks and he was supposedly fully weaned. By this time I had begun to realize that handfeeding and weaning problems were the major cause of many of the behavioral problems I saw in young parrots. During the in-home consultation, it became obvious to me that the frantic young bird was desperate to be fed. His lunging and agitation was not based on aggression — it was based on the insecurity of not enough nutritious food to sustain his growing body. How would a novice caregiver know that hunger was the problem — especially when "experts" told her that the baby was weaned and not to handfeed him again or she would spoil him? How could she have known that the only solution to her baby parrot's "aggression" was regression feeding? She needed to start handfeeding him again — both for nutrition and security. Over the years I have heard so many stories about baby parrots with serious "behavioral problems" and to this day, new caregivers are still given the horrendous advice not to hand feed the baby again once he is weaned or he will be spoiled. Poor early socialization, gavage (tube) feeding, power syringe feeding, inadequate and insufficient handfeeding, and forced weaning have diminished or ruined the pet potential of far too many companion parrots. Unfortunately many novice caregivers have no idea how to get their parrots past the problems caused by poor early socialization and improper handfeeding protocols.

⮑ Aggression can also be an indication of illness or injury. If your parrot's aggression comes on suddenly or even gradually worsens, look carefully for other signs of a health problem. Any time a parrot exhibits a drastic change in behavior, he or she should be seen by an avian veterinarian. In the last week or so of my elderly African Grey Bongo Marie's life, she became uncommonly aggressive towards me. This broke my heart because I knew this was her way of telling me that she was in too much pain to be handled and it was time for her to go. We shared a wonderful life together for over a quarter of a century.

⮑ On pages 57-59, I wrote about sexual behavior in companion parrots and on page 47, explained parrots in "overload" being perpetually "pumped up." After conversations with avian veterinarian Dr. Tammy Jenkins, Rebecca Fox from U.C. Davis and others, I want to merge this information. We need to provide our parrots with the best care we can — highly nutritious food, a well-lighted environment with lots of humidity, a roomy habitat with lots of enrichment including toys to shred and chew, and, if accepted by our avian companion, lots of love and physical affection. Aren't these the same things that stimulate sexual behavior in parrots? Yes but, does this mean we have to stop giving our parrots optimal care during the time when their hormones exacerbate sexual behavior? Is our good care contributing to "hormonal toxicity" in our companion parrots and, if so, what long-term influence does this have on their behavior and health? As I finish this book, this is a relatively new concept involving companion parrots and I don't have all the answers but I could NEVER recommend providing less then optimal care. We need to pay close attention to our parrots and if we notice that their sexual behavior is too intense for too long, we need to modify their environment until they get past this type of behavior. During these times, it makes sense to cut back on the length and intensity of light and, perhaps, the richness of food. It may also help to remove anything that could be perceived as a nest box or nesting material from their habitat. Most of all, we need to determine if the way we are handling our parrots is actually keeping them in hormonal overload and contributing to both behavioral and health problems. Observant caregivers will eventually learn to manipulate and balance their parrots' environment and handling to prevent prolonged stress and/or breeding behaviors.

THE BEAK BOOK INDEX

• 1. Moluccan Cockatoo • 2. African Grey • 3. Caique • 4. Budgie • 5. Senegal • 6. Slender-billed Conure • 7. Quaker • 8. Lovebird • 9. Cockatiel • 10. Lory • 11. Mitred Conure • 12. Red-lored Amazon • 13. Hyacinth Macaw

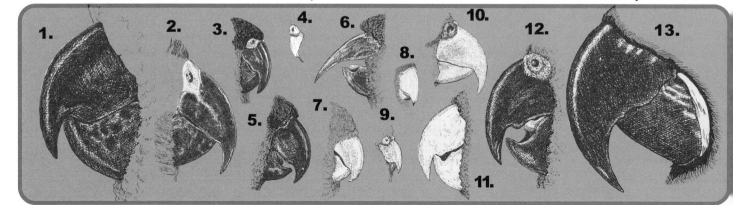